CAI

Rent Rolls
of
Somerset County Maryland

1663-1723

Note: These rent rolls were copied as written; however, the location of the lands was not always included or it was in error. In these cases I attempted to supply the information but could not be completely accurate.

Transcribed by

Ruth T. Dryden

HERITAGE BOOKS
2010

HERITAGE BOOKS
AN IMPRINT OF HERITAGE BOOKS, INC.

Books, CDs, and more—Worldwide

For our listing of thousands of titles see our website
at
www.HeritageBooks.com

Published 2010 by
HERITAGE BOOKS, INC.
Publishing Division
100 Railroad Ave. #104
Westminster, Maryland 21157

Originally published 1989

— Publisher's Notice —

Page 92 does not exist. No text is missing; this page number was missed when the book was created.

All rights reserved. No part of this book may be reproduced or transmitted in any form or by any means, electronic or mechanical, including photocopying, recording or by any information storage and retrieval system without written permission from the author, except for the inclusion of brief quotations in a review.

International Standard Book Numbers
Paperbound: 978-1-58549-133-9
Clothbound: 978-0-7884-8428-5

CALVERT PAPERS

RENT ROLLS OF

SOMERSET COUNTY

MARYLAND

1663-1723

Note; These rent rolls were copied as written
however, the location of the lands was
not always included or it was in error.
In these cases I attempted to supply the
information but could not be completely
accurate.

transcribed by

Ruth T. Dryden
2414 Front St. #25
San Diego, Ca. 92101

SOMERSET COUNTY MARYLAND
1666-1723

The lands of Baltimore100, Nanticoke 100, the upper tip of Pocomoke 100 may now be in Sussex Co. Deleware. Also those listed in Mattapany 100 and lower Pocomoke 100 may include parts of tracts in Accocomac Co. Virginia.
Time and tides have altered the islands off the Atlantic and Chesapeake Bay, and also the adjacent lands so that some no longer exist or have been absorbed by floods or swamps.

CALVERT PAPERS
Rent Rolls, Somerset County Md.
1663-1723

ACRES	TRACT	SURVEY DATE-BY WHOM	LOCATION
650	COLEBURN	18 Aug 1663 Stephen Horsey, in Annamessex River at mouth of Coulburn creek possessed- 150a.-Nathaniel Horsey 250a.-Isaac Horsey 150a.-Samuel Horsey	Annamessex 100
550	DIXONS CHOICE	19 Aug 1663 Ambrose Dixon- on south side of Annamessex River, possessed by Capt. Thomas Dixon	Annamessex 100
200	HEARTS EASE	1663 Robert Hart- on south side of Annamessex River at head of Hearts Creek, belongs to Robert Coleburns orphans in Manokin	Annamessex 100
300	WILLIAMSTON	4 Sep 1663, Thomas Williams- adjacent land of Mich'll Williams, possessed by Thomas Williams	Annamessex 100
1280	WATERS RIVER	5 Sep 1663-William Watters- on north side Annamessex River between Assateage Creek and Swansey Creek, possessed- 150a. Thomas Tull Sr. 700a. John Waters 430a. Richard Waters	Annamessex 100
600	STRAIGHTS	4 Sep 1663- George Johnson - on south side Annamessex River, land belonging to George Johnson's heirs in England, possessed- 300a. John Heath 300a. Thomas Beauchamp	Annamessex 100
300a.	JOHNSTOWN	5 Sep 1663- George Johnson- on south side Annamessex River near Beaver Dam. The land belongs to Johnson's granchild in England. Capt. Thomas Dixon is attorney.	Annamessex 100
350	BOSTONTOWN	20 Aug 1663- Henry Boston- on s/s Annamessex River and resurveyed 30 March 1682 for Wm. Palmer(Planner) and found to contain within the bounds, 800a, the whole tract possessed by William Palmer son and heir of William Palmer	Annamessex 100
500	CHEAP PRICE	4 Sep 1663- Thomas Price - on s/s Annamessex River, in possession of William Palmer(Planner) to whom it doth belong as heir to said William	Annamessex 100
300	WILLIAMS CONQUEST	-Michael Williams - on south side Annamessex River, possessed by William (Planner)Palmer to whom right belongs	Annamessex 100

ACRES	TRACT	SURVEY DATE-BY WHOM	LOCATION

100a. WAREPOINT 13 Mar 1663 -Germon Gillett Annamessex 100
by Pocomoke River, possessed
  150a. John Outen
  50a. in right of Phillip Conner's child
by Widow Conner

100a. YORKSHIRE ISLAND-William Wilkinson- Annamessex 100
by Annamessex Bay, since found to be 150a.
the right in Samuel Horsey, in the present
occupation of Rice Morgan. Surv. date 2 Jun. 1664

300a. DIXONS LOTT 1664-Ambrose Dixon -   Annamessex 100
on west side of Morumsco Creek, possessed by
  150a. George Wilson
  150a. William Wilson

300a. BOYCES BRANCH, 9 Apr 1664, William Boyce- Annamessex 100
on north side of north br. of Annamessex River,
Possessed by Ed. Stockdell in right of his
wife the heir of Boyce

300a. HALLS CHOICE 6 Jun 1665- Charles Hall- Annamessex 100
on north side Annamessex River, possessed by
widow Alice Hall

100a. PLANNERS ADVENTURE-William Planner- Annamessex 100
possessed by the widow, a relict of Furbey Rugg
surveyed-6 Apr 1664

150a. WATKINS POINT- 20 Feb 1664-John Horsey, Annamessex 100
at mouth of Johnsons Creek, possessed by
Stephen Horsey to whom it belongs

300a. EMESSEX 10 Feb 1663, Benjamin Summers- Annamessex 100
near land of Cornelius Ward, and resurveyed
for said Summers and found to be but 250a.

150a. MAKEPEACE 9 Feb 1663, John Roach, Annamessex 100
at small gut dividing from land of John Smith

200a. JOHNSONS LOTT, 12 Feb 1663, John Johnson- Annamessex 100
by creek dividing from land of Stephen Horsey,
possessed by-John Cullens by gift from Johnson

400a. BOSTONS ADVENTURE, 1 Feb 1664-Henry Boston- Annamessex 100
on west side Morumsco Creek at pine dividing
from Ambrose Dixon's. Possessed by-
  250a. John Long
  150a. Helena relict of Jeffrey Minshall

400a. HARTFORD BROAD OAKE, 26 Oct 1666, Robert Catlin-Annamessex 100
at head of Annamessex, possessed by William Catlin
heir to Robert.

400a. THE DESERT, 10 Mar 1665, Stephen Horsey- Annamessex 100
at north point of Annamessex River, Possessed by,
  246a. Thomas Walston
  154a. John Tull

300a. CONTENTION-resurveyed 1 Feb 1666-Edward Dickenson-Annam. 100
at head of Annamessex near land of Robert Catlin,
the land held by Somerset Dickenson the heir.
Possessed by Thomas Beauchamp

ACRES	TRACT	SURVEY DATE-By Whom	Location
100a	MATTUX HOPE	14 Jan 1666 Lazarus Maddux	Annamessex 100
200a.	SALSBURY	3 Apr 1667 John Rhodeson N/S Annamessex River near land of M.Waters possessed by Nathaniel Roach in right of James Curtis the purchaser	Annamessex 100
200a	ARMSTRONGS PURCHASE	3 April 1667 for Matthew Armstrong on N/S Annamessex- possessed by Samuel Handy	Annamessex 100
300a.	ARMSTRONGS LOTT	10 April 1666 Matthew Armstrong on N/S Annamessex- Annamessex 100 Possessed -250a. James Curtis 500a. Samuel Handy	
50a.	LONDONS GIFT	3 Jan 1667 William Furnace- assigned George Johnson, in a neck of land called the Desert, belonging to heirs of George Johnson, a minor in England under the guardianship of Capt.Thomas Dixon, Attorney.	Annamessex 100
50a.	LONDONS ADVISEMENT	3 Jun 1667 William Furnace. assigned to George Johnson, in neck called Desert, belongs to heirs of George Johnson, in guardianship of Catp.Thomas Dixon,Attorney.	Annam.100
200a.	JOHNSONS FIRST CHOICE	2 Jun 1667 William Stevens- assigned to George Johnson above head of the Annamessex River, belongs to orphans in England, guardianship assigned Capt. Dixon, Attorney	Annam.100
16a.	TEAGS DOWN	6 Sep. 1667 Ambrose London- at point of neck between Annamessex and Manokin, together with the Last Choice, in all 26a. Belongs to Samuel Handy who purchased from Thomas Newbold who purchased from London.	Annamessex 100
16a.	BLACK RIDGE	5 Sep.1667 Ambrose London- between Annamessex and Manokin Rivers possessed by Samuel Handy	Annamessex 100
10a.	STAKERIDGE	6 Sep 1667, Ambrose London- between Annamessex and Manokin Rivers, belongs to Samuel Handy who purchased of Thomas Newbold who purchased from Ambrose London	Annamessex 100
25a.	LONDONS ADVENTURE	5 Sep 1667 Ambrose London- belongs to Samuel Handy	Annamessex 100
150a.	DISCOVERY	2 May 1668, William Cheesman- assigned to George Johnson. at head of Annamessex River. belongs to heirs of George Johnson, guardian Capt. Dixon, Attorney	Annamessex 100
300a.	COLEBURNS PURCHASE alias SCOTLAND	1 Mar.1668- William Coulbourn at w/s Beaver Dam. First belonging and possessed by William Scott	Annamessex 100
100a.	CONDOQUE	4 Nov 1668 William Stevens- Assigned to Phillip Conner, on w/s Morumsco Creek possessed-50a. by widow of Phillip Conner 50a. by John Outon	Annamessex 100

ACRES	TRACT	SURVEY DATE-By Whom	Location
100a.	JONES ISLAND	19 Mar 1669-Leonard Jones-Annamessex 100 near Cagers Island at a point by Ocupation Creek, the land possessed lies near CAGERS STRAIGHTS, in possession George Hopkins in right of Robert Hopkins Sr.	
200a.	KIRKS PURCHASE	29 May 1668-John Kirk, Annamessex 100 near Watkins Point at a point dividing it from the land of John Horsey-possessed by John Kirk.	
150a.	HILLS FOLLY	18 Aug 1672, John Hill- Annamessex 100 on s/s of Back Creek, near moth of Annamessex. Possessed by Thomas Stockwell in right of his wife, heir to Hill	
100a.	LONG ACRE	9 Oct 1673, Alexander Draper-Annamessex 100 being an Island in a marsh on the s/s Annamessex. Possessed by Cornelius Ward and included in a lot, survey made for said Ward, called Long Acre 115a. surveyed 1701	
50a.	HOPKINS DESTINY	27 Feb 1673, George Johnson-Annamessex 100 N/S at mouth of Annamessex River. Thomas Everndon refuses to pay rent, who was possessed in right of his wife, the heir and minor in England.	
200a.	RECOVERY	3 Nov 1676, William Stephens- Annamessex 100 assigned John Kirk on n/s Pocomoke. Possessed by John Kirk	
200a.	MOREWORTH	18 Sep.1676, William Stevens and John Horsey near Watkins Point. Possessed- Stephen Horsey 132a. Anthony Bell pur/o Horsey Heir- 68a.	
350a.	BEAR NECK	19 Sep 1676-William Stevens-Annamessex 100 assigned to Robert Dukes, between Annamessex and Morumsco. The land possessed called BEARDS NECK and held by Robert Dukes son of Robert Dukes	
300a.	BOSTON	16 Sep 1676, William Stevens- Annamessex 100 assigned to Thomas Cottingham on N/S Morumsco. possessed by Charles Cottingham son of Thomas	
50a.	STANDS STEADS ABBY	4 Dec 1677, William Stevens-Annamessex 100 Assigned by him to Richard Barns and John Sterling in Annamessex Neck near Apes Hole. Possessed-25a. Richard Barns 25a. John Sterling son of John	
200a.	PRICES VINEYARD	resurvey 25 Jun 1676-Annamessex100 James Price, near Pocomoke Bay on w/s Johnsons creek. Possessed by Mary Price widow of James	
100a.	CHEESEMANS CHANCE	28 Jun 1676-John Freman- Annamessex 100 Assigned to William Freeman, on n/s Morumsco Creek about 2 miles in the woods Possessed-40a. George Hey 60a. Joseph Evans	

ACRES	TRACT	SURVEY DATE-BY WHOM	LOCATION
100a.	LITTLE USK	4 July 1677-William Stevens- assigned William Jenkins, n/s Possessed by Cornelius Ward's sons in the right of Nathaniel Daughertys Child	Annamessex 100 Annamessex River
150a.	LONG TOWN	8 Jan 1676-William Stevens, assigned Thomas Shollites, near Pocomoke Bay Thomas Shollites deceased without heirs. Now in possession and claim, supposed it is Long Ridge, held by Thomas Davis	Annamessex 100
100a.	CHESTNUT RIDGE,	4 July 1677,William Stevens, assigned Cornelius Ward, at mouth of Annamessex possessed by Cornelius Ward	Annamessex 100
150a.	COW QUARTER,	13 July 1677, Stephen Horsey, assigned John Horsey, on Watkins Point on the north side Pocomoke possessed by Stephen Horsey	Annamessex 100
200a.	MIDDLE RIDGE,	9 July 1677,William Stevens, assigned Stephen Horsey, two miles from Pocomoke bay Possessed by John Gunby	Annamessex 100
300a	UNDUE,	18 July 1677-Col.Wm.Stephens assigned to Stephen Horsey, near Watkins Point Possessed by Thomas Davis	Annamessex 100
200a.	VULCANS VINEYARD,	10 March 1677, Thomas Cottingham. at Beaver Dam Branch. at head of Blamors Creek Possessed by Charles Cottingham son of Thomas	Annam.100
200a.	FIRST CHOICE,	4 March 1677-Thomas Dixon North side Pocomoke Bay at head of Planners creek. possessed by said Dixon	Annamessex 100
100a.	DANIELS DEN,	3 March 1674-Daniel Donohoe, at mouth of Morumsco Creek Possessed by Alexander Mattux	Annamessex 100
500a.	CORK	12 Sept.1678-William Stevens, assigned to Cornelius Ward on south side of Annamessex	Annamessex 100
300a.	WOOD STREET,	13 Nov 1677-John Emmett, Assigned to Thomas Jones. resurveyed by a special warent for 850a. to WOOD STOCK by Thomas Jones but supposed it was returned by the name of LITTLE BOLTON 26 Oct 1688. Now held by Robert Catherwood in right of Jone's orphan.	Annamessex 100
150a.	WEBLY	18 Nov. 1677, Josias Leonard, assigned to Donnick Dennis, in Morumsco Creek Possessed by John Outen	Annamessex 100
100a.	LINSEN GREEN,	25 July 1679, William Stevens, assigned to Josias Seaward. On north side Morumsco creek, possessed by Samuel Tomlinson	Annamessex 100

| ACRES | TRACT | SURVEY DATE-BY WHOM | LOCATION |

3000a. DOUBLE PURCHASE-19 Nov 1679, Randolph Revell, Annamessex 100
s/s Nanticoke, at a neck of land called
Orracoco. 2800 a. surv. 19 Nov 1679 adj.
Double Purchase. 5000 a. land surv. 17 Nov.
1679 by Randall Revell
Possessed by-
1160a. Randall Revell
250a. Thomas Mitchell
250a. Ann Colburn
500a. Stephen Horsey
500a. Nathaniel Horsey
300a. Mary King
1570a. Capt. John West
200a. William Foxon
125a. Andrew Thompson
75a. Abell Wright
340a. William Banaster
245a. James Furnace
240a. Stephen Horsey
45a. Abell Wright

100a. MARTINS HOPE, 16 Aug 1679- William Green, Annamessex 100
assigned Francis Martin, on south side Annam.
near Apes Hole. Held by William Brittingham
in Virginia, who married the widow of said
Francis Martin

50a. STERLING CHOICE, 17 Jul 1679-John White, Annamessex 100
assigned John Sterling, in Annamessex Neck.
Possessed by John Sterling son of John

50a. ADAMS GREEN, 24 Jun 1679, William Stevens, Annamessex 100
assigned Phillip Adams, on north side Morumsco
creek. Possessed by Thomas Adams

200a. THE EXCHANGE, 24 July 1679, William Stevens, Annamessex 100
assigned John Rockson, on south side of Annam.
possessed by John Roach Sr.

150a. MERCHANTS TREASURE, 9 June 1679, Stephen Coffin, Annamessex 100
assigned Daniel Donohoe, on N/S Pocomoke River
Possessed- 102a. John Outen
48a. Phillip Conner

150a. FIRST CHOICE, 17 June 1679-William Stevens, Annamessex 100
assigned to Robert Cattlin. on s/s Beaver Dam
at head of Annamessex River.
Possessed by William son and heir of Robert Catlin

50a. HEARTS CONTRACT-3 May 1677-William Stevens, Annamessex 100
assigned William Coleburn, on S/S Annamessex.
Belongs to Robert Coulburns orphan in Virginia

150a. DOUBLE PURCHASE, 10 Mar.1679-William Stevens-Annamessex 100
assigned WIlliam Planner, at head of RedCap Creek
possessed by William Planner son and heir

100a. HOLLWELL 13 March 1679-William Stevens, Annamessex 100
assigned Thomas Sewell on E/S main branch of
Annamessed. Possessed by Jeffrey Long in right
of his wife

ACRES	TRACT	SURVEY DATE-BY WHOM	LOCATION

200a. DICKENSONS FOLLY-21 April 1680 Wm.Stevens — Annamessex 100
assigned John Kirk, near Duffs Creek

300a. BRICKLEHOE 23 Aug.1679-John White, Annamessex 100
assigned John Carter, in Annemessex neck near
Watkins Point. Possessed by John Carter Jr.

100a. HOPEWELL 23 Aug 1679-John Garrott Annamessex 100
in Annemessex Neck between head of Hearts Creek
and head of Johnsons Creek.
Possessed by Thomas Davis

1400a. POMFRETT resurveyed 13 June 1679 Wm.Coleburn-Annemessex 100
a neck of land on the south side of Annamessex
near the mouth of Coleburns Creek. Possessed by,
  50a. Robert Coleburns orphans in Accocomack
  200a. William Coulbourn by Escheat
  66a. John Taylor
  50a. Mitshall Holland
  250a. Widow Ann Coleburn

400a. MITCHELLS LOTT- 1679 Col.Wm.Stevens Annamessex 100
assigned Randall Mitchell on west side Dams
at head of Morumsco Creek. Possessed by,
  150a. Richard Mitchell
  150a. John More
  100a. John White

250a. HALLS ADVENTURE-4 Feb 1679, Wm. Stevens Annamessex 100
assigned Charles Hall on north side Annamessex
Possessed by the widow Alice Hall

100a. HALLS HUMMOCK-22 Dec.1680-Charles Hall Annamessex 100
on north side of the Annamessex River
Possessed by the Widow Alice Hall

100a. LONGS LOTT 26 Apr 1680-Wm.Stevens Annamessex 100
assigned Samuel Long, on the west side Beaver
Dam branch at head of Morumsco.
Possessed by his son John Long

150a. HORSEYS DOWN 29 Apr 1680-Wm.Stevens Annamessex 100
assigned Stephen Horsey on north side Watkins Point
possessed by Anthony Bell 68a. by sale from Horsey
Stephen Horsey- 82a.

100a. BAY BUSH HALL 14 Mar 1680- William Stevens Annamessex 100
assigned John Hill, between Annamessex and
Pocomoke Bay. William Jenkins was possessed of
this land, who made it over to Amos Cook who
dying without heirs it escheats to the property

100a. HOGES HUMMOCK 14 Apr 1681-William Stevens Annamessex 100
assigned to Robert Duke on the north side
Pocomoke Bay in Annamessex Neck
Possessed by Robert Dukes son of Robert

150a. CHERRY HINTON,14 Mar 1680-William Stevens Annamessex 100
assigned Francis Martin, between Annamessex and
Pocomoke Bay.
Possessed by William Brittingham by marrying the
widow Martin

ACRES	TRACT	SURVEY DATE-BY WHOM	LOCATION
150a.	CABBIN SWAMP	19 Mar 1680-William Stevens assigned to John Roach, between the Annamessex and Pocomoke Bay. Possessed by same	Annamessex 100
200a.	BALD RIDGE	19 March 1680-William Stevens assigned John Roach, on south side Annamessex and south side of a great Savanna possessed by same.	Annamessex 100
150a.	WHITE OAK SWAMP	1 March 1680-William Stevens assigned Cornelius Ward, between Annamessex and Pocomoke Bay. Still possessed by Ward.	Annamessex 100
350a.	BEARDS NECK	19 Sep 1676- Assigned Robert Dukes, The same with Board Neck before	Annamessex 100
150a.	GALLOWAY	20 April 1680-John Kirk in Annamessex 100 neck on north side Pocomoke Bay Possessed by said Kirk	
250a.	LONGE HEDGE	25 Feb 1679-John Carter in Anamessex Neck on north side Pocomoke Bay Possessed by John Carter Jr.	Annamessex 100
150a.	RAGLAND	15 May 1683-William Scott possessed by same.	Annamessex 100
300a.	MACKEE MEADOW	11 Jun 1683-James Price possessed by Mary widow of said Price	Annamessex 100
100a.	THE AGREEMENT	6 June 1683-James Price Possessed by Mary widow of said Price	Annamessex 100
100a.	UNITY	23 May 1683-Samuel, Nathaniel and Jessee Horsey. Possessed by Samuel and Nathaniel Horsey	Annamessex 100
50a.	SCOTTS FOLLY	15 Mar.1683-William Scott Possessed by same	Annamessex 100
150a.	REST	7 June 1683-Joseph Gray who denys payment of rent professingit to be taken away by an older survey	Annamessex 100
200a.	FERRY BRIDGE	10 May 1685-Col. Wm. Coleburn possessed by Ann Coleburn relict and heir of Wm.	Annamessex 100
200a.	MUSKETTA HUMMUCK	26 Sept. 1683-Benjamin Summers, possessed by same	Annamessex 100
1100	HACKLAND	18 Oct 1662-John Vankack on south side Money Creek Possessed by Levin Denwood	Money 100
800a.	MANNINGS RESOLUTION	16 Oct.1662-Thomas Manning, in Money Creek. Possessed by, 150a. Samuel Covington 400a. Daniel Jones 250a. William Jones	Money 100
500a.	MITCHELLS CHOICE	2 March 1663-George Mitchell, on north side Little Money Creek. Possessed by, 250a. George Downs 250a. Thomas Dashiell	Money 100

ACRES	TRACT	SURVEY DATE-BY WHOM	LOCATION
300a.	BOSMANS CHOICE	2 Mar.1663-William Bozman on south side of Great Money Creek Possessed by Lazarus Maddox by the name of MOTHERS CARE	Monney 100
400a.	MARCOMBS LOTT	7 Mar 1663-John Marcomb in Little Money Creek Possessed by George Betts	Monney 100
300a.	SWEETWOOD	12 Feb.1663-John Elzey on the north side Money River possessed by Phillip Covington	Monney 100
300a.	COVINGTONS VINEYARD	1 Mar.1663-Nehemiah Covington, on the north side Great Money. Possessed by same.	Monney 100
300a.	CHANCE	1 March 1663-Stephen Horsey on the south side of a brach of Money Creek at a point dividing it from the land of William Jones. Possessed by the ??Duck, and George Downes	Monney 100
300a.	THE SUCESS	26 Feb.1663- Thomas Bloyd on the south side of Little Money Creek possessed by Bloice Wright, heir of Thomas Bloyd	Monney 100
50a.	THE WORST IS PAST	35 Oct.1666-James Nicholson, upon the ridge between Manokin and Little Money Possessed by James Langrell in behalf of orphans	Monney 100
300a.	WALLERS ADVENTURE	1 Nov 1666-John Waller on south side Little Money Possessed by William Waller son and heir.	Monney 100
100a.	BETTS PURCHASE	1 Jun 1666-George Betts on the north side Money, on west side of Cockrells Creek. Possessed by same	Monney100
100a.	IGNOBLE QUARTER	1 Nov 1666 George Andrews, on south side Little Money Possessed by John Panter	Monney 100
150a.	BLOYCES HOPE	1 Nov 1666-Thomas Bloyd east side of the backcreeek of Little Money Possessed by Bloyd Wright	Monney 100
300a.	CARYS ADVENTURE	20 Nov 1666 Thomas Cary at head of gr. Money on north side Main Branch Possessed by same	Monney 100
200a.	THE SECOND CHOICE	14 Feb.1666-Henry Hayman on the north most side of the head of gr.Money Possessed by Phillip Covington son and heir of John Covington who purchased of Hayman	Monney 100
150a.	DAM QUARTER	22 Feb 1666-William Stevens assigned to Thomas Ball on the south side of the point of Wiccomico River. Possessed by John White	Monney 100
200a.	PANTHERS DEN	11 Nov 1666-John Panther in Little Money, Possessed by same	Monney 100

| ACRES | TRACT | SURVEY DATE-BY WHOM | LOCATION |

250a. LUNN'S IMPROVEMENT-3 June 1667 Wm.Stevens   Money 100
       assigned Edward Lunn, called
       Island Quarter, being an island
       possessed- 200a. George Hutchins
                  50a. Mrs.Mary Woolford

300a. FRIENDS CHOICE-24 Feb 1666-Percival Reed,   Money 100
       assigned to Thomas Gerr Garrott,
       on the south part of Wicomico on Dam
       Quarter. It hath been escheated for
       John White and Richard Wallace

150a. GOLDEN QUARTER-1 July 1667, Thomas Ball   Money 100
       on southmost bounds of Wicomico at
       the mouth of the thoroughfare,
       Possessed by Ephraim Pollock who purchased
       from Col. James Allerton of Virginia in
       whom the right was assigned

100a. CARNYS ORDER-6 June 1667-Thomas Carny, marriner-Money 100
       in Great Money Creek near the land of Henry
       Hayman. I know not the land nor where it
       is supposed cut off by other surveys.

100a, DAVIDS DESTINY-21 May 1668-David Williamson,   Money 100
       upon an Island called Denis Quarter
       Possessed by widow Ann Roberts

200a. ELLIOTTS CHOICE-20 May 1668, Stephen Elliott,   Money 100
       on Dam Quarter near west side of Williamsons
       Creek, Possessed by widow Ann Roberts.

150a. LUNS ENCREASE-20 May 1668, Edward Lunn,   Money 100
       on Golden Quarter on north side of a
       gut thru thoroughfare possessed by Mrs.
       Mary Woolford

700a. JONES' CHOICE-resurveyed 20 Feb 1699, Wm.Jones,   Money 100
       between Gr.Money Creek and Little Money Creek
       Possessed by-350a. John Jones
                   175a. William Turpin
                   175a. Robert Jones

100a. CONTENTION 9 Feb 1762-John Ranshah(Renshaw)   Money 100
       at a corner of Thomas Boyces
       possessed by Joshua Austin

150a. WASHFORD   6 Feb.1672-Henry Hayman,   Money 100
       at head of main branch of Money Creek
       Possessed by-75a. John Webb
                   75a. Thomas Cary

50a. SHAPLEIGHS NEGLECT-1 May 1672-Henry Hayman   Money 100
       at head of Money Creek. I do not know who
       claims this land, nor the land

100a. WHITE OAK SWAMP-18(none) 1673- Richard Cary,   Money 100
       at head of main branch of Money Creek
       Possessed by Joy Hobbs whose father purchased
       from Cary.

100a. THE DOWNS-5 Sep 1675-Francis Roberts   Money 100
       on north side of Quarter near Manokin.
       Possessed by widow Ann Roberts.

ACRES	TRACT	SURVEY DATE-BY WHOM	LOCATION
50a.	HABNAB	2 Nov.1675- George Betts at head of Littley Money at head of land of John Markham. Possessed George Betts	Money 100
200a.	COX'S MISTAKE	27 Aug.1677- William Green, assigned Cornelius Johnson, on north side of Money River Hill. Possessed by William Jones	Money 100
100a.	WHITE MARSH	28 Feb 1674- Nehemiah Covington-assigned Thomas Covington, on north side Great Money, Land possessed by Nehemiah Covington. He denys the rent pretending it is included in older survey	Money 100
170a.	LOWER WOOD	28 Aug 1677- William Green, Assigned Richard Book, on north side Money River. Possessed by Phillip Covington	Money 100
50a.	STONIDGE	4 Apr.1680- Nicholas Smith, on south side Great Money Creek and included in later survey of 300a. by Levin Denwood, the farm not including any land in those lines made by a Special Warrent	Money 100
200a.	RAMSBURY	10 Nov.1679- Thomas Walker west side of Little Creek that leads to Money. Possessed by Thomas Shaw who purchased from Walkers heir.	Money 100
100a.	SAUCERS FOLLY	5 Jul.1679 -Benjamin Saucer, on south side of Money Creek.Possessed by same	Money 100
50a.	PENNY WISE	24 Jul 1679- Thomas Bloyd, on south side of Little Money Creek. In possession of Bloyd Wright heir of Thomas Bloyd	Money 100
100a.	ROBERTS LOTT	27 Aug 1679- Francis Roberts, assigned Charles Williams, at Dam Quarter Possessed by Charles Williams	Money 100
50a.	HANSLAP	28 June 1679- Gilbert James. assigned John Panther, on south side of Money Creek. Possessed by John Panther	Money 100
50a.	HAYMANS CHANCE	15 May 1680- Josias Swaward, assigned to Edward Hayman, near head of Great Money . Possessed by Joy Hobbs whose ancestors purchased from Hayman	Money 100
50a.	LITTLEWORTH	3 Aug 1681-Edward Williams, assigned to John Panther, on south side Money Bay. Possessed by John Panther	Money 100
140a.	MARLBOROUGH	22 Dec 1681-Samuel(no other name)- assigned Thomas Walter, on south side of Little Money Creek. Possessed by Thomas Shaw who purchased of Walter's heirs.	Money 100
50a.	JONES ADVENTURE	Dec. 1682. Assigned Samuel Jones, in possession of Samuel Jones	Money 100

| ACRES | TRACT | SURVEY DATE-BY WHOM | LOCATION |

1000a. NOBLE QUARTER -8 Sep.1663- John Taylor, Money 100
on north side of the Wicomico River
near land possessed by Capt.Nichols Evans.
It is in error, it is the tract below Capt.
Evans. Possessed 300a. There was a survey
by a special warrent for Thomas Shiles and
now in possession by his son Thomas. 550a.
for Nicholas Rice by the name of IGNOBLE
QUARTER possessed by Richard Crockett

1000a. RICE LAND-8 Sept.1663-Nicholas Rice. Money 100
on north most side of Wicomico River,
on east side Taylors Creek. Possessed
by Nicholas Evans to whom it descended
by the oath of his father John Evans who
was possessed with the right

1000a. DISPENCE 8 Dec 1663- David Spence, Wicomico 100
on south side of Wicomico River. Possessed by-
250a. James Spence son of David
250a. John Spence son of David
242a. Thomas Walker by the name of WOODBRIDGE
The remainder cut off by an older survey
after sold to Thomas Holbrook

250a. JONES HOLE-8 Sept.1663- James Jones, Wicomico 100
on north side Wicomico River. Possessed
by Capt.Nicholas Evans who bought of James
Jones heir. Possessed by Mary Day

550a. KELLUMS FOLLY-6 Jun 1665-John Ingram, Wicomico 100
on north side Wicomico Creek. Resurvey
8 Feb 1682 Thomas Pemberton for 900a.
Possessed by Richard Stevens who purchased
of Pemberton.

250a. ERLINDLEY 20 May 1663- John Elzey, Wicomico 100
on north west side Wicomico River. Possessed
by John Renshaw who purchased older rights
of C. Ballard.

300a. GINSON 9 Jun 1665- William Bosman Jr. Wicomico 100
on south side Wicomico River. Possessed
by Isaac Noble son and heir of Isaac Noble
who had the right.

300a. STEPHENS CONQUEST- 6 Jun 1665-Richard Stevens-Wicomico 100
on the north side Wicomico River, dividing
land of Robert Ingram. Possessed by Richard
Stevens.

300a. WHITTYS LATTER INVENTION-10Apr.1666-Richard Whitty-Wic. 100
north side Cuttamachico near land of Whittys.
Possessed by-100a. James Mackmorie
200a. John Winder

300a. WHITTYS INVENTION-7 April 1666, Richard Whitty-Wicomico 100
north side Cuttamachico nearland of George
Johnson. Possessed by James MacMorie who purchased
of Thomas Winder son and heir to John Winder
who had the rights.

| ACRES | TRACT | SURVEY DATE-BY WHOM | LOCATION |

300a. WHAT YOU PLEASE-1 Dec.1668-William Keen, Wicomico 100
    on north side Wicomico near the mouth
    of Michaels Branch. Possessed by-
    250a. Joseph Venables
    50a. John Gosslin

300a. MITCHELLS LOTT-4 Apr.1666-Alexander Mitchell-Wicomico 100
    assigned to William Elgate on north side
    of Cuttamachico. Possessed by-
    96a. Joseph Venables who purchased from William
    Lour?? who had Elgates right.

300a. HOPEWELL 1 July 1669-John Manlove. Wicomico 100
    assigned John Marrott in Cuttamachio River
    Possessed by Alexander Carlisle who purchased
    of Thomas Humprheys who had the right.

300a. SECOND PURCHASE- 19 Sep.1672-John Woolford- Wicomico 100
    on the south side of Wicomico. Possessed by-
    150a. Benjamin Wales
    150a. Robert Dashiell

300a. KEENS LOTT-19 Sep 1672-William Keen, Wicomico 100
    on the Wicomico River. Possessed by
    Thomas Humphreys

150a. GLOUCESTER-18 Nov. 1672-John Keen Wicomico 100
    at the head of Wicomico River. Possessed by-
    70a. John Smith
    50a. George Baily

250a. BENNETS ADVENTURE-7 Jun 1665-Richard Bennett Esq.Wicomico 100
    on north side Wicomico Creek at a point
    dividing it from Richard Stevens. Apportains
    to Col.Charles Scarboroughs children in Virginia

300a. WALLEYS CHANCE-9 Jul.1665-Thomas Walley- Wicomico 100
    at head of Wicomico Creek. Possessed by
    George Goddard

300a. TAUNTON DEAN-27 Jul.1666?-Capt.William Thorne-Wicomico 100
    on south side Wicomico Creek. Possessed by
    Benjamin Nesham who married Ben.Cottman's widw
    who was vested in the right and holds for orphans
    of Cottman

400a. THE HAZARD-2 Nov.1664-William Thomas Wicomico 100
    Two Islands with Wicomico marshes, possessed
    by Capt.Charles Ballard

100a. THE ADVENTURE-2 Nov 1664-William Thomas, Wicomico 100
    being the north point of Wicomico River.
    Possessed by Sumner Adams the right heir,
    Capt. John MacLoysters

300a. JOHNSONS LOTT-20 Oct 1664- George Johnson, Wicomico 100
    north side Wicomico Riber. Possessed by Robert
    Dashiell who married the coheir of Daniel Hast
    who had the right.

| ACRES | TRACT | survey date-by whom | LOCATION |

300a. KIKOTAN CHOICE-2 APR.1666- John Winder Wicomico 100
on north side Cuccmachico at an oak
dividing it from the land of Richard Whitty.
Possessed by John Winder son of John

500a. HORSEYS BAILYWICK-26 Mar.1664- Stephen Horsey-Wicomico 100
possessed by-
100a. Richard Phillips
150a. Phillip Askew
250a. purchased by Robert Ridgley and included
with offers of 200a. made by special
warrent for said Ridgley called BOLLAU?

300a. BARBERS REST-6 April 1666- Robert Hardy, Wicomico 100
on north side Cuttamachico next to land
of Daniel Hast. possessed by James Hardy his son.

300a. VULCANS VINEYARD-6 Apr.1666- Thomas Cottingham-Wicomico 100
on north side Cuttamachico at oak dividing
from land of Thomas Carey Jr. Possessed by
Richard Nicholson for many years, who purchased
from Cottingham

300a. AVERYS POLICY- 31 Mar.1666, John Avery, Wicomico 100
on north side Cuttamachico at an oak dividing
from land of Thomas Cottingham. The land
possessed including a resurvey of 480a. for
William Elgett by Special Warrent.

300a. DANIELLS ADVENTURE- 2 Apr.1666 Daniel Hast. Wicomico 100
on north side Cuttamcahico. It has been re-
named by the name of Daniells Down, now
belongs to Hulls orphans in Virginia

200a. HEMANS HILL-5 Apr.1666-Henry Heman, Wicomico 100
on north side Cuttamachico. This land not known

300a. CARNYS DELIGHT-6 Apr 1666. Thomas Carney Jr. Wicomico 100
on north side Cuttamachico near land of
Henry Haman.

250a. HIGH MEADOW-2 Dec 1672, Edward Surman. Wicomico 100
near head branch of Wicomico River
Possessed by Richard Chambers

200a. LONG ACRE 23 Oct. 1672-James Jones, Wicomico 100
north side Wicomico River
possessed by John Cauthray

600a. BELEAN 26 Nov 1675-Robert Ridgeley, Wicomico 100
at Wicomico River at mouth of Koons Branch
included in tract called BELEAN containing
1200a. mistake the land in possession of
George Hutchins. 500a. possessed Ephraim Wilson

50a. HOG QUARTER-24 Nov 1574-Thomas Shiles, Wicomico 100
north side Wicomico River. Possessed by
John Shiles son of Thomas

200a. CATTLE HAVEN-5 Apr 1673- Henry Haman, Wicomico 100
on south side Rokiawalkin River. Possessed
by Ed. Ruttledge in right of Passwaters orphan.

ACRES	TRACT	SURVEY DATE - BY WHOM	LOCATION
150a.	COXES CHOICE	20 Mar.1673 Thomas Cox, on the south side of the Wicomico River	Wicomico 100
250a.	SPENCE'S CHOICE	17 Mar.1673 David Spence apportioned to James Spence in North Carolina. No rent paid	Wicomico 100
250a.	SECOND PURCHASE	21 Mar.1673-Francis Roberts, On the south side Wicomico, belongs to the heirs of Edward Gibbs. In possession of John Green?, ordered for town land in Wicomico the said to be bought by Samuel Worthington	Wicomico 100
500a.	EVERSHAMP	16 Mar.1673- Thomas Hallbrook and John Holland, on the north side of Rockawalkin in possession of Thomas Walker but sold, not conveyed, to Alexander Adams	Wicomico 100
50a.	BARBERS ADDITION	17 Mar. 1673- Robert Harding, on the north side of Rockawalkin River possessed by James Harding son of Robert	Wicomico 100
450a.	HOGGS DOWN	10 July 1679- George Southern, on the south side of Cuttamachico possessed by Graves Jarrett who with his brother Richard, purchased of Southern by Richard. His death falls to Graves	Wicomico 100
150a.	HACHILAH	30 Sept.1674-William Elgate on the south side Cuttamachico. Possessed by same	Wicomico 100
300a.	COVINGTON CHOICE	28 Oct 1675. Thomas Covington, on the north side of main branch of Rockawalkin in possession of Samuel Covington	Wicomico 100
300a.	BERETONS CHANCE	10 Nov 1675-William Brereton, on the north side of Wicomico, possessed by William Brereton son of William	Wicomico 100
300a.	LITTLE MOSLEY(Marshley)	13 Sep.1678-Wm.Stevens, assigned to William Keen on the north side of Rockawalkin River. Possessed by-100a. Pascoe Bartlett 200a. Thomas Lucas, both marrying Keens daughters.	Wicomico 100
354a.	MUNSLEY	26 Jan.1694- William Elgate, on the north side Rockawalkin near Cottinghams creek	Wicomico 100
500a.	SUNKEN GROUND(The)	10 Apr.1677- James Jones on the north side Wicomico River. Possessed by Capt. Evans who bought of Howell Jones heir to James. The remainder by Mary Day who claims 350a. purchased from Howell Jones	Wicomico 100
300a.	SECOND CHOICE	23 Apr.1675-Samuel Smith near main branch of Wicomico River. Resurveyed and found that 377a. belongs to John Parsons	Wicomico 100
200a.	WHITE CHAPPEL	23 Oct 1676-William Stevens, assigned to Robert Crouch, near head of Wicomico River. Possessed by Robert Crouch	Wicomico 100

| ACRES | TRACT | SURVEY DATE-BY WHOM | LOCATION |

400a. MIGHT HAVE HAD MORE-10 Mar.1676, James Jones, Wicomico 100
on the north side Wicomico, on west side
of Taylors creek. Possessed-
200a. Richard Crockett
200a. Capt. Nicholas Evans for Williams orphan

550a. WILTON 23 Oct.1676-William Stevenes, Wicomico 100
assigned to James Cox, at head of Wicomico
River. Possessed by Thomas Cox

300a. MAIDENHEAD 24 Oct.1676-WIlliam Stevens Wicomico 100
assigned Daniel Clark. four miles west of
Wicomico River where it divides. Possessed
by John Caldwell

50a. HICKORY RIDGE-22 Sep.1676-William Stevens Wicomico 100
assigned to John Shiles, near the mouth of
the Wicomico River. Possessed by John Shiles

325a. ROBINSONS LOTT-28 June 1676-William Robinson, Wicomico 100
on the south side of Wicomico River near
the land of David Spence. Possessed by-
295.a. Benjamin Cottman for Robinsons heirs
30a. by John Hollands heirs

150a. NEWBURY 26 Nov 1676- William Stevens Wicomico 100
assigned Richard Kimball, on the south side
of the Wicomico River. Possessed by the widow
of Thomas Shurman who gave it to said by will.

1200a. LITTLE BELEAN-3 Jan 1677-Robert Ridgeley, Wicomico 100
on the south side of Rewastico. Possessed by-
525a. John Davis
400a. John Pearce
75a. Robert Grudman?

100a. WINTERBURN 4 Oct 1677- John White Wicomico 100
assigned Isaac Noble on the south side Wicomico,
given to Isaac Nobles,son and heir to Isaac

100a. COXES LOTT 6 Oct 1677- John White Wicomico 100
assigned to Thomas Cox, on south side Wicomico
River in possession of Patrick Conner who purchased
from Cox.

200a. SUFFOLK 10 Oct 1677-Thomas Walker Wicomico 100
on north side ROckawalkin River, in possession
of Walker but sold to Alexander Adams.

1450a. HIGH SUFFOLK-10 Oct. 1677, Thomas Walker, Wicomico 100
on north side Rockawalkin River. Possessed by
Adam Heath who purchased of Walker.

150a. TOCITTER 5 Oct 1677- John White, Wicomico 100
assigned to Daniel Hast, on north side Wicomico
River. Possessed by Benjamin Wales marrying one
of the coheirs of Hast.

100a. FORTUNE 19 Oct 1677-William Stevens Wicomico 100
assigned to Daniel Hast, on the north side of
Wicomico River, possessed by Benjamin Wales in
right of marrying one of the coheirs of Hast.

ACRES	TRACT	SURVEY DATE-BY WHOM	LOCATION
600a.	GODDARDS FOLLY	10 Oct.1677-John White- assigned Richard Stevens, on south side Wicomico River. Possessed by Stevens	Wicomico 100
150a.	BERKS	3 Oct.1677-John White, assigned to Benjamin Cottman, on east side of Stevens back Brook, possessed by Cottmans heirs or Benjamin Nesham in their right who married the widdow.	Wicomico 100
500a.	CHANCE	2 Oct 1677- John White assigned to Benjamin Cottman, on east side of Stevens Back Creek. 300a. possessed by John Booth 200a. belongs to William Rodolphus in Accocomac Va. Their guardian refuses payment of rent pretending the land was cut off by an older survey.	Wicomico 100
50a.	SIDNEY	5 July 1677- William Stevens, assigned to Thomas Roe, John Evans, Richard Crockett. on north side Wicomico, Possessed by Richard Crockett by surviorship	Wicomico 100
250a.	TROUBLE	13 Oct 1677- Thomas Strawbridge, near the head of the Wicomico River. Possessed by William Alexander Jr., a purchaser from Strawbridge	Wicomico 100
50a.	CANTERBURY	20 July 1677- John Parsons, assigned Alexander Mitchell, on the south side of the Wicomico River. Possessed by Isaac Noble by desent from his father.	Wicomico 100
44a.	ANGOLA	29 Aug.1677- William Green, assigned to John Johnson a negro. on the south side of the Wicomico River. No heir so land escheat to his Lordship	Wicomico 100
150a.	DAVENTRY	19 July 1677- John Parsons, on the south side of the head of Wicomico River. Possessed by John Parsons but since held by William Alexander Jr.	Wicomico 100
200a.	DOWGATE	17 July 1679- John Rixon, on the south side Rokawalkin River, possessed by David Shahee purchased from Rixon's heirs.	Wicomico 100
200a.	BETTYS CHOICE	29 Oct 1679-John Richardson, on the south side Rokawakin River. Possessed by John Wood who ran away or deserted the country and since dead. No heir appearing	Wicomico 100
25a.	BLACKMAIL	16 June 1679- William Elgate, on the north side Rokawalkin River. Possessed by Joseph Venables who purchased.	Wicomico 100
25a.	THE SUPPLY	25 June 1679- William Elgate on the south side Rokawalkin River. Possessed by Joseph Venables who purchased it.	Wicomico 100

ACRES	TRACT	SURVEY DATE-BY WHOM	LOCATION
200a.	HEREAFTER	1 Oct.1679- Thomas Roe assigned to John Spence and James Spence on the south side Wicomico River. Possessed 100a. John Spence, 100a. James Spence.	Wicomico 100
100a.	SARAHS NECK	18 April 1680-John Winder assigned to Phillip Carter, on the south side Rokiawalkin, possessed by David Shehee.	Wicomico 100
100a.	WRIGHTS CHOICE	19 July 1679- Thomas Bloyes, assigned to William Wright, near the mouth of the Wicomico River. Possessed by William Wright's relict.	Wicomico 100
50a.	EASON	20 July 1679- Thomas Bloyes, assigned to William Wright. Possessed by the widow of William.	Wicomico 100
50a.	VENTURE	20 July 1679- Thomas Bloyce. assigned to William Wright, on the south side of the Wicoomico River. Possessed by Widow of Wm.	Wicomico 100
110a.	DEPTFORD	10 Mar.1679- William Stevens Assigned to John Winder, on the west side of Rewastico, Possessed by John Winder son of John	Wicomico 100
40a.	LINCHOYLE	10 Mar.1679- William Stevens, assigned to John Winder, on the north side of Rewastico. Possessed by John Winder son of John	Wicomico 100
50a.	GREENWICH	4 Mar.1 679- William Stevens. assigned to Daniel Hast, on the north side of Rokawalkin on north side Jones Creek. Possessed by Robert Dashiell one of the coheirs of Hast.	Wicomico 100
300a.	RUM RIDGE	1 Apr.1680- Thomas Walker, assigned to Thomas Cox. 2 miles from the fork of Rokawalkin. Belongs to Matthew Wallace who is now removed to Cecil County or thereabouts.	Wicomico 100
500a.	COLLINS ADVENTURE	19 Apr. 1680- Thomas Walker, assigned to George Collins, on the north side of the main branch of Rokawalkin. Possessed by Nehemiah Covington	Wicomico 100
250a.	TAMEROONS RIDGE	28 Jun.1679- Gilbert James, assigned to Phillip Ascue, in the woods at head of the Wicomico River. Possessed by Phillip Ascue son of Phillip	Wicomico 100
150a.	ACCUES CHOICE	7 Nov 1679 Edward Dickenson, assinged to Phillip Ascue on the north side of the main branch of Passandike Creek. Possessed by Phillip Ascue.	Wicomico 100
50a.	WOULD HAVE HAD MORE	29 Apr.1680-John Richardson, on the south side Rokawalkin. Possession and land unknown	Wicomico 100
50a.	GREENHILL	22 Apr. 1680- William Stevens, assigned to Thomas Humphreys on the north side of Rokawalkin. Possessed by Alexander Carlisle who purchased of Humphreys.	Wicomico 100

ACRES	TRACT	SURVEY DATE-BY WHOM	LOCATION
100a.	ELGATES LOTT	25 April 1680- William Stevens, assigned to William Elgate, on north side of Rokawalkin, possessed by William Elgate	Wicomico 100
50a.	COTTMANS POINT	29 Apr.1680, William Stevens, assigned to Benjamin Cottman, at the Wicomico River, possessed by Benjamin Nesham who married the widow Cottman.	Wicomico 100
25a.	MILE END	20 May 1680, William Stevens, assigned to William Brereton, in fork at head of the Wicomico River. Apportains to said William Brereton who is in Virginia at present.	Wicomico 100
250a.	WHETTSTONE	19 Mar.1680- William Stevens, Assigned to Phillip Carter, on the north side Rokawalkin on north side of Cottinghams branch possessed by Phillip Carter.	Wicomico 100
50a.	TROY	21 Mar.1680- William Stevens, assigned to John Evans, on the north side of Wicomico, possessed by Capt. Nicholas Evans son and heir to John Evans.	Wicomico 100
200a.	HARRINGTON	16 Mar 1680- William Stevens, assigned to Thomas Collbrook, in fork of Dashiells Creek, Possessed by same.	Wicomico 100
350a.	CRAMBURN	2 Apr. 1680-William Stevens, assigned to George Goddard, on the south side of the Wicomico. 100a. belongs to Peter Surman 250a. possessed by George Goddard	Wicomico 100
150a.	SUFFOLK NECK	5 Apr.1681, William Stevens assigned to John Covington, on the north side of Money River, the land is called Sassafras Neck and is in possession of Phillip Covington to whom it doth belong	Wicomico 100
100a.	WHITTYS CONTRIVANCE	16 Mar.1680, William Stevens, Assigned to Thomas Sheills, Possessed by- 86a. Thomas Dashiell 14a. John Shiells.	Wicomico 100
100a.	HUNTING QUARTER	17 Mar.1680, William Stevens, assigned to Cornelius Anderson, between the head of Wicomico and Manokin. Possessed by William Alexander or son.	Wicomico 100
150a.	GUERNSEY	1 Mar.1681- William Stevens, Assigned to Nicholas Toadvine between the head of Wicomico and Rokawalkin. Possesssed by same.	Wicomico 100
300a.	CAMP	10 Apr.1680- for Col.Stevens, at head- of Rokawalkin. Possessed by- 150a. Richard Wallace 150a. James Smith	Wicomico 100
850a.	STAINS	10 Apr.1680-Col.William Stevens, 4 miles from fork of Rokawalkin, Possessed by Samuel Layfield heir to George Layfield who bought the right.	Wicomico 100

| ACRES | TRACT | SURVEY DATE-BY WHOM | LOCATION |

50a. MIGHT A HAD MORE-9 Jan 1679- John King   Wicomico 100
　　　　Assigned Daniel Hast, at head of Jones Creek.
　　　　Possessed by Benjamin Wales in right of his
　　　　wife, daughter and coheir of Daniel Hast.

400a. MIDDLE NECK-10 April.1680, Col. William Stevens, Wicomico 100
　　　　Assigned to Thomas and Susanna Walker, near head
　　　　of Rokawalkin, Possessed by Thomas Walker and
　　　　Capt. Nicholas Evans who married Susanna

1100a. CASTOWAY   2 Apr.1680- William Stevens,   Wicomico 100
　　　　Assigned to Thomas and Susanna Walker, hear headof
　　　　Rokawalkin. Possessed by Thomas Walker and Capt.
　　　　Nicholas Evans who married Susanna.

700a. WHITFIELD 2 Apr.1680, William Stevens,   Wicomico 100
　　　　Assigned to Thomas and Susanna Walker, near the head
　　　　of Meadow Branch. Possessed by Thomas Walker and
　　　　Nicholas Evans who married Susanna

100a. THE ADDITION-6 Apr.1680- Richard Keen,   Wicomico 100
　　　　Assigned to Thomas Walker and by him assigned to
　　　　his son Thomas, on south side Wicomico River.

200a. COCKMORE   30 May 1681- Richard Chambers,   Wicomico 100
　　　　on the south side Wicomico. Possessed by same.

700a. PEMBERTONS GOOD WILL-3 Sep.1682-John Winder,   Wicomico 100
　　　　In the fork at head of Rokawalkin.
　　　　700a. belongs to William Winder in Virginia
　　　　350a. possessed by John Winder

200a. ANDERSONS INVENTION-3 Sep.1682-Cornelius Anderson, Wicomico 100
　　　　He deserted this county long since and it was
　　　　assigned to Daniel Hast, Now possessed by
　　　　Benjamin Wales and Robert Dashiell, each 100a.

50a. BILBOA   21 Sep.1682- Cornelius Anderson,   Wicomico 100
　　　　He deserted thecounty. Land not known

350a. WOODFIELD-2 Apr.1682, Thoms and Susanna Walker-Wicomico 100
　　　　Possessed by Walker but said to be sold to
　　　　Alexander Adams but not conveyed.

1000a. SAMUELLS ADVENTURE-7 Jan 1665-Col.Samuel Smith, Wicomico 100
　　　　in Virginia. Above Wicomico Bridge. Possessed-
　　　　367a. Ann Brereton
　　　　133a. not found when come to be divided
　　　　50a. Peter Presley possessed by Jonathan Raymond

1000a. THE LOTT   Nov.1664, William Thomas,   Wicomico 100
　　　　on east side of Wicomico River. Possessed by-
　　　　892a. William Harris son and heir of William.
　　　　108a. belongs to Thomas Dashiell

300a. TONYS VINEYARD-10 Oct.1665, Stephen Horsey,   Wicomico 100
　　　　on south side Wicomico Creek. All now possessed in
　　　　right of John Orhines widow for the orphan.

300a. FRIENDS CHOICE-6 Feb.1672-William Layton,   Wicomico 100
　　　　on the north side Rokawalkin River.
　　　　Possessed by Thomas Ralph who purchased of Layton

ACRES	TRACT	SURVEY DATE-BY WHOM	LOCATION
50a.	CARYS ADVANCE	-no date, Edward Cary, Possessed by Richard Cary.	Wicomico 100
50a.	WHITE CHAPPELL GREEN	-no date-Assigned to Adrain Gordon, Possessed by Robert Crouch Sr.	Wicomico 100
50a.	ISLAND MARSH	-9 Feb 1682-William Brereton Possessed by William Brereton son and heir to Wm.	Wicomico 100
200a.	COXS CHOICE	-16 May 1683- Anthony Underwood, Capt.Henry Smith the last possessed who died and land not known.	Wicomico 100
100a.	CHEVELEY	12 Jun 1682-Assigned William Keen, Possessed by Pascoe Bartlett, given him in consideration of his daughters marriage	Wicomico 100
200a.	THE FATHERS CARE	-3 July1683,Assigned to Thomas and Susannah Walker. Possessed by Thomas Walker and Capt. Nicholas Evans who married Sussanah	Wicomico 100
300a.	HOGGNECK	1 Oct 1683-Assigned Francis Jenkins, Possessed by John Croutch. Purchased of Jenkins but not conveyed.	Wicomico 100
150a.	HOGGSDOWN,	10 July 1682-Richard Stevens. Possessed by Madam Mary King.	Wicomico 100
50a.	FOXSTALL	-4Oct 1682. Assigned to John Evans, Possessed by Capt.Nicholas Evans	Wicomico 100
350a.	RHOODY	1 Feb 1682, Assigned John Singleton, Possessed by Robert Dashiell by Marrying Daniel Hast's daughter who was entitled to the land.	Wicomico 100
500a.	SUMMERFIELD,	no date. Thomas Pemberton, Assigned by John Roach Jr. who purchased it.	Wicomico 100
900a.	PEMBERTON	-29 Sept.1680 assigned none Possessed by Wm. Whittingham	Pemberton-Wicomico 100
750a.	THE SUPPLY	5 July 1683-Isaac Foxcroft. belongs to the widow of Sampson Waters in New England but left to management of James Dashiell	Wicmico 100
100a.	MONSHAM	3 Jul.1683-assigned John Christopher, Possessed by John Christoper	Wicomico 100
350a.	HERMON	8 Feb 1682-John Parker, possessed by John Booth	Wicomico 100
100a.	SALLOP	no date. Surv. John Davis Davis long since dead. John Squires last possessed. is said to deserted this county.	Wicomico 100
50a.	BATTLEFIELD	-8 Feb.(none) assigned John Davis,	Wicomico 100
150a.	BEDLAM GREEN,	5 Oct 1683-assigned Robert Croutch. In Possession of Robert Croutch Sr.	Wicomico 100
550.a.	COLEBROOK	20 Oct.1662, William Cole, on east shore in Manokin River. Possessed by William Turpin in right of George Jone's orphans, who married Richard Whitteys heir to whom it belongs.	Wicomico 100

ACRES	TRACT	SURVEY DATE-BY WHOM	LOCATION

600a. THORNTON 2 Nov.1662- William Thorn   Wicomico 100
               In Manokin River. Possessed by
               Alexander Brown

300a. BROWNSTONE 6 Mar.1666-John Westlock,   Wicomico 100
               On thenorth branch of the Manokin River.
               Possessed by Arthur Denwood

1200a. MORE AND CASE IT-11 Nov 1662-William Bozman, Wicomico 100
               On the north side of Manokin River, East side
               of Goose Creek. Possessed by-
               600a. John Boseman
               600a. Luke Valentine

200a. BARNABYS LOTT-12 Mar.1663-James Barnaby   Wicomico 100
               on the south side Back Creek on Manokin River
               Possessed by-146a. John Henderson
                          54a. James Willin

300a. OWENS CHOICE-9 Mar.1663- Owen Magrah   Manokin 100
               On the Manokin River. Possessed by the
               widow Mary Magraugh

300a. FOUNTAINS LOTT-12 Mar.1663-Nicholas Fountain, Manokin 100
               Possessed by Nicholas Fountain

300a. DIEP (Deep) 8 Mar,1663- John Shipway.   Manokin 100
               At the head of Manokin, Possessed by-
               150a. Henry Dorman
               150a. John Lokey

600a. DAVIES CHOICE-14 Mar 1663, James Davis, Manokin 100
               Between 2 branchs of upper fork of Manokin River
               150a. belongs to C.Mary Smith who died. Paid
                     since 1685
               330a. John Fisher
               120a. Ephraim Wilson and Peter Dent

300a. CANES CHOICE-18 Mar 1683-James Cane,   Manokin 100
               on the north side of Manokin. Possessed by
               Lazarus Mattux

300a. NELSONS CHOICE-22 Mar.1663-John Nelson, Manokin 100
               On the Manokin River, Possessed by
               Matthew Dorman

600a. BERRERS LOTT-13 Mar.1663, Phillip Berrer, Manokin 100
               On the south side Back Creek in Manokin River.
               Possessed by William Davis

300a. FURNIS'S CHOICE-12 Mar.1663, Wm. Furniss Manokin 100
               On the south side of Back Creek of Manokin River
               Possessed by James Furniss son and heir to James.

200a. ELLARDS CHOICE-14 Mar.1663 Stephen Ellard Manokin 100
               On Manokin River, Possessed by Matthew Dorman

500a. GLANVILLS LOTT-11 Mar.1663, William Glanvill, Manokin 100
               On the south side Manokin River. Possessed of
               Peter Dent in the Right of C.Kings. orphan.

300a. DAVIES CONQUEST-14 Mar.1663, WIlliam Davis, Manokin 100
               On the south side of back of Manokin.
               Possessed by Ephraim Wilson

| ACRES | TRACT | SURVEY DATE-BY WHOM | LOCATION |

400a. ST.PETERS NECK-2 May 1663, Peter Elzey, Manokin 100
On westmost side Manokin, on west side Cockrells
Creek, resurveyed lines for 750a. and still in
possession of Peter Elzey

1000a. ALMADOINGTON-10.Nov.1663-John Elzey, Manokin 100
The petition in name of Arnold and John Elzey.
Possessed by Capt. Arnold Elzey

210a. THE FIRST CHOICE-23 Sep.1663, Richard Acworth, Manokin 100
On the north side Manokin River. Possessed of
Arthur Denwood purchased of Acworths heir.

300a. SOUTH BETHERTON-15 Sep.1665, William Thorn, Manokin 100
On the north side Manokin River at oak dividing
from the land of Christopher Nutter. Possessed
by John Brown given by Thomas Widow who had the
right

150a. NUTTERS DELIGHT-23 Sep.1665, Christopher Nutter, Manokin 100
On the north side Manokin River. In possession
of Arthur Denwood

200a. WINDERS PURCHASE, 1 Apr. 1666, John Winder, Manokin 100
On back Creek of Manokin River. Possessed by
Marcy Fountain by deed from Nicholas Fountain
who purchased of Winder

150a. KILMANAN-18 Oct 1665, Christopher Nutter, Manokin 100
At the head of a branch of Manokin River.
Possessed by John Gray

150a. NICHOLSONS ADVENTURE, 23 Oct 1666, James Nicholson, Manokin 100
At the head of St.Peters Creek near land of Peter
Elzey. Possessed by George Febus

300a. OXHEAD, 1 Oct 1666, James Price, Manokin 100
At head of Kings Creek near the land of William
Glanville, Possessed by Peter Dent

300a. CARNYS CHANCE-14 Feb 1666, Thoms Carney, Manokin 100
By a branch at the southwest end of a ridge between
the Manokin River and Gr. Money. Possessed by
Joy Hobbs by the name of Carlisle

300a. NUTTERS PURCHASE-6 Mar 1666, Christopher Nutter, Manokin 100
On the north side of head of Manokin River.
Possessed by Capt. Charles Ballard

300a. POOLLS HOPE-15 Apr. 1667, Thomas Pooll Manokin 100
At head of back creek of the Manokin River. Possessed,
100a. James Furniss
200a. Gideon Tilman

150a. GOLDEN QUARTER, 25 Apr.1667, John Smith, Manokin 100
At the head of Manokin River. Possessed by
WIlliam Pollock

300a. WOOLFORDS CHANCE-22 Nov.1667, Roger Woolford, Manokin 100
In Manokin River at head of Goose Creek, Possessed
by Mrs. Mary Woolford relict of Roger.

250a. MANLOVES DISCOVERY, 20 Jun.1668, Thomas Manlove, Manokin 100
At head of Manokin River. Possessed by Samuel Worthington

ACRES	TRACT	SURVEY DATE-BY WHOM	LOCATION
100a.	SMALL HOPES,	28 no date. William Stevens, Assigned William Thorns. Possessed and rent paid by Gideon Tilghman	Manokin 100
150a.	NEW RANNEY	10 Aug.1669, John Winder, Between Manokin and Annamessex. Possessed by Nicholas Fountain	Manokin 100
150a.	OWEN IMPROVEMENT,	24 Apr. 1667, Owen Magraugh, On Manokin River. Possessed by Mary relict of Owen Magraugh.	Manokin 100
50a.	NORMANDY	Nov.1670- Nicholas Fountain, Possessed by Nicholas Fountain	Manokin 100
50a.	THORNS INTENTION-	8 May 1671, David Brown, Possessed by Alexander Brown	Manokin 100
50a.	JESHIMON,	6 Dec.1662, David Brown, On the north side of Manokin. Possessed by Alexander Brown	Manokin 100
100a.	MANLOVES VENTURE,	19 Nov 1692, Richard Ackworth, Assigned and pattented to John Manlove. Possessed by Richard Chambers.	Manokin 100
200a.	ELLIOTTS IMPROVEMENT,	9 Mary 1673, Thomas Manlove, Near the Nanticoke River. Possessed by Matthew Dorman	Manokin 100
1100a.	BRIDGES LOTT-	resurveyed 1673, Joseph Bridges, On the south side Manokin. Possessed by Robert Catherwood in right of Thomas Jones' orphans	Manokin 100
900a.	AMITY	13 Oct.1673, Alexander Draper, On the south side Manokin near head of Trading Branch. Possessed by- 200a. William Turpin 700a. James Furniss	Manokin 100
300a.	GRAVES END	22 Nov 1673, Thomas Shollites, Near the mouth of Manokin, Possessed by Francis Gradie? in right of Thomas Roe's orphans	Manokin 100
300a.	FRIENDS CHOICE,	14 Oct none. Thomas Jones On the south side Manokin River in Indian Neck, North side of Trading Branch. Possessed by 150a. John Polk 150a. Thomas Everton	Manokin 100
90a.	CHANCE	16 Feb.1673, Henry Smith, On the south side Manokin River. North side of Trading Branch. Know not the right of possession of this land unless John King is intermarrying with Ursula Whittington	Manokin 100
160a.	GULLITS ADVISEMENT-	14 Jan.1673, John Brown, On the south side of Manokin River. Possessed 50a. John Brown 50a. Peter Dent in right of Thomas Wilsons orphans 50a. Ephraim Wilson	Manokin 100

ACRES	TRACT	SURVEY DATE-BY WHOM	LOCATION
100a.	KINGS CHANCE	16 Feb 1673, John King, Possessed by Dennem O'Lannum	Manokin 100
100a.	CONTENTION	5 Feb.1674, John Bosman, Assigned Lazarus Mattux, near south bounds of James Cane, Possessed by Lazarus Mattux	Manokin 100
300a.	THE NORTH FORELAND	28 Apr.1675, Thomas Walker, Assigned Thomas Roe on Devills Island. Possessed by John Laws in right of his brother George Laws	Manokin 100
50a.	SOUTHFORELAND	28 Apr.1675, Thomas Walker Assigned Thomas Roe, a small Island at mouth of the Manokin River. Possessed by Graves Jarrett	Manokin 100
100a.	DESERT	April 1675, David Brown, At head of Manokin River. Possessed by Alexander Brown	Manokin 100
100a.	OWENS DELIGHT	8 Sept.1675, Owen Magraugh, At the head of Manokin River. Possessed by Mary relict of Owen Magraugh	Manokin 100
150a.	WOOLWICK	28 Feb.1677, William Stevens, Assigned Henry Leaton, on Devills Island. Possessed by John Windsor	Manokin 100
36.a	CROSS	29 Aug.1677- William Green, Assigned Thomas Row, on the southmost part of Devills Island. Possessed by Francis Gradon in right of Thomas Row's orphan	Manokin 100
50a.	SPRINGHEAD	Feb.1677, WIlliam Stevens, Assigned Thomas Row, between upper and middle streights near Hollands Island, Possessed by Francis Gradon in right of Row's orphan	Manokin 100
50a.	GREENWICH	28 Feb 1677, WIlliam Stevens, assigned John Laws, on Devills Island, in Possession of Thomas Laws	Manokin 100
70a.	POYK	9 July 1679, Henry Smith On the south side Back Creek in Manokin. Possessed, 10a. Nicholas Fountain 60a. Michael Gray	Manokin 100
250a.	WEBLEY	resurveyed Dec.1679, Henry Smith, Assigned Andrew Whittington, part of Thomasons Purchase and Naswaeton, on south side Manokin River. Possessed by John King	Manokin 100
100a.	WANSBOROUGH	20 Nov.1679, Thomas Manlove near the head of the Manokin River. Possessed by Madam Mary King	Manokin 100
50a.	HOCKLEY	20 Nov.1678, Thomas Manlove Near the head of Kings Branch. Possessed by Richard Plunkett	Manokin 100
150a.	WEATHERLYS CHANCE	16 Dec.1679, James Weatherly, Possessed by Arthur Denwood	Manokin 100
150a.	MATTUX ADVENTURE	20 Aug 1679, John White, Assigned Alexander Mattux, on south side of Manokin at head of Keens Creek. Possessed by Lazarus Mattux.	Manokin 100

ACRES	TRACT	SURVEY DATE-BY WHOM	LOCATION
50a.	TROUBLE	20 Aug 1679, John White assigned to Henry Miles, on east side of Possessed by heir, belongs to Alice Miles	Manokin 100
125a.	CONEY WARREN,	29 Oct 1674, John King, on the south side Manokin River. Possessed by John King	Manokin 100
125a.	TURKEY COCK HILL,	29 Oct 1679, John King, Assigned to John Bounds, at head of King's Creek Possessed by William Duncan	Manokin 100
300a.	THE FAIR SPRING,	4 Feb.1679, William Stevens, Assigned to William Furniss, on south side Back Creek. Possessed by James Furniss	Manokin 100
100a.	NOVA FRANCIA,	25 Aug.1679, John White, Assigned to Nicholas Fountain on south side Back Creek, in possession of Nicholas Fountain.	Manokin 100
100a.	DAVISE CHOICE,	25 Aug 1679, John White, Assigned to Richard Davis on the south side Back Creek. Possessed by Ephraim Wilson	Manokin 100
none	NORWICH	10 Apr.1681, Thomas Shank Between the branch of Manokin and Wicomico. The said Shank dead without ehirs, the land Escheatable	Manokin 100
50a.	DOUBLE PURCHASE,	20 Oct 1680, Nicholas Fountain, On the south side Nanticoke River. Possessed same.	Manokin 100
20a.	NEWFOUNDLAND,	30 Oct 1680, Nicholas Fountain, On south side Nanticoke River, Possessed by same.	Manokin 100
700a.	WOOLFORDS LAND,	11 Nov 1672, Roger Woolford, Possessed by Mary Woolford relic of Roger.	Manokin 100
70a.	MAIDENSTONE,	28 Apr.1680, WIlliam Stevens, Assigned to Elizabeth Davies, on south side Back Creek. Possessed by Ephraim Wilson	Manokin 100
250a.	SHIPWAYS CHOICE,	25 Apr.1680, William Stevens, Assigned to John Shipway, in fork of Manokin above the Wading Place, Possessed by Henry Dorman	Manokin 100
100a.	MATTUX INCLOSURE,	24 May 1680, William Stevens, Assigned Lazarus Mattux, on south side Back Creek. Posssessed by Lazarus Mattux	Manokin 100
250a.	TOTNESS	21 Mar.1680, William Stevens, Assigned to William Turpin, on south side Back Creek Possessed by John Turpin	Manokin 100
100a.	VULCANS FORGE-	16 Mar.1680, William Stevens, Assigned Richard Chambers, on south side Smiths Branch. Possessed by Richard Chambers	Manokin 100
100a.	ROWLEY RIDGE,	16 Mar 1680, William Stevens, Assigned Richard Chambers, on north side Smiths Branch in Indian Neck. Possessed by Richard Chambers	Manokin 100
150a.	WOODLAND,	21 Mar.1680, William Stevens, Assigned Andrew Whittington, on north side Kings Branch in Manokin. Possessed by Robert Dent in right of Thomas Wilsons orphans.	Manokin 100

| ACRES | TRACT | SURVEY DATE-BY WHOM | LOCATION |

500a. BECKFORD 24 Nov.1679, Col.William Stevens Manokin 100
Assigned Edmond Howard, at the Wadding Place
near the head of the Manokin. Possessed by
Peter Dent.

50a. LONGVILE 28 Sept. 1681, John Johnson, Manokin 100
Assigned James Johnson, at head of Shipways
Branch. I know no such person but said to be
long since dead.

50a. CORPORALLS RIDGE, 3 Aug 1687, Charles Jones, Manokin 100
Assigned Henry Smith, on south side Manokin
Possessed by William Smith

50a. DEMINICE 7 Oct.1687, Matthew Scarborough, Manokin 100
Assigned Danain O'Lannum, on south side Kings Branch
onthe south side Manokin, Possessed by same.

100a. RICHINS ADDITION, 3 May 1682, John White, Manokin 100
Assigned John Richins, on the south side Manokin
Possessed by MadDanoll Polk

100a. WOOLVER 3 Oct 1681, Nathaniel Daugherty, Manokin 100
Assigned Andrew Whittington, near head of Kings
Branch. Belongs to William Fassick and John King

150a. DORMANS PURCHASE, 29 Nov 1682, Phillip Carter, Manokin 100
Assigned Matthew Dorman on north side of head of
Manokin, Possesssed by Matthew Dorman

50a. FLINT 29 Jul.1679, WIlliam Stevens Manokin 100
Assigned Edward Jones, on south side Back Creek
Possessed by Miles Gray

900a. ILLCHESTER, 25 May 1683, Capt. Henry Smith, Manokin 100
Possessed by-150a. John King
100a. Margaret Goldsmith
75.a William Knox,theother part being 75a.total 150a
500a. James Strawbridge.

100a. SMITHS HOPE, 25 May 1683, Capt. Henry Smith, Manokin 100
Possessed by Henry Phillips

350a. SMITHS RESOLVES, 29 May 1683, Assigned Henry Smith Manokin 100
Possessed, 250a. William Pollock
100a. William Smith

250a. WHITE OAK- 30 July 1683, Henry Miles Manokin 100
In Annamessex and Manokin Neck. Possessed by
Samuel Miles his son.

100a. GULLETTS ASSURANCE, date unknown. Assigned to, Manokin 100
William Gullott. In Possession of Wm. his son

50a. SALLKIRK 1 June 1683, Assigned James English, Manokin 100
Possessed by John Ervin

150a. PARTNERS CHOICE-8 July 1682, Assigned Arnold Elzey,Manokin 100
Possessed by Robert Horsey

150a. COME BY CHANCE-14 June 1682,Assigned Christopher Nugent.
Possessed by widow Margaret. Manokin 100

100a. KINGS CHANCE-4 Jun.1683, Assigned John King, Manokin 100
Possessed by Upshur King

ACRES	TRACT	SURVEY DATE-BY WHOM	LOCATION
100a.	MIDDLE	16 May 1683- assigned Owen Mongraugh-Manokin 100 Possessed by Mary Macgraugh	
100a.	CROLLERS	FOLLY-No date. John Croller- Manokin 100 Land escheatble and entered by Robert Wilson for whom it is reserved	
100a.	FLANFREE	POINT-2 July 1683-Thomas Highway, Manokin 100 on north side of Manokin. Possessed by Highway	
125a.	DULBIN	4 June 1683-assigned Denum Olannum Manokin 100 Possessed by Denum Olannum	
200a.	HOGG	RIDGE-5 May 1683, assigned Thomas Manlove, Manokin 100 In possession of Mrs. Mary King	
20a.	FISHING	ISLAND-no date. Surveyed by George Lane-Manokin 100 the mouth of Manokin River. Possessed by Dennis Lane widow of said George.	
200a.	COLRANE	2 Feb. 1682, assigned James Conner, Manokin 100 Knows not this land nor rent paid. Conner pretends the right not in him.	
120a.	TURKEY	COCK HILL-29 Sep.1683, Edward Tedbury, Manokin 100 No rent paid. The person dead and know no heir.	
50a.	CANDEE	ISLAND-5 Jul.1683, assigned John King, Manokin 100 Possessed by Benjamin King.	
150a.	HARTHBERRY-29 May 1683-assigned Capt.Henry Smith, Manokin 100 In possession of William Polk, vide William Smiths accounts.		
100a.	HEATH	QUARTER-28 May 1683-assigned Abraham Heath, Manokin 100 Possessed by William Heath, vide, Anthony Goldsmith account	
300a.	HOPEWELL-15 Nov 1683-assigned William Berry, Manokin 100 Possessed by James Berry		
200a.	ST.GILES	12 June 1683-Assigned George Betts, Manokin 100 Possessed by George Betts	
150a.	DURHAM	2 July 1663- John Mears, Manokin 100 No rent paid. Know not the land	
50a.	GULLETTS	HOPE-no date-Assigned Wm. Gullett, Manokin 100 Does not hold any such land or know of it.	
50a.	CHANCE	1 Oct.1683- Assigned Peter Elzey Manokin 100 Possessed by Peter Elzey	
100a.	KENDALL	21 July 1683-apportained to Bonnard Ward, Manokin 100 who is dead and no heirs in county, nor none in Possession of the land.	
50a.	FLODDERS	2 July 1683-possessed by Arthur Smith, Manokin 100	
250a.	WASSAWOMACK-March 1663, Surveyed by Henry Elliott, Manokin 100 on s/s Pocomoke R. Know not such land nor possessed by Col.Jenkins. Return not to be found		
300a.	OWEN	GLANDORE-1 Mar.1663- Garman Gillott, Manokin 100 on s/s Pocomoke River. Garman Gillett in his life is included in a survey for John Waghab of 800a. called Piney Point.	

ACRES	TRACT	SURVEY DATE-BY WHOM	LOCATION

700a. BLAKES HOPE-9 Mar 1663, Joel Blake, Pocomoke 100
on the west side of Pocomoke, Possessed by-
233 1/3a. by Edward Stevens
233 1/3a. by William Stevens
233 1/3a. by John Stevens and his mother

250a. ARRACOCO 9 Mar.1663, William Price, Pocomoke 100
on the east side Pocomoke River. Possessed by
William Morrill

400a. PRICES GROVE-10 Mar 1663-William Price, Pocomoke 100
on west side Pocomoke River. Possessed by
Ralph Milburn.

800a. PINEY POINT, 13 Mar.1663, John Waughop, Pocomoke 100
on the south side Pocomoke River, Belongs to
John Waughops orphan in St. Mary's County

100a. COBHAM 13 Mar.1663, James Jolly, Pocomoke 100.
No such land to be found nor in former survey

350a. EDWIN 3 June 1664- William Edwin, Pocomoke 100
In Pocomoke River by Morumsco Creek. Possessed
by William Matthews.

150a. ELGATE 3 June 1664-William Elgate, Pocomoke 100
on north side Pocomoke River. Possessed by
John Ellis

200a. LAURENCES- June 1664- John Laurence, Pocomoke 100
on north side Pocomoke River. No such land is
found.

700a. GOLDEN LYON, March 1663-Thomas Harwood, Pocomoke 100
on east side Morumsco Creek by Pocomoke River
Possessed-200a. Teague Riggen Jr.
100a. John Riggen
100a. John Andrews
300a. Teague Riggin Sr.

1000a. WILLIAMS HOPE,13 Mar.1663, William Smith, Pocomoke 100
on the west side Pocomoke River. Capt. Smith
claimed this alnd but lay in dispute with
several others.

150a. STEVENSON,16 Nov 1664- Christopher Stevenson,Pocomoke 100
Assigned and patented for William Smith, on
the south side Pocomoke River. Know not the land
nor who possessed

300a. THE LANUM DEVORY-18 Nov 1664-Richard Gaines, Pocomoke 100
patented in the name of Mary Gaines, his relict
in Pocomoke. Know not such land

1000a. SMITHS FOLLY-13 Mar.1663-William Smith, Pocomoke 100
on west side Pocomoke. Possessed by-
700a. Donnock Dennis Sr.
300a. John Dennis

200a. ACQUINTICA-26 Aug 1665-George Wall, Pocomoke 100
on south side Pocomoke River. Possessed by
William Powell.

| ACRES | TRACT | SURVEY DATE-BY WHOM | LOCATION |

150a. ACCOMPSON-28 Aug.1665- Robert Jones,   Pocomoke 100
on south side Pocomoke River. No such land
now nor in former surveys.

300a. PIMMO   20 Jan 1665- Mark Manlove   Pocomoke 100
on the north side Pocomoke River. Possessed by
70a. Peirce Bray
200a. Thomas Jones' orphans
30a. John Wallburn an inhabitant in Pennsylvania

300a. THE KINGS NECK-20 Nov.1665- Jenkins Price.   Pocomoke 100
on north side Pocomoke River near land of
Nicholas Guythor. Possessed by Samuel Collins

150a. SEAMANS CHOICE-4 July 1665-Thomas Ball,   Pocomoke 100
assigned and patented by John Hyland. on south
side Morumsco Creek. Possessed by Teague Riggin Sr.
who refuses payment pretending it was cut by a
former survey

1000a. REHOBETH   18 July 1665- William Stevens,   Pocomoke 100
by the Pocomoke River in Pungahoy Creek.
Possessed-600a. Stevens White
400a. Col. Francis Jenkins

100a. DUBLIN   5 Nov 1665, John Mackitt,   Pocomoke 100
In the north side Pocomoke, East side Morumsco
Creek. Possessed by the widow Taylor

100a. HUDSONS FORTUNE-7 Nov 1665, Henry Hudson   Pocomoke 100
On the east side Morumsco Creek. No such land.

1000a. THORNSBURY-Aug 1665, Henry Piesley,   Pocomoke 100
On north side Pocomoke near land of Wm. Smith.
No such land to be found nor in former survey

150a. THE IRISH GROVE-6 Nov 1665-Daniel Quillan,   Pocomoke 100
On east side Morumsco Creek, North side Pocomoke
River, Possessed by Peter Carsley

300a. HIGNOLLS CHOICE-8 Feb 1667, Robert Hignoll,   Pocomoke 100
at head of Morumsco Creek, at a pine dividing
it from John Kings land. Possessed by-
150a. Edward Dykes
150a. Major John Cornish

300a. LITTLE TOWN- 7 Nov 1663- Ralph Linzey,   Pocomoke 100
for William Merrill

300a. CRANBROOK   21 Dec.1663- Catherine Price   Pocomoke 100
on north side Pocomoke by land of William Smith
100a. supposed to be possessed by Robert Worth
100a. by John Dennis in the name of HUDSONS
FOLLY. The remainder taken into older survey.

1500a. KENT   18 Mar 1665-Col. Edward Carter,   Pocomoke 100
on north side Pocomoke. West side Poshumunson
Creek. Held by Madam Carter in London. No rent
ever paid nor the land well known.

300a. ACQUINTICA-20 Nov 1665, Jenkins Price,   Pocomoke 100
on the north side Pocomoke River. Possessed
by Thomas Newbold.

| ACRES | TRACT | SURVEY DATE-BY WHOM | LOCATION |

150a. THE IRISH GROVE-10 Nov 1665, Morris Lysten-Pocomoke 100
    on the north side Pocomoke, west side Morumsco Ck.
    Possessed-22½a. Alexander Mattux
              22½a. Phillip Conner
              100a. Sampson Wheatly

3000a. BENEFIELD 3 Aug 1666- Richard Bennett,   Pocomoke 100
    by the north side Pocomoke. Possessed by
    John Kellum in right of Col. Charles Scarboroughs
    children.

450a. NEWTOWN   2 Oct 1665- Jenkins Price,   Pocomoke 100
    by Acquintica Swamp. Resurveyed for William Hobbs.
    Possessed by-225a. Alexander Mattux
                 225a. John Perkins

1000a. CHUCKALUCK-28 Oct.1665-Robert Pitts.   Pocomoke 100
    on north side Pocomoke River. Possessed by
    Thomas Layfield, purchased by George Layfield
    of Robert son and heir of Robert Pitts and
    given to said Thomas Layfield.

400a. THE ADVENTURE-10 Feb. 1665- Jeffrey Minshull. Pocomoke 100
    at head of Morumsco Creek. At head of small branch
    assigned. Col. Stevens who by resurvey made it
    450a..Possessed by Samuel Layfield by survey
    made it 450a.

100a. KINGS NORTON- 16 July 1665-Thomas White,   Pocomoke 100
    Assigned William Stevens on the north side
    Pocomoke River. Belongs to William White but is
    in Possesseion of the Indians of Askimmi ____Town

200a. CONNERS GROVE-13 Feb 1666, Phillip Conner,   Pocomoke 100
    on north side Pocomoke near land of Richard
    Bennett Esq. Cut off by older survey

300a. MANLOVES IMPROVEMENT-15 Jan 1666-John Manlove, Pocomoke 100
    On northmost side of Pocomoke. Northmost side
    Dividing Creek, The land unknown and supposed
    to be taken in older survey.

300a. COVENTRY   5 Jan.1666, Samuel Young,   Pocomoke 100
    onnorth side Dividing Creek. Land unknown.

400a. MEANT MORE 15 Jan.1666, William Stevens,   Pocomoke 100
    on north side Pocomoke and west side Dividing
    Creek. Land not known

500a. COLEMANS ADVENTURE, 25 Jan 1666, John Coleman, Pocomoke 100
    on uppermost side Pocomoke River and West side
    Dividing Creek. Possessed by-
    200a. George Tull
    300a. Richard Tull

100a. ALLENS CONTEST-4 Sept.1666, Richard Allen,   Pocomoke 100
    on east side Morumsco Creek, near land of
    John King. Possessed by Robert Wood

150a. HILLIARDS DISCOVERY-1 Apr.1667, John Hyland, Pocomoke 100
    Assigned Henry Hudson. on East side Morumsco Creek
    Possessed by Teague Riggin Sr.

ACRES	TRACT	SURVEY DATE-BY WHOM	location

500a BRINGINGHAM-2 Jun.1664, William Smith   Pocomoke 100
on north side Pocomoke River, the land not known and so formerly returned by C.Jenkins.

400a. MINSHALLS ADVENTURE-16 Jan.1667, Jeffrey Minshall-Pocomoke 100
on west side Dividing Creek, near head of Phillips lines. Claims this land but is within other surveys.

300a. CHANCE 17 June 1667, Roger Woolford, Pocomoke 100
on the west side Dividing Creek, near Indian field in the Possession of Mrs.Mary Woolford

300a. AFRICA 7 June 1667, John King, Pocomoke 100
on east side of Dividing Creek in Pocomoke River, possessed by Cornelius Morris

500a. CALDICITT 30 Jun 1667- William Stevens. Pocomoke 100
at upper end of Pawmonky, Possessed by Stevens White

100a. THE EXCHANGE-2 July 1667, Robert Jones, Pocomoke 100
on the north side Pocomoke River near land GREENWELL, in possession of widow Sharrott

100a. FRIENDSHIP 3 July 1665- George Wale, Pocomoke 100
on the north side Pocomoke at Acquintice. Possessed by Thomas Newbold

170a. HINDERSONS SECOND CHOICE-7 Sep.1668,James Henderson-Pocomoke 100
On the south side Pocomoke. Possessed by widow Honner Small in her childs right

130a. LANDING RURCHASED-8 Spt. 1668, James Hinderson, Pocomoke 100
On the south side Pocomoke 4 miles below Purchased Landing, Possessed by Walter Taylor for the orphans of John Henderson

250a. BRUMSPCAPS FIELD-28 Sep.1667, Daniel Dennis, Pocomoke 100
on the south side Pocomoke River. Possessed by John Mills in right of David Jones' orphans

200a. HUDSONS FOLLY, 2 Nov.1667, Henry Hudson, Pocomoke 100
assigned Nicholas Hudson on the east side of Morumsco Creek. No such land. Supposed it is the tract before called CRAMBURN.

500a. MORESLACK 4 Nov 1668, William Stevens, Pocomoke 100
assigned James Henderson, at the mouth of a small gut on the south side Pocomoke. Possessed by his son John Henderson. It is sold by commissioners for C.Smith's land unto Jacob Adams who is in posses--'on

500a. SNOW HILL 2 Nov.1668, William Stevenson Pocomoke 100
on the south side of Pocomoke
Possessed by-250a. Henry Bishop
            250a. Thomas Peterkin in right of George Bishop

100a. THE NEW YEARS GIFT-7 Jun. 1670,John Hilliard Pocomoke 100
on north side Pocomoke River at Nasuatax by an Indian Path, Possessed by the Widow Quillan.

ACRES	TRACT	SURVEY DATE-BY WHOM	LOCATION
100a.	ADAMS GARDEN-	18 May 1670 Phillip Adams, In Morumsco Creek, Possessed by Thomas Adams	Pocomoke 100
350a.	MORRICES HOPE-	8 Feb.1670, Morris Lestor, On Pocomoke Bay. 94a. being but off by older survey which is in possession of Michael Clifton. No more left.	Pocomoke 100
200a.	COVENTRY-	27 Mar.1671, John Hilliard, on west side Pocomoke River at Naswattux neck. Possessed by Eliza Townsend	Pocomoke 100
300a.	ACTON	21 Mar 1671, John Freeman, in Acquintica. Possessed by Walter Taylor	Pocomoke 100
100a.	SCOTTS FOLLY,	15 Sep. 1672, William Scott, on the south side Pocomoke. Possessed by William Scott. It is a mistake. It is in Possession of John Houlston	Pocomoke 100
250a.	SECOND PURCHASE-	surv.1674, George Betts, On the south side Pocomoke. Possessed by Bernard Runsley	Pocomoke 100
200a.	THE LODGE-	28 Mar.1674, George Betts, Possessed by William Quinton	Pocomoke 100
300a.	GOODWILL	30 Mar.1674, John Laws, near land of George Carter, in Possession of Robert and George Laws.	Pocomoke 100
100a.	LITTLE ACTON	4 Feb 1672- John Freeman, On the north side Pocomoke in Acquantica Neck. Possessed by John Broughton	Pocomoke 100
100a.	ADVENTURE	20 Jan 1673-William Brittingham, On the south side of Pocomoke. The right in WIlliam Merrill who denys the payment of rent claiming older survey hath taken it away.	Pocomoke 100
100a.	BENSTONS LOTT-	21 Oct.1673, Henry Smith. On the north side Pocomoke River. Possessed by Francis Benston in Virginia.	Pocomoke 100
100a.	MOUNT HOPE	12 Dec.1673, Henry Smith On the north side Pocomoke River. Possessed by Benjamin Bockburn	Pocomoke 100
300a.	MILTEN	3 Dec 1673, Henry Smith on the north side Pocomoke, 4 miles from River Possessed by-50a. Rowland Bevan Jr. 250a. Thomas Peale	Pocomoke 100
150a.	SMITHS CHANCE,	12 Dec.1663, Henry Smith. on the north side of Pocomoke. Possessed by Dorman Donnaked	Pocomoke 100
400a.	PATTENTED	5 Oct.1674, Thomas Davis,Taylor, on the south side Pocomoke River at Davis point. Possessed-200a. Widow Pitt 200a. Robert Blades	Pocomoke 100

| ACRES | TRACT | SURVEY DATE-BY WHOM | LOCATION |

300a. WINTER QUARTER-26 Oct 1674, William Stevens,   Pocomoke 100
near Nasawattuxe, Possessed by Thomas
Quillan, vide Christopher Taylors acct.

100a. SECOND CHOICE-15 Jun.1674, Robert Holston,   Pocomoke 100
3 miles from Pocomoke. Claimed and rent
paid by same.

300a. GADSHILL   25 Jun.1675, Thomas Jones,   Pocomoke 100
assigned Morgan Thomas on south side Pocomoke
on east side James Creek. The person is dead
and no heirs appear nor rent ever paid.

220a. LEVERTON-   4 Feb.1674- John Bozman,   Pocomoke 100
assigned William Pozman. Possessed by
John Bozman

300a. MANLOVES LOTT-25 Nov.1678, William Manlove   Pocomoke 100
Assigned Cornelius Morris on south side of
a path of marsh in Pungateage. Possessed
by Samuel Tomlinson

500a. KINGLAND   20 July 1678-William Stevens   Pocomoke 100
near division line between Maryland and Virginia.
Possessed by-200a. Richard Bally in Amonckin Va.
  100a. Siland Chapman
  200a. George Hopes son in Va.

100a. CLAINFASTING-18 Nov 1677, Josias Seaward,   Pocomoke 100
Assigned Daniel Quillain, in Naswattux.
Possessed by the widow Quillan and Hugh Porter.
Porter pays the rent

50a. THE LINE LOTT-28 Oct 1674, William Stevens,   Pocomoke 100
at division line where Maryland and Virginia
cross Pocomoke River. Possessed by William
Brittingham Sr. who lives in Virginia

50a. ELLIS'S LOTT-3 Dec 1676, William Stevens   Pocomoke 100
Assigned John Ellis, on the south side Morumsco.
Possessed by John Ellis

500a. FOOLKS CHOICE-23 Sep.1676, William Anderson,   Pocomoke 100
on the south side Pocomoke near Divisional line.
Possessed-250a. Isaac Piper
  250a. John Paradise in right of Phillip
    Parker of Annamokin in Virginia

400a. SEWARDS PURCHASE, 1 Nov 1677, John Emmett,   Pocomoke 100
Assigned Josias Seward, on east side Morumsco Ck.
Possessed-200a. Adrain Marshall
  200a. Esau Boston

200a. CARTERS LOTT-29 Mar.1674, George Carter,   Pocomoke 100
on south side Pocomoke River, Possessed by
the widow Timmons

200a. DESART   1 Sep.1675, John Anderson,   Pocomoke 100
Possessed by Samuel Layfield, vide Benjamin
Layfields account.

ACRES	TRACT	SURVEY DATE-BY WHOM	LOCATION

150a. HARDSHIFT 18 Dec.1678, John Rowsaloe, Pocomoke 100
on the south side Pocomoke. Possessed by
Richard Wharton in right of Humphrey Roads
orphans

50a. PERSIMMON POINT-28 Nov 1678, Walter Lane, Pocomoke100
Assigned William Manlove, on south side of
Pocomoke Bay. Know not who holds the land.
One Richard Lestor who ran into Virginia was
the last that claimed it.

500a. CHERRYTON- 18 July 1678, William Stevens, Pocomoke 100
Assigned John Henderson, on the south side of
Pocomoke. Possessed by William Smith

500a. BEARPOINT 10 July 1679, William Stevens, Pocomoke 100
Assigned Stephen Coffin, on west side Dividing
Creek. Possessed by-350a. Peter Benton in his
    wife's right
  150a. William Townsend

100a. ADAMS GARDEN-23 July 1679, William Stevens, Pocomoke 100
Assigned Phillip Adams, on the south side Morumsco
Creek. Possessed by Thomas Adams son and heir
to Phillip.

100a. TOWNSENDS DISCOVERY- 17 Jun 1679, William Stevens,Pocomoke 100
Assigned John Townsend, about 3 miles from the
Pocomoke River, Possessed by John Townsend son
of said John.

300a. DICKENSONS FOLLY, 28 Jul 1679, William Stevens, Pocomoke 100
Assigned William Dickenson, on south side of
Morumsco Creek. Possessed by-
  40a. Peter Dickenson
  260a. Sommersett Dickenson

50a. HAM 24 June 1679, Samuel Collins, Pocomoke 100
At the mouth of Grillon? Ck. Possessed by same.

400a. DALES ADVENTURE, 9 July 1679, Devid Dale, Pocomoke 100
on the north side Pocomoke, between land of
Jenkins Price and Gwithors. Possessed by-
  200a. Samuel Collins
  200a. Gideon Tillman but is cut off by an
    older survey

1000a. SUFFOLK 11 June 1679, William Stevens, Pocomoke 100
on the south west side of Dividing Creek.
Possessed by-446a. Robert Heath
    75a. held by Arch.Smith in right of
      Tripshaws orphan
    200a. John Tull who hath sold to
      WIlliam Mills, vide, Samuel
      Morris acct. Bal. taken up by
      older survey.

600a. HARRISONS ADVENTURE, 12 Jun.1679, John Harrison,Pocomoke 100
on the west side of the main branch of Dividing Ck.
Possessed by John Harrison

| ACRES | TRACT | SURVEY DATE-BY WHOM | LOCATION |

1300a. CONVENIENCE-11 June 1679, William Stevens,   Pocomoke 100
At mouth of Parting Creek. Possessed by-
200a. Stephen and William White
50a. John Watts, Laurence Riley
50a. William Matthews, in their wife's right
100a. Alexander White
50a. William White
150a. John Watts in Virginia
100a. Edm.d Howard
200a. Richard Wharton
650a. Samuel Layfield

600a. THE LATE DISCOVERY, 22 Nov 1679, John Robins, Pocomoke 100
near Gwithors Island at a marked pine of Jenkins
Price's. Possessed by Samuel Collins

700a. SMITHS RECOVERY-resurveyed 2 Dec 1679, Henry Smith, Pocomoke 100
was part of THOMPSONS PURCHASE and HASWORTHYS CHOICE
in the Indian Neck. Possessed by-
150a. Phillip Fitzgerald in the right of Edward
Wheelers orphan
150a. John Pollock
300a. John Tunstall
100a. Thomas Everdon

100a. OLD TOWN   18 Nov.1677-Josias Seward.   Pocomoke 100
Assigned Roger OKeen in Acquntica Neck. Know not
who possessed this land since OKeen long since
dead without heir

200a. BECKLES   1 Jun.1679, William Harper,   Pocomoke 100
on the south west side Dividing Creek. Possessed by-
100a. George Tull
100a. Edward Harper

500a. NORFOLK   11 Jun 1679, William Harper,   Pocomoke 100
on the south side Dividing Creek. Possessed by
the widow of said Harper

1350a. HOGG QUARTER, 12 June 1679, John Anderson,   Pocomoke 100
at the mouth of Holdstens Creek. Possessed by-
500a. Francis Thorogood
800a. Samuel Layfield

150a. COSTINS TROUBLE, 11 Jun 1679, William Furnice, Pocomoke 100
Assigned Henry Coffin(Costin) on the south west
side of Dividing Creek. Possessed by-
150a. John Tull of Ann.
300a. Peter Benton

300a. GOSHEN   20 Mar.1679, Samuel Cooper,   Pocomoke 100
Assigned Edward Wright, near Parrahawkin Possessed
by-150a. John Winn, now by Randall Smullin but not
Conveyed
150a. Ambrose Riggin

1000a. PITCHCRAFT-7 Jun 1679, William Stevens,   Pocomoke 100
Assigned Henry Smith on island of broken woodland
Possessed by-200a. John Evans in Virginia
200a. John Taylor
600.a to be sold for payment of Smith's
debt.

ACRES	TRACT	SURVEY DATE-BY WHOM	LOCATION
500a.	JERSEY,	4 Mar.1679, William Stevens, Assigned to Phillip Hammond, on the south side Pocomoke near Mattapony. Claimed by Madam Littleton in Virginia.	Pocomoke 100
200a.	WINTER QUARTER	6 Aug.1679, John Goddin, Assigned Walter Powell, on south side St. Martins, and south side Herrig Creek. Possessed by Charles Townsend in right of John Powell in Accocomac Va.	Pocomoke 100
100a.	VENTURE	6 July 1679, John Borwn, Assigned Robert Smith about 3 miles from the Pocomoke River. Possessed by Samuel Tomlinson, vide Richard Chambers	Pocomoke 100
50a.	GOOSE MARSH	7 Nov.1679, Edward Dickenson, at mouth of Morumsco Creek. Possessed by Summerset Dickenson.	Pocomoke 100
150a.	THE LUYS	28 Feb.1679, Timothy Pead on the south side Pocomoke at a white oak by the river side. The land not in anyone's possession. No heir appears.	Pocomoke 100
400a.	WARWICK	20 Jun.1679, John White Assigned Rowland Beven, on north side Pocomoke in neck of land by a Cypress swamp. Possessed by Rowland Beven.	Pocomoke 100
200a.	WOODHALL	24 Aug 1679, John White, Assigned John Woodward, on the west side of a branch of the north side Pocomoke. Possessed by Moses Fenton	Pocomoke 100
100a.	CORK	16 Apr.1680- John Winder, Assigned Walter Lane, in Naswattux Neck. Possessed by Walter Lane	Pocomoke 100
100a.	THE OLD HEAD	16 Apr.1680, John Winder, Assigned Walter Lane,in Naswattux Neck. Apportions to John Lane in Europe and not Possessed. land now returned	Pocomoke 100
450a.	WATERFORD	26 June 1679, Roger O'Keen, Assigned John Mackett	Pocomoke 100
350a.	LEDBOURN	8 Mar.1679, Col. William Stevens, On the south side main branch, at head of Morumsco Creek. Possessed by- 100a. Dockett Beauchamp 150a. John Heath 100a. Edward Beauchamp	Pocomoke 100
50a.	GEORGES MARSH,	6 Apr.1680, William Stevens, Assigned George Manlove, on north side Pocomoke, on north side a glade of marsh. Possessed by John Clark in right of John Waltum in Pennsylvania	Pocomoke 100
350a.	SALEM	20 Dec.1680, Samuel Cooper, about 5 miles from Pocomoke. Possessed by Jonathan Cooper	Pocomoke 100

| ACRES | TRACT | SURVEY DATE-BY WHOM | LOCATION |

450a. MIDDLESEX 28 Apr.1680, William Harris   Pocomoke 100
             on south side Pocomoke near Dividing Creek.
             Possessed by-200a. Griffith Thomas
                      250a. in right of William Morris, if not cut
                            off by an older survey

150a. WHITBY   28 Apr.1680, William Stevens,   Pocomoke 100
             Assigned Thomas Cole in Naswattux Neck. Cole
             dead without heirs and escheats to his Lordship

200a. HARPERS DISCOVERY-21 Mar.1680, William Stevens,Pocomoke 100
             Assigned William Harper on west side Dividing Creek.
             Possessed by-100a. William Duncan
                          100a. William Warwick

800a. COWLEY   15 Mar.1680, William Stevens,   Pocomoke 100
             Assigned Mark Manlove, on south side Pocomoke at
             a corner tree of Timothy Pead. Possessed by-
             100a. William Bradshaw, last possessed of.Dead in Pa.
             700a. William Brittingham

150a. LIMRICK 10 Mar.1680, William Stevens,   Pocomoke 100
             Assigned Daniel Quillan, in Nasattux, Possessed
             by Hugh Porter and widow Liddia Quillan, Edmond
             Dickerson

350a. DONAHO'S SECOND CHOICE-1 Apr.1681,Wm. Stevens, Pocomoke 100
             Assigned Daniel Donahoe, on the east side Dividing
             Creek. Possessed by Dorman Donahoe son of Daniel

50a. UNLOOKT FOR-8 Apr.1681, William Stevens,   Pocomoke 100
             Assigned Daniel Donahoe, 4 miles from Pocomoke.
             Possessed by Dorman Donahoe

200a. HARRISONS VENTURE-5 Apr.1680, William Stevens, Pocomoke 100
             Assigned John Harrison, on west side Dividing Creek
             in Possession of John Harrison

700a. TRUE BRIDGE-11 Mar.1680 William Stevens,   Pocomoke 100
             Assigned Christopher Stanby, on north east side
             of Winter Quarter, Possessed by-
             400a. William Williamson
              50a. Jeremiah Carey
             250a. Richard Webb

150a. WOOTEN UNDEREDGE- 11 Mar.1681, William Stevens,Pocomoke 100
             Assigned Timithoy Pead, on south side Pocomoke.
             Apportains to William Twyford in Accoc. Va.

400a. RAVENSTON 17 Mar.1680, William Stevens,   Pocomoke 100
             Assigned to William Bradshaw. A little to the north
             of Acquin... a. The land lies in Quapamco Neck
             and surveyed by Matthew Scarborough. Possessed by
             Capt. Edward Hammond.

150a. TOSSITER 18 Mar.1680, William Stevens.   Pocomoke 100
             Assigned William Bradshaw, A little north of
             Acquntica. Possessed by William Noble

300a. CHANCE   23 Oct.1681, Roger Woolford,   Pocomoke 100
             on north side Pocomoke, on north side Indian Path.
             Possessed by Mrs. Mary Woolford

ACRES	TRACT	SURVEY DATE-BY WHOM	LOCATION
50a.	DUDLEY	28 Sep.1681, Elizabeth Smith, Assigned Abraham Heath, on north side Dividing Creek. Knows not the land. Abraham Heath's heir denies any such land	Pocomoke 100
200a.	WINDSOR CASTLE-	28 Sep.1681, William Winslow, On the north side of a branch of Dividing Creek William Winslow the heir denies the land and hath paid no rent. Possessed by Capt. John West	Pocomoke 100
150a.	LANGTON	29 Sep.1681, Thomas Hall, On the south side of Pocomoke River, 2 miles back in the woods from the river. Possessed by Francis Thorogood blt is now rented	Pocomoke 100
200a.	BASHAW	25 Oct.1681-Samuel Cooper, on the east side main branch of Dividing Creek. Assigned to Thomas Wallis. Possessed by same.	Pocomoke 100
100a.	COME BY CHANCE-	14 Feb.1681, Peter Waples, 3 miles from Pocomoke. None possessed. The heir in Pennsylvania	Pocomoke 100
50a.	HANDYS MEADOW-	9 May 1681, James Slaughtor, Assigned Samuel Handy, near the mouth of the Pocomoke in Possession of Samuel Collins	Pocomoke 100.
300a.	HARNSWORTH	3 Apr.1682, William Stevens. Assigned Roger Woolford, on the west side of the main branch of Dividing Creek. Possessed by Mrs. Mary Woolford	Pocomoke 100
850a.	THE ENTRANCE-	25 Apr.1683, Edward Howard, On the north side and westmost side of Pocomoke Bay Possessed by-400a. William White 450a. Thomas Williams in right of Edward Howard	Pocomoke 100
300a.	ASSACIMACO	10 June 1664, William Smith, On the north side Pocomoke. Said to go to the right of Capt. Henry Smith deceased but possessed by the indians of Askimmoton Town	Pocomoke 100
2000a.	PARTNERS CHOICE-	17 July 1665, William Stevens, On the north side Pocomoke near the land of Thomas White. This land is in the Indian Town Asquiminicomton and belongs to William White, Laurence Ryley, William Mastors, John Watts	Pocomoke 100
500a.	LOYDS GROVE,	18 Nov.1665, Richard Lloyd, Assigned Charles Oldfield, on north side Prices Creek. Possessed by-250a. John Laws 250a. Capt. Henry Smith	Pocomoke 100
500a.	LEDBURN	1 Mar.1665, William Stevens, On the north side Pocomoke at southmost bounds of Phineas White in Asquimacton Indian Town and possessed by the Indians. Samuel Layfield claims.	Pocomoke 100
500a.	NORTHFIELD	8 Nov.1663, Jenkins Prince On the north side Pocomoke at a marked Cypress tree. In the former returns said to be seated by indians in Acquinmacton Indian Town	Pocomoke 100

ACRES	TRACT	SURVEY DATE-BY WHOM	LOCATION
100a.	MIDDLE	28 Aug 1683- Robert Jones on the south side of Pocomoke in Possession of the widow Mary Starrett	Pocomoke 100
300a.	TEASE	20 Jan.1675- Mark Manlove On the north side of Pocomoke. Possessed by John Clark in right of John Wallburn of Pa.	Pocomoke 100
300a.	KINGS LOTT	-10 Feb1663,John King at head of Morumsco Creek. Possessed by Thomas Adams	Pocomoke 100
1350a.	STANLEYS	24 July 1663, Hugh Stanley At the east side Pocomoke River. This land by the death of John Stanly heir apparent is inflated. 500a. said to be possessed by John Brittingham 250a. Possessed by Robert Holston supposed of Va. Some part held by and possessed by John Williams and Robert Houlstone	Pocomoke 100
150a.	WOOLVER MARSH	-20 Apr.1680, John Kirk On the eastmost side Duffs Neck in Pocomoke Bay Possessed by John Kirk	Pocomoke 100
400a.	MILLSBRANCH	- 31 May 1683, Assigned George Russell Possessed by-200a. Thomas Marplus 200a. to orphans of Wm. Major in Va.	Pocomoke 100
200a.	MERRILL HALL	-8 Oct 1683, Col.Wm.Stevens, Possessed by Samuel Layfield	Pocomoke 100
200a.	NEW MACHIR	- 3 July 1683, assigned John Lonster, Possessed by John Gillett who purchased of Lonster	Pocomoke 100
500a.	FREEMANS DISCOVERY	, 10 Jul.1682, Assigned Joseph Freeman Joseph Freeman the heir in Pa.	Pocomoke 100
175a.	MIDDLETON	-12 May 1683, Assigned John Harrison, Possessed by John Harrison	Pocomoke 100
150a.	MIDDLE PLANTATION	-12 May 1663-assigned Wm.Harper, Possessed by widow Harper	Pocomoke 100
700a.	SHAFTSBURY,	1 Oct 1681, Edward Hammond Lies on Pocomoke in Poquoderanto 100, Possessed by Edward Hammond	Pocomoke 100
300a.	VENTURE	18 May 1683, assigned Peter Whaples, Possessed by Lodowick Fleman	Pocomoke 100
150a.	WEST RIDGE,	18 May 1680, assigned Timothy Poad, Timothy dead at the south, No heirs apparent	Pocomoke 100
100a.	PAXEN HILL,	14 Jun 1682, assigned Wm.Winslow, William Winslow the heir declaims it	Pocomoke 100
400a.	BODDAM	3 July 1683, James Langstor, Apportains to James Langster son and heir of James	Pocomoke 100
50a.	TILLMANS ADVENTURE	12 Sept. 1682, assigned Gideon Tillman Declaimed by Tillman pending a cut by elder Survey	
150a.	HOLSTONS CHOICE	- 10 May 1683,assigned Robert Holston, and Wm. Brittingham. Possessed by Wm. Brittingham by surviorship	Pocomoke 100

| ACRES | TRACT | SURVEY DATE-BY WHOM | LOCATION |

200a. BACON HILL, 16 Oct 1683, assigned Francis Jenkins-Pocmoke 100
　　　　In Possession of John Smith who purchased

109a. SHOEMAKERS MEADOW-6 May 1685, John Rowell,　　Pocomoke 100
　　　　Know not the land, Rowell dead

200a. LITTLE DERRY, 3 Aug 1684, John Rousells,　　Pocomoke 100
　　　　It is the same with the land below

200a. PROVIDENCE- 3 Aug 1684, John Rousells,　　Pocomoke 100
　　　　Held by Somerset County, where the court House stands

300a. GOOD SUCESS-2 May 1685, James Rownd,　　Pocomoke 100
　　　　in the present possession of William Hickman.
　　　　Since alienated to William Noble 150a. and 150a.
　　　　to Robert Mitchell

300a. CATTLE GREEN, 3 Oct 1683, Francis Jenkins,　　Pocomoke 100
　　　　in Acquminicompton Indian and in the Indians
　　　　Possession. 125a. possessed by William Nelson

100a. BENGILL　15 Sep.1683, John Marks,　　Pocomoke 100
　　　　Possessed by Richard Lamberson. Supposed this
　　　　land is escheatable. John Marks died without
　　　　heirs and not alienated to Lamberson

100a. HARPERS INCREASE, 1 Oct.1683,Assign. Wm.Harper,　Pocomoke 100
　　　　50a. Possessed by Wm. Denehou
　　　　50a. William Warwick

100a. ACWORTHS CHOICE, 16 Feb 1664, Richard Acworth,　Nanticoke 100
　　　　on the east side Nanticoke River, east side of
　　　　Barren Creek. Possessed by James Weatherly

300a. ACWORTHS PURCHASE, 19 Feb 1664. Richard Acworth, Nanticoke 100
　　　　On the east side Nanticoke on north side Rowa-
　　　　ttiquott Ck., Possessed by James Weatherly

300a. ACORTHS FOLLY, 18 Feb.1664, Richard Acworth,　Nanticoke 100
　　　　on the east side Nanticoke near Rowattiquott Ck.
　　　　Possessed by James Weatherly

200a. WHITE MARSHES CHANCE-9 Feb.1664,Richard Whitemarsh, Nanticoke 100
　　　　on the east side Rowasticutt Creek in Nanticoke
　　　　No such land to be found

300a. WHITEMARSHES DELIGHT, 18 Feb 1664, Richard Whitemarsh,Nantiko 100
　　　　On the east side Rowasticutt Creek
　　　　150a. possessed by Robert Given by the name of Givens
　　　　Lott
　　　　150a. possessed by James Given

300a. MEECHS RIGHT, 20 Apr.1667, John Meech,　　Nanticoke 100
　　　　On the southmost side of Nanticoke on the west side
　　　　ofWetepkin Creek. Possessed by Capt.James Dashiell

300a. LONG HILL-23 July 1668, Samuel Jackson,　　Nanticoke 100
　　　　on the south side of Nanticoke, on east side
　　　　Wetepkin Creek. Possessed by Capt.James Dashiell

200a. MEECHS DESCARTS, 22 Aug 1668, John Meech,　Nanticoke 100
　　　　on the south side Nanticoke, on west side Wetepkin
　　　　Creek. Possessed by Capt. James Dashiell

| ACRES | TRACT | SURVEY DATE-BY WHOM | LOCATION |

300a. MEECHS HOPE, 14 Sep.1668, Thomas Meech,   Nanticoke 100
      on the south side Nanticoke, East side Wetepkin Ck.
      Possessed by-150a. widow of Thomas Shurman
                  150a. Benjamin Nesham

200a. NUTTERS ADVENTURE, 5 Dec 1670, Christopher Nutter,Nanticoke 100
      On the south side Nanticoke River, and east side
      of Quantico Creek. Possessed by-
      100a. Christopher Nutter
      100a. Matthew Nutter

250a. TRUELOCK GRANGE-23 Mar.1672, Phillip Ascue,   Nanticoke 100
      In Nanticoke River, in Quantico Creek on the
      south side of the creek. Possessed by-
      100a. Thomas Rolph Jr.
      75a. John Bougher
      75a. James Russell

250a. SALOP   23 Nov 1672, John Windsor,   Nanticoke 100
      near the Nanticoke River on a branch of QUantico
      Creek. Possessed by William Giles Jr.

200a. SALISBURY PLAIN, 28 Nov 1672, Isaac Noble,   Nanticoke 100
      on the south side Nanticoke at head of Manquah
      Creek. Possessed by Charles Nutter in right of
      Piper's orphans

750. WEATHERLYS PURCHASE, 28 Nov 1672, James Weatherly,Nanticoke 100
      near the Nanticoke on south side Rowestico
      Possessed by-225a. James Train
                  200a. Charles Nutter in right of Wm.Pipers orphans
                  325a. James Weatherly

200a. WRENGTON, 29 Nov 1672, Samuel Simmons,   Nanticoke 100
      Near the Nanticoke at a corner had of John
      Windsor. Possessed by Benjamin Nesham marrying
      the widow of Benjamin Cottman

150a. YEARS LAND, 27 Nov.1672, John Round,   Nanticoke 100
      near Nanticoke on north side Wetpquin Creek.
      Possessed by John Bound

150a. MOUNT HOPE, 2 Dec 1672, William Wright,   Nanticoke 100
      In Nanticoke River. possessed by-
      75a. William Bennett
      75a. Thomas Larramor

100a. ACWORTH DELIGHT, 20 Nov.1672, Richard Acworth,Nanticoke 100
      In Nanticoke in Rowastico Neck, near fresh
      water run. Possessed by heirs of Thomas Acworth

200a. OAKHALL   21 Nov.1672, Richard Acworth,   Nanticoke 100
      near the Nanticoke River on south side Barren Ck.
      Possessed by James Weatherly, alias John Gilly

200a. HOGG QUARTER, 21 Nov.1672, Richard Acworth,   Nanticoke 100
      near Nanticoke River, on south side Barren Creek.
      Possessed by Richard Acworth

300a. FANNINGHAM, 22 Nov 1672, Richard Acworth,   Nanticoke 100
      on the north side Barron Creek, near head of the
      creek. Apportains to Michael Williams orphans

| ACRES | TRACT | SURVEY DATE-BY WHOM | LOCATION |

240a. PARTNERS CHOICE-22 Nov.1672, John Craycroft, Nanticoke 100
Assigned to William Green, on south side
of Nanticoke, Possessed by William Green

250a. WHICH YOU PLEASE, 22 Nov 1672, John Craycraft, Nanctioke 100
Assigned William Green, on south side of
the Nanticoke, Possessed by Wm. Green

50a. MANLOVES ADVENTURE, 28 Nov 1673, John Manlove, Nanticoke 100
Near Nantocoke on the south side, Possessed
by James Weatherly

300a. BENTLEY, 2 April 1672, Thomas Walker, Nanticoke 100
on the south side Nanticoke, on southmost side
Quantico Creek. Apportains to the widow of
Sampson Waters in Boston, New England, but
managed by James Dashiell

100a. WOODGATE DOCK, 19 Mar. 1672, William Woodgate, Nanticoke 100
On the Nanticoke River, at a great pine on the
south side. Possessed by Capt. John MaClestor

350a. CHELSEY 19 Nov 1672, Charles Hutchins, near Nanticoke
on Quantico Creek on the north side. Possessed by
100a. Daniel Macgunis
100a. John Tully
150a. Stephen Tully

200a. HARTFORD 19 Nov 1672, Charles Hutchins, Nanticoke 100
Assigned Richard Samuell, on south side of
Nanticoke River, Possessed by Richard Samuell

300a. MIDDLESEX, 30 Nov 1672, Charles Hutchins, Nanticoke 100
Assigned Robert Willson, on south side of
Nanticoke at a point of land by a marsh, Possessed
by David Howard in right of John Willson's orphans

300a. SHADWELL 30 Nov.1672, Charles Hutchins. Nanticoke 100
Assigned John Pearce, on the south side Nanticoke
at a marked white oak by a branch. Possessed by
150a. Robert Collier
150a. Sidney Brown

50a. WOOLF TRAP NECK, 23 Nov.1673, James Dashiell, Nanticoke 100
on the south side Nanticoke River, at a line
from John Meech's. Possessed by Capt. James Dashiell

100a. ABERGAVENY, 10 May 1673, Roger Phillips, Nanticoke 100
on south side of Nanticoke, on south side Quantico
Creek. Possessed by Jonathan Jackson

100a. MANLOVES DELIGHT, 20 Nov 1672, Richard Acworth, Nanticoke 100
assigned James Weatherly, on south side of Nanticoke
Possessed by tge heirs of Thomas Acworth

300a. WARE 13 June 1674, William Woodgate, Nanticoke 100
assigned Richard Samuell, on the south side of
Nanticoke on Roaring Point. Possessed by Samuell

200a. ST ALBANS 18 June 1674, William Woodgate, Nanticoke 100
Assigned Richard Townsend, at mouth of Salmon
Gutt, the north east bounds of Francis Hutchins.
Possessed by widow of John Ailworth

| ACRES | TRACT | SURVEY DATE-BY WHOM | LOCATION |

200a. WARWICK 14 Sep.1674, John Squire, Nanticoke 100
on the south side Nanticoke on the south side of
Quantico, The person long since dead and no heir
appears and must escheat

200a. BATCHELLORS ADVENTURE, 5 Oct.1674, Robert Collier,Nanticoke 100
Assigned Isaac Foxcroft, on the south side Nanticoke
River, 2 miles from the River, Apportains to the
widow Waters in Boston New England. Capt. James
Dasheill manages the concern

200a. ILLINGWORTHS HOPE, 9 Apr.1674, Stephen Cannon, Nanticoke 100
Assigned Richard Illingsworth, on Wetepkant Creek,
on the south side Jackson's Creek. Possessed by
Robert Nicholson

150a. DOUGHTYS LOTT, 8 Apr.1674, Stephen Cannon, Nanticoke 100
on the east side Nanticoke on south side of Wetepkin
Creek. Possessed by William Wainright and co-heirs
of Stephen Cannon 150a. and 100a. poss. by Peter
Doughty

300a. CANNON SHOTT, 8 Apr.1674, Stephen Cannon, Nanticoke 100
on the south side Wetpkin Creek. Possessed by
William Wainright as marrying the coheir of Stephen
Cannon

300a. CANNONS CHOICE, 8 Apr.1674, Stephen Cannon, Nanticoke 100
Assigned John Furrs on the east side Nanticoke on
Wetepkin Creek. Since resurveyed for,
188a. Peter Doughty
182 a. Thomas Larramer

300a. JESHIMON 28 Sep.1674, William Stevens, Nanticoke 100
Assigned Isaac Foxcroft, on the south side of
Nanticoke. Apportains to the widow Waters in Boston
New England. Manager Capt.James Dashiell

300a. MONMOUTH 31 Oct.1674, John Evans, Nanticoke 100
on the south side Nanticoke, on north side Quantico
Creek. Possessed by Oliver South in the right of
one Webb in Northumberland Co. Virginia

100a. ACWORTHS CONTRIVANCE, 26 Feb.1674, Richard Acworth,Nanticoke 100
on the south side of Nanticoke, on the northside of
a fresh water run. Possessed by James Weatherly

200a. EGYPT 13 Oct.1674, James Jones, Nanticoke 100
on the south side Nanticoke on south side Quantico
Creek. Possessed by Edward Bennett

100a. DUDLEY 17 Nov 1675, Stephen Cannon, Nanticoke 100
Assigned John Peasy, on the south side Nanticoke
near Oyster Creek. Possessed by-
80a. James Collier
20.a Robert Collier

100a. NEWCASTLE 16 Sep.1675, Stephen Cannon, Nanticoke 100
assigned Joseph Thompson, on the south side Oyster
Creek. Possessed by James Langrell

ACRES	TRACT	SURVEY DATE-BY WHOM	LOCATION
300a.	STANNAWAY	16 Nov.1675, Joseph Aylwood, on the south side Nanticoke at the corner tree of Charles Hutchins. Possessed by said John Aylworths widow.	Nanticoke 100
200a.	LYONS DEN	26 June 1676, John Lyon, on the east side Nanticoke River. at a marked tree. Possessed by the widow Marrutt, relict of John Marrutt	Nanticoke 100
100a.	MORRIS'S LOTT,	16 Nov.1675, Jenkins Morris, on the south side Nanticoke at the head of Momonquak. Possessed by-50a. Christopher Nutter 50a. Matthew Nutter	Nanticoke 100
100a.	TICKNELL	23 Jun.1676, Leonard Jones, about 2 miles from Walopkewant Creek, near Tyaskin. Possessed by- 50a. Thomas Larramor 50a. widow of Samuel Fleuelyn	Nanticoke 100
600a.	BEWDLEY,	24 June 1676, Leonard Jones, on the south side Nanticoke. Possessed by Capt.James Dashiell	Nanticoke 100
100a.	THE SMALL LOTT,	21 Oct.1676, Samuel Jackson, on the south side Quantico near the land of Roger Phillips. Possessed by Jonathan Jackson son and heir of Samuel	Nanticoke 100
220a.	SHIELDS CHOICE,	21 Sep.1676, William Stevens, Assigned Alice Shields, on the north side Quantico Creek. Possessed by-110a. Christopher Nutter, 110a. Matthew Nutter.	Nanticoke 100
150a.	FISHERMANS QUARTER,	24 Nov.1676, William Stevens, Assigned Lewis Beard, on the south side Nanticoke on the north side of a Small Branch. The land is not known, the party long since dead	Nanticoke 100
100a.	FAIR RIDGE	26 June 1676, John Windsor, Assigned Richard Samuell, near the mouth of the Nanticoke River. Possessed Capt. James Dashiell vide, Richard Samuell Sr.'s account	Nanticoke 100
200a.	COVENT GARDEN,	12 MAY 1676, Robert Collier, on the east side Nanticoke, a little southward of Quantico, Apportains to the widow Waters in Boston, New England, Management of the escheat is in James Dashiell	Nanticoke 100
150a.	LYONS FOLLY	26 Nov.1678, John Lyon, on the north side of Rewastico Creek, at the side of a branch. Possessed by John Cheesman	Nanticoke 100
100a.	WILTON	6 Nov.1678, Charles Nutter, on the south side Manumquak. Possessed by Charles Nutter in the right of Capt. Piper's orphans	Nanticoke 100
100a.	THE FATHERS DELIGHT,	7 Dec.1678, John Manlove,. on the north side Rewastico Branch. Possessed by James Weatherly	Nanticoke 100

| ACRES | TRACT | SURVEY DATE-BY WHOM | LOCATION |

200a. MIDFIELD   29 Sep.1678, Henry Morgan,   Nanticoke 100
                  on the east side Nanticoke on the south side
                  Quantico Creek. Possessed by Nathaniel Abbott
                  in right of JohnLucklys orphans

300a. PARRAMOURS FIRST CHOICE,2 Dec.1678, John Parramour,Nanticoke 100
                  on the south side Quantico Creek near the head.
                  Possessed by William Giles Jr.

50a. ROSS   6 Dec 1678, John EVANS,   Nanticoke 100
                  on the east side Nanticoke and north side Quantico
                  Creek. Possessed by James Russell and John Brougher
                  marrying the coheirs of Alexander Thomas

50a. SONS CHOICE 7 Dec 1678, John Manlove,   Nanticoke 100
                  on the south side Rewastico Branch. Psssessed
                  by Thomas Acworths heir

150a. PARIS   18 July 1679, John White,   Nanticoke 100
                  assigned Peter Doughtey, on the south side
                  Peteqkowant, Possessed by Peter Doughtey

600a. PHARSALIA   18 July 1679, John White,   Nanticoke 100
                  Assigned Mark Manlove, at head of Rewastico Creek.
                  Possessed by Col. Francis Jenkins who owns it

300a. TURNSTILE   19 July 1679, William Stevens,   Nanticoke 100
                  Assigned John Brown, between Wetepkwant and the
                  mouth of Nanticoke. Possessed by-
                  150a. Peter Doughty
                  150a. Thomas Larrimor

200a. GREEN RECANTATION, 28 July 1679, William Stevens,Nanticoke 100
                  Assigned William Green, on the north side of the
                  main branch of Quantico. Possessed by the widow
                  Lucy Burkum

200a. VENTURE   17 July 1678, Magdalen Westlock,   Nanticoke 100
                  on the south side Quantico near the land of
                  Phillip Ascue, Possessed by Nathaniel Abbott, in
                  the right of John Lucklys orphans

700a. HOGG QUARTER, 10 Jun 1677, William Stevens,   Nanticoke 100
                  assigned William Green, to the northward of
                  Wetepkowant. Possessed of John White of Nanticoke Rive

1400a.THE WESTERN FIELD, 4 Jun 1680, WIlliam Stevens,Naticoke 100
                  Assigned Robert Ridgly, between Rewastico Branch
                  of Back Creek. Belongs to one of the sons of
                  Robert Ridgley, Not possessed by anyone

533a. WESTLOS NECK. 9 Dec.1676, John Spat,   Nanticoke 100
                  on the east side Nanticoke on the south side Quantico
                  Possessed by-300a. George Betts
                                233a. orphans of Capt.Thomas Winder in Va

100a. LITTLE MONMOUTH, 27 Aug 1679, Thomas Brereton,   Nanticoke 100
                  on the south side Quantico in a swamp. Possessed by
                  John Evans

50a. WARRINGTON 20 Oct.1676, William Stevens,   Nanticoke 100
                  Assigned Gilbert Jones, on the south side Quantico.
                  Possessed by James Jones.

ACRES	TRACT	SURVEY-DATE, BY WHOM	LOCATION
300a.	WEATHERLYS ADVENTURE	4 Apr.1680, William Stevens, Assigned James Weatherly, On the northmost branch of Quantico. Possessed by James Weatherly	Nanticoke 100
500a.	BEDFORD	4 Apr.1680, William Stevens, Assigned James Weatherly, at head of Barren Creek. Possessed by James Weatherly	Nanticoke 100
200a.	WOODSTOCK	15 June 1679, Robert Twerley, On the north side Rewastico Branch, Possessed by William Langsdon	Nanticoke 100
100a.	FERRY HALL	2 Apr.1680. John Smith, In marshes and hummocks of land on the south side of Nanticoke. Possessed by relict of John Marriett	Nanticoke 100
300a.	WEATHERLYS RESERVE	16 Dec.1679, James Weatherly, On the north side Rewastico Creek. Possessed by James Weatherly	Nanticoke 100
1000a.	SPRINGHILL	3 Mar.1680, William Stevens, Assigned Francis Jenkins, on the south side of Nanticoke back in the woods. Possessed by the Honorable Francis Jenkins	Nanticoke 100
100a.	MARSH HOOK	15 Dec.1679, James Weatherly, Being marshy land at the bottom of a neck made by the Rewastico and Mannumquak Creek. Possessed by James Weatherly	Nanticoke 100
200a.	WEATHERLYS RIDGE	15 Dec.1679, James Weatherly, On the north side Rewastico Creek. Possessed by James Weatherly	Nanticoke 100
100a.	SANKY ISLAND	15 Dec 1679, James Weatherly, An island on the north side of the mouth of Rewastico Creek. Possessed by James Weatherly	Nanticoke 100
50a	PASTURAGE	14 Dec 1679, James Weatherly, On the south side Rewastico Creek, north side of Lyons Creek. Possessed by same	Nanticoke 100
50a.	SLIPE	14 Dec.1679, James Weatherly, between Rewastico and south west side Lyons Lyons Creek. Possessed by same	Nanticoke 100
100a.	ONCE AGAIN	14 Dec 1679, James Weatherly, Between Rewastico and Manumquak. Possessed same.	Nanticoke 100
250a.	WEATHERLYS CHANCE	8 Apr.1681, James Weatherly, on the south side Barren Creek. Possessed same.	Nanticoke 100
200a.	WARRINGTON	28 Feb.1680, Thomas Halse, On the south side Nanticoke by LYONS DOWN. Possessed by John Kemp	Nanticoke 100
150a.	FAIRHAM	30 July 1681, Edward Bennett, on the south side of the head of Quantico Creek Possessed by- 50a. James Tully 50a. Stephen Tully 50a. Edward Bennett	Nanticoke 100

ACRES	TRACT	SURVEY DATE-BY WHOM	LOCATION

350a. DARBY   3 Mar.1680, William Stevens,   Nanticoke 100
               Assigned Thomas Wilson, on the south side of
               the main branch of Barren Ck. Possessed by same

200a. WESTON   12 Mar.1680, William Stevens,   Nanticoke 100
               Assigned John Richards, on northward of
               Wetepkowant. Possessed by John Reed

300a. WEATHERLYS CONTRIVANCE,12 Apr.1681. Col. William Stevens
               Assigned James Weatherly,   Nanticoke 100
               On the south side of Rewastico Branch. Possessed
               150a. the heir of Thomas Ackworth
               150a. James Weatherly

400a. OLDBURY 1 Apr.1681, William Stevnes,   Nanticoke100
               Assigned Francis Jenkins. on south side of
               the main branch of Quantico. Possessed by same.

100a. KINGSTON, 1 Oct 1681, Thomas Chapwell,   Nanticoke 100
               Between Quantico and Nanticoke River. Chappell
               hath an heir in Accomomak. The land unseated
               and no rent paid.

150a. BECKNAM 20 Nov.1681, Andrew Jones,   Nanticoke 100
               Assigned James Dashiell, On the south side
               of Wetepkwant Creek. Possessed by Thomas Dashiell

250a. PECHINGO RIDGE, 20 Nov.1681, Owen Macraugh, Nanticoke 100
               Assigned James Weatherly, on the south side of
               Rewastico Branch. Appertains to the heir and
               orphan of Thomas Acworth, who is in possession

500a. MANLOVES GROVE, 5 Apr.1680, William Stevens, Nanticoke 100
               Assigned Luke Manlove, on the south side of
               Nanticoke. Possessed by-
               250a. James Caldwell
               250a. George Hutchins by the name of FIRST CHOICE

130a. TOSSWANDOCK,3 June 1682, WIlliam Stevens, Nanticoke 100
               Assigned Charles Nutter. At the head of the
               Nanticoke River. Possessed by Charles Nutter

1200a.ATTAWATTAQUAQUO,2 Jun.1682,William Stevens, Nanticoke 100
               Assigned to Charles Nutter. at the head of
               Nanticoke. 400a. appertains to the orphans of
                         John Nutter at Delaway Bay
               800a. Possessed of Charles Nutter

300a. VENTURE 2 Nov.1682, Samuel Jackson,   Nanticoke 100
               On the north side Chickawant Branch or creek.
               Possessed by Jonathan Jackson

100a. CANNONS LOTT, 8 Sept.1681, James Sangster, Nanticoke 100
               Assigned to Stephen Cannon, on the south side
               of Wetepkowant Creek. Appertains to Patrick
               Quatermass who lives in Dorset County

100a. NATH   8 Sep.1681, James Langster,   Nanticoke 100
               Assigned to Julian Meseck. On the north side of
               Wetepkowant. Possessed by Julian Meseck

| ACRES | TRACT | SURVEY DATE-BY WHOM | LOCATION |

600a. WETEPKEWANT-1 July 1664, Stephen Horsey,   Nanticoke 100
On the east most side of Nanticoke where there is no such land and so hath been formerly returned by C.Jenkins.

500a. CLOSEFORK, 12 Oct.1671, Richard Whitty,   Nanticoke 100
In Quantico Branch on the south side of the creek. Since resurveyed by the name of RECOVERY. Possessed by George Dasheill

300a. CAMBRIDGE, 26 Nov.1672, George Smith,   Nanticoke 100
Near Nanticoke at a corner tree of John Craycrofts. Claimed by Thomas Gordon

300a. MORRIS'S DELIGHT-26 Nov.1672, Jenkins Morris, Nanticoke 100
Near Nanticoke at a marked Gum and a corner tree of George Smith's. Noone in possession. Former returns said to be possessed by Indians

900a. GETHSEMANE, 3 Oct.1674, William Stevens,   Nanticoke 100
On the south side Nanticoke in Quantico Creek.
Possessed by-300a. Samuel Worthington
           300a. John Hamblin
           300a. John Kemp

200a. TAYLORS HILL-3 June.1683, John Gladston,   Nanticoke 100
Possessed or claimed by Robert Laws, by gift from John Pantor who purchased of Gladston

100a. GLADSTOWER, 13 Jun.1682, for Gladston,   Nanticoke 100
Possessed by John Gladston in Dorset County

150a. TURKEY COCK HILL-6 June1683, Manasses Morris. Nanticoke 100
Possessed by William Giles Jr.

250a. BATCHELORS DELIGHT, 8 Jun.1683, James With and Marmaduke Mastors. Those persons have deceased the county long since and said to be dead. No heirs appear or rent ever paid.

250a. BATCHELORS INVENTION, The land as before,   Nanticoke 100
150a. BATCHELORS CONTRIVANCE, The land as before,   Nanticoke 100

550a. CRANE RIDGE, No time when surveyed,   Nanticoke 100
Assigned James Weatherly, Possessed by same.

200a. MARISH POINT, 11 May 1683, James Weatherly,   Nanticoke 100
Possessed by Richard Ackworth

600a. PARTNERS CHOICE, 12 Jun.1682, Assig.Wm. Keen, Nanticoke 100
Possessed-200a. William Keen
          200a. Edmund Macnamary
          200a. Orphans of Wm. Keen Jr.

350a. CARTERS LODGE,14 May 1683,Assign. George Carter,Nanticoke 100
Apportains to George Trotter

300a. CHANCE 19 May 1683, Assign. John Parramour,   Nanticoke 100
No one in possession or know not the land unless James Weatherly possesses it

2500a.GREENLAND, 5 Apr.none ,Col.William Stevens,   Nanticoke 100
Assigned William Green. Possessed by William Green an inhabitant of Dorset County

| ACRES | TRACT | SURVEY DATE-BY WHOM | Location |

200a. BOWER   2 Dec.1682, Assigned Thomas Farnall, Nanticoke 100
              Possessed by Thomas Farnall

30a. TARRKILL HUMMOCK,5 Oct.1683, David Howard   Nanticoke 100
              in right of John Wilsons orphans

100a. GLADSTEANS DELIGHT,3 Jun.1682,John Gladstean,Nanticoke 100
              Possessed by John Gladstean who lives in Dorset.Co.

300a. JOHN GLADSTEANS LAND,24 Apr.1684,John Gladstean,Nanticoke 100
              Possessed by same who lives in Dorset Co.

750a. THE SUPPLY, 5 July 1683,Assigned Capt.Isaac Foxcroft.
              Belongs to the widow Waters in Boston, New England
              the estate managed by Capt.James Dashiell, Nanticoke 10

100a. LYONS LOTT, 21 May 1683, Assigned John Lyon, Nanticoke 100
              Possessed by James Givan

150a. BASSLEGG,1 Oct 1683, assigned Francis Jenkins, Nanticoke 100
              Possessed by Col.Frand s Jenkins

320a. COLLIERS GOOD SUCESS,15 Apr.1684,Possessed by, Nanticoke 100
              James Collier son of Robert thefirst taken up.

2400a. PARSALIA, 25 Jun.1675, South Littleton,   Matapany 100
              On the seaboard side at Wanscutt,alias Great
              Matapany Creek. Possessed by-
              300a. Madam Susannah Littleton in Virginia
              200a. John Purnell
              300a. Daniel Gore in his wife's right
              400a. Richard Waters
              400a. William Whittingham Jr.
              300a. Henry Harman in Accocomac Va.

550a. PURNELLS LOTT-(no date)no find whom.   Matapany 100
              On the northeast side Little Mony Creek and is
              named Fresh Water Branch. Possessed by John Purnell

800a. TRANSLVANIA, 22 Sep.1676, William Stevens, Matapany 100
              Assigned William Waltton on the seaboard side
              at Mattapony in a branch. Possessed by-
              100a. Widow Carroll
              400a. Fisher Walton
              300a. Stephen Walton

200a. BATCHELLORS LOTT,9 Nov.1676, John Smock   Matapany 100
              At seaboard side between Poquedernorten and
              Assateage. Possessed by Henry Smock son and heir
              to John.

100a. RUMLEY MARSH, 3 June 1676. Ambrose White   Matapany 100
              On the seaboard side where Mattapany and Assawoman.
              Possessed by Thomas Powell

400a. MUSKETA POINT-29 Nov.1676, William Cord,   Matapony
              by assignment from William Stevens. On the seaboard
              side at Mattapany, at the mouth of a small gut.
              Possessed by William Cord son and Heir of Wm.

1550a. INGLETEAGE,13 Oct 1675, John Robins,   Matapany 100
              On the seaboard side near Mattapany Creek. Possessed
              by Thomas Robins.

300a. HEADLY HILL, 14 Apr.1676, William Stevens,   Matapany 100
              assigned Henry Hall near Poquerdernorten about 4
              miles from the salt water,.Possessed by Henry Hall

| ACRES | TRACT | SURVEY DATE-BY WHOM | LOCATION |

200a. BURMUDA HUNDRED, 9 Apr.1674, Nathaniel Wasey,   Mattapony 100
   On the seaboard side, by the head of a small
   branch that runs into Swansire Creek. Possessed
   by Nathaniel Basey

200a. PAGGAN, 26 July 1679, WilliamStevens.   Mattapony 100
   Assigned Timothy Pade, on seaboard side near
   Mattapony. Possessed by Afrad⁰ Johnson

200a. TIMBER QUARTER, 25 July 1679, William Stevens,Mattapony 100
   Assigned Thomas Purnell, on the seaboard side near
   Mattapony. Possessed by-50a. Affradosa Johnson,
   150a. John Purnell

250a. BASTABLE, 15 July 1678, Daniel Selby,   Mattapony 100
   On the seaboard side near the head of Mattapony
   Creek. Possessed by Phillip Selby

300a. MIDDLETON, 16 Sep.1675, Henry Hall,   Mattapony 100
   near Poqudernorten, at the head of Assawoman Branch
   Possessed by-100a. Henry Hall Jr.
   200a. John Hall

200a. BATCHELORS ADVENTURE, 19 Jun.1679 George Hafford,Mattapony 100
   On the seaboard side on the west side Turpin Branch.
   Possessed-150a. Richard Holland
   500a. William Holland

100a. HOGGHILL, 28 Aug 1679, Jacob Hill,   Mattapony 100
   Assigned Thomas Clifton, on the seaboard side, on
   the west side Swansticutt Creek. Possessed by
   Abraham Hill.

250a. PETERSON, 16 May 1680, Peter Watson,   Mattapony 100
   On the west side Swansicutt Creek. Possessed by
   Rowland Hodgson

100a. THE KEY,6 Mar.1680, Bowman Littleton, John Robins-Mattapony 100
   Thomas Purnell,Daniel Selby,William Survile, Gearge
   Hamlin,William Hearn, Nathaniel Goosey,Thomas
   Profitt, Francis Williams,William Cord, William
   Walton,William Stevenson. On the south side
   Pocomoke River. Possessed by Joseph Anderson in
   the right of Col. John Robins in Virginia

300a. JOHNSONS HOPE, 10 Mar.1680, William Stevens, Mattapony 100
   Assigned Robert Johnson, on the seaboard side
   near Mattapony. Possessed by Robert Johnson

300a. WAKFIELD, 26 Mar.1687, Assigned Francis Jenkins, Mattapony 100
   Near the divisional line on the west side Sumerset
   Branch, Possessed by James Smith who lives in Accocomac

200a. WEST CHESTER, 29 none 1681, Wm. Stevens   Mattapony 100
   Assigned John Rust, on the west side main branch
   of Swansicutt. Possessed by John Rownslee in right
   of Robert Bouchers orphan

250a. TIMBER QUARTER, 5 Dec 1680, Matthew Scarborough, Mattapony 100
   Between seaside and Pocomoke. Possessed by same

250a. THE LOCK, 15 Dec.1680, Matthew Scarborough, Mattapany 100
   Assigned to George Baynum, near Mattapony Key. Possessed by Thomas Murphy

| ACRES | TRACT | SURVEY DATE-BY WHOM | LOCATION |

350a. NUNSGREEN-5 Oct.1681. Matthew Scarborough, Mattapony 100
near Middleton at a corner tree of Durham.
Possessed by Matthew Scarborough

350a. CARAGANASTICK-2 Jan 1682, Thomas Jones Mattapony 100
Assigned Daniel Selby, at the head of Mattaony
Branch. Possessed by-
200a. Phillip Selby
150a. by heirs of Parker Selby

200a. BRIDGEWATER, 16 Dec 1682, Walter Read, Mattapony 100
Assigned John Jones, on the south side of Pocomoke
back in the woods. Possessed by John Aydelott

100a. READS CONTRIVANCE, 23 Nov.1682, Walter Read, Mattapony 100
Assigned John Jones on the north side of Pocomoke.
Possessed by John Aydelott

1400a. BANTRY 18 Apr.1674, Daniel Selby, Mattapony 100
Possessed by-200a. Phillip Selby
1200a. John Purnell and William Selby in right
of the heirs of Parker Selby

50a. GEORGES MARSH, 10 Apr.1674, George Hamlin, Mattapony 100
On the seaboard side near Mattapony Creek.
Possessed by John Purnell

300a. SPEEDWELL, 10 Apr.1674, William Collins Mattapony 100
On the west side of Swansicutt, Not possessed or
claimed by anyone. Suppose the land was surveyed
for John Collins who thought the certificate
was not returned.

200a. PARNALLS ADVENTURE, 7 Apr.1674, Thomas Purnell, Mattapony 100
Near Mattapony Creek. Possessed by John Purnell,
vide John Holland's account

300a. CEDAR GROVE, 10 Apr.1674, John Pike, Mattapony 100
Near Mattapony Creek. This land resurveyed by a
special Warrent for 280a. for and in the name of
Sarah and John Starrett, he in marrying the said
Sarah who was Pike's heiress and by whom assigned
to Daniel Selby for valuable consideration but the
certificate and assignment both miscarried in the
Revolution. The land Possessed by Phillip Selby.

250a. ACCOMPSICK ISLAND, 16 Apr.1675. James Mills, Mattapony 100
On the seaboard side near Poquedernorten. Possessed
by John Watts in Virginia

725a. TIMBERLAND, 16 Apr.1679, James Mills. Mattapony 100
Assigned to David Watts, on the seaboard side near
Mattapony. Possessed by John Watts in Virginia

200a. ST.LEONARDS, 11 Jun 1682, Assigned to Tobias Pepper, Mattapony
Possessed by Tobias Pepper 100

200a. FALMOUTH, 11 June 1682, Assigned Thomas Clifton, Mattapony 100
Possessed by Peter Watson

200a. TEMPLE COMB, 10 Jun.1682, Assigned John Cupman, Mattapony 100
Possessed by-100a. William Ainsworth in his wife's
right. 100a. claimed by Mary Cupman

ACRES	TRACT	Survey date- by Whom	Location
150a.	TANNERS HALL,	26 May 1683, Assigned Wm.Waite, Possessed by Nathaniel Waite	Mattapony 100
500a.	ROME	17 May 1683, John Pope, Possessed by John Pope	Mattapony 100
200a.	NEW YARMOUTH,	29 May 1683, William Barnes, Apportains to George Russell in Accocomac Virginia vide Thomas Hogintons account	Mattapony 100
150a.	CARTWHEEL,	28 Sep.1683, Richard Pepper, Possessed by Walter Read	Mattapony 100
325a.	COLDHARBOR,	15 Dec 1683, Thomas Purnell Possessed-235a. Affradozi Johnson 90a. John Purnell	Mattapony 100
200a.	OLDBURG,	22 Dec 1683, Thomas Acworth Possessed by Thomas Acworth alias Ackford	Mattapony 100
400a.	THORNBURY,	21 Dec.1683, Thomas Ackford Possessed by same	Mattapony 100
275a.	MATTAPANY MARSH,	27 Dec 1683, Thomas Purnell, Possessed by John Purnell	Mattapony 100
200a.	VALE OF EASOM,	18 Dec.1682, John Mark who is dead and no heirs appears	Mattapony
100a.	SCILLY	18 Dec.1683, Thomas Ackford Apportions to Rowland Shephard who removed up the bay.	Mattapony 100
200a.	MILLBURG HEATH,	22 Dec 1683, Tobias Pepper Possessed by same	Mattapony 100
150a.	SHRENSBURY,	17 Dec 1688, Henry Rogers Possessed by Capt.John Westland	Mattapony 100
200a.	MOTILACK,	17 Dec 1683, Richard Webb Possessed by Capt. John Westland	Mattapony 100
200a.	SHAFTSBURY,	17 Dec.1683, Assigned John Pope, Possessed by John Pope	Mattapony 100
150a.	GOODHOPE	8 Oct 1683, Assigned John James, Possessed by Nathaniel Hopkins	Mattapony 100
300a.	THE BLACKRIDGE,	13 Sep.1684, Thomas Wellbourne, Apportains to Daniel Willbourn in Virginia	Mattapony 100
300a.	DUBLYN	13 Sep.1684, Daniel Selby Apportains to William Selby in Virginia	Mattapony 100
100a.	LUTTERWORTH	10 Sep.1684, Francis Joyce Possessed by Francis Joyce	Mattapony 100
77a.	DURDAN DOWN,	16 Jun 1684, Richard Holland Belongs to John Holland son of Richard	Mattapony 100
160a.	LITTLE	3 Apr.1683, Col.William Stevens Possessed by Samuel Layfield	Mattapony 100
300a.	FON	The same day for Col.Stevens apportains to Samuel Layfield	Mattapony 100
300a.	UNITY	10 Mar.1666, James Jones Assigned Edward Smith, at seaboard side at a marked tree by a glade near the land of John Smith. Claimed by Benjamin Scholfield in the right of one of Smith's coheirs.	Mattapony 100

| ACRES TRACT | SURVEY DATE-BY WHOM | LOCATION |

1000a. MORDIKE 27 Aug.1668, Paul Marsh   Mattapany 100
           On the south side of Pocomoke River over
           against Ascomonoconson on the middle ground.
           Possessed by Matthew Scarborough

500a. NEWPORT PAGNELL, 10 Sep.1668, Wm.Stevens   Poquadenorton 100
           Assigned John White, on the seaboard side near
           Assateage Point on the north side of Marsh's
           Creek since by resurvey made 760a. It contains
           750a. Possessed by-375a. Laurence Riely in his
                wife's right
           375a. by John Watts in Virginia

150a. BUCKINGHAM, 27July 1679 resurvey John White   Poquadenorton 100
           At the seaboard side at Assateage Point on the
           north side March Creek. Possessed by-
           360a. Francis Thorogood
           350a. William Massey
           400a. William White
           400a. Stephen White

600a. PATTENTED, 20 Feb 1673, Alexander Williams, Poquadenorton 100
           between the land of Robert Richardson and Thomas
           Selby. Possessed by-163.a John Rickett
                           437a. John Webb

2000a. MOUNT EPHRAIM, no date, Robert Richardson   Poquadenorton 100
           On the seaboard side Possessed by-
           650a. Thomas Thompson in right of Selby's orphan
           1200a. Charles Richardson
           100a. James Bratten

700a. SMITHS FIRST CHOICE, no date, Edward Smith   Poquadenorton 100
           At the seaboard side on the north east side of
           Robert Richardson's land. Possessed by Benjamin
           Schoolfield

1050a. ROBINSONS INHERITANCE, no date or who   Poquadenorton 100
           At the seaboard side at a neck of woodland ground
           and marsh bounded by Hearn Creek. Possessed by-
           500a. Johnson Hill
           550a. John Sturgis

1500a. PARRAMOURS DOUBLE PURCHASE, 1666, John Parramour, Poquadernorton
           Between Weefua?? on the north east and Hearn Creek
           on the south west. Possessed by-
           550a. John Porter in the right of Thomas Parramour
                in Virginia
           550a. John Standors i n ditto right
           200a. Thomas Ackford
           200a. Richard Pepper Sr.

600a. PURGATORY,1 May 1675, Robert Johnson,   Poquadernorton 100
           On the north side of Parramour, at the seaboard
           side. Possessed by Robert Johnson

1250a, SIMPLETON, no date.Thomas Selby   Poquadernorton 100
           On the north side of Henry Bishop's land, part
           thereof being a point of marsh and trees. Possessed
           by-520a. John Owton
              200a. John Bishop
              530a. Thomas Selby

ACRES	TRACT	SURVEY DATE-BY WHOM	LOCATION	

2300a. DURHAM HOUSE, 20 Dec.1675 Henry Bishop Sr.   POQUADENORTON 100
At the seaboard on the north side of Poquadenorton
Bay and brook. Possessed by-
1000a. Matthew Scarborough
1300a. Ephraim Wilson

1000a. ASSATEAGE FIELD, alias WREXHAM   Poquadenorton 100
12 Nov.1675, Edward Wall. On the seaboard side
of west side of Mobjack Bay. This land is by
resurvey included in 1200a. of WREXHAM. Possessed
700a. Ebenezer Croper
500a. John Croper

500a. COW QUARTER, 30 Jun.1677, Ambrose White   Poquadenorten 100
on the seaboard side near Assawoman. Possessed by-
250a. Richard Woodcraft
250a. William Robinson

450a. FAIRHAVEN, 2 July 1677, Willian Nock   Poquadenorton 100
near Assawoman. Possessed by-
150a. William Ricketts
150a. John Ricketts
150a. William Robinson

150a. ASSAWOMAN, 2 July 1679. William Nock   Poquadenorton 100
On the seaboard side at an Indian Path. Possessed by-
75a. William Robinson
75a. William Ricketts

800a. FAIRFIELD, 21 Nov.1676, William Stevens   Poquadenorton 100
Assigned Thomas Purnell, on the seaboard side near
the east bounds of Edward Smith. Possessed by
Thomas Purnell son of Thomas

50a. GREEN MEAD, 1 May 1677, William Stevens   Baltimore 100
assigned Robert Johnson on the south side of the
St.Martins River. Possessed by Robert Johnson
Jr. of Baltimore 100

400a. THE FRIENDS DENYALL, 26 Oct.1676, John Smock, Baltimore 100
Assigned Robert Johnson, near the mouth of Dividing
Creek. In possession of Robert Johnson Jr.

200a. THE ENDEAVOUR, 16 Jun 1675, John Emmett   Baltimore 100
Assigned James Winderson, on the south side of an
Island at the mouth of St.Martins. Possessed by
Wrixum White

150a. RICHARDSONS FOLLY, 23 July 1677, Robert Richardson, Baltimore 100
Near the head of the St.Martins River about 2 miles
from the water. Possessed by Thomas Powell by the
name of Richardsons Folly

300a. BURLEY, 6 July 1672, William Stevens   Baltimore 100
Assigned William Tomkins, on the seaboard side
near the head of Assatagae Creek. Possessed by
William Faucett

300a. DISCOVERY, 18 Oct.1677, John Emmett   Baltimore 100
Assigned Henry Bishop at Quapomqua near the head
of Pocomoke. Possessed by Devorez Drigors in the
right of Henry Bishop's children

1100a. ST LAURENCE NECK, 16 Oct.1677 John Emmett, Baltimore 100
Assigned Thomas Pointer, on the west side of Mojack
Bay, to the northward of Capatole. Possessed by
450a. Jeremiah Pointer, 650a. Argalas Pointer

ACRES	TRACT	SURVEY DATE-BY WHOM	LOCATION

600a. DEALL   17 Oct.1677, John Emmett   Baltimore 100
              Assigned to William Junis Jr. on the west side of
              Mobjack Bay, northward of Capatotoe Creek.
              Possessed by, 200a. Corn. Junis
                            400a. Benjamin Stockfield

250a. SALEM   5 Sep.1676, Ellis Coleman   Baltimore 100
              Near the head of the Pocomoke River. Possessed
              by William Robinson at Snow Hill, Merchant

500a. COLICKMORE, 29 Dec.1677, James Rownd   Poquadenorton 100
              At seaboard side at Assateage. Possessed by Madam
              Mary Edgar vide John Hamton account

600a. DIOCESS 14 July 1677, John Emmett,   Poquadenorton 100
              Assigned Henry Bishop, on the north
              west side of
              Assateague River. Possessed by Benjamin Burton

250a. EXON   16 July 1677, John Emmett   Poquadenorton 100
              Assigned Henry Bishop, about 2 miles from Poquade-
              norton Landing. Possessed by William Stephenson

600a. WATTS CONVENIENCE, 22 Apr.1678, John Watson, Poquadenorton 100
              On the westmost side Poquadenorton Bay. Possessed
              by John Macally tenent to John Watts in Virginia

450a. WELLBECK, 12 Apr.1678, William Stevens,   Poquadenorton 100
              Assigned William Tomkins, in Sinepuxon Neck.
              Possessed by William Turvill

1500a. GOSHEN 16 Nov.1676, William Stevens,   Poquadenorton 100
              Assigned to Francis Jenkins, in Sinepuxon Neck.
              On the west side Newhaven Sound. Possessed by
              William Faucett

400a. EXCHANGE, 25 Feb.1677, William Stevens   Poquadenorton 100
              On the seaboard side near Sinepuxon. Possessed
              by John Franklin

200a. BENGRAVE, 16 Apr.1678, William Stevens,   Poquadenorton 100
              Assigned Edward Smith, on seaboard side, 2 miles
              in the woods. Possessed by Robert Peirce

600a. HIGHFIELD, 25 Nov.1676, William Stevens   Poquadenorton 100
              Assigned Thomas Pointer, on seaboard side near
              Assateage, Possessed by Thomas Pointer

200a. LANDOWN 30 Aug.1676, Henry Morgan,   Poquadernorton 100
              Near the head of Pocomoke. Possessed by Edward Hammond

600a. TEUXBURY, 28 June 1678, William Stevens   Poquadenorton 100
              Assigned Edward Smith, on seaboard side alittle to
              the northward of Assateage Fields. Possessed by-
              100a. Walter Evans
              100a. Enock Griffin or John Green in his right
              400a. orphans of William Wouldhave

300a. EDWARDS LOTT- 9 Sep.1678, William Stevens   Poquadenorton 100
              Assigned Thomas Pointer, on Poquadenorton and
              Assateage. Possessed by Edward Pointer

400a. SHERBORN, no date. John White   Poquadenorton 100
              Assigned to Matthew Scarbrough, near the head of
              Pocomoke River in Ropunque. Possessed by Capt.
              Edward Hammond

ACRES	TRACT	SURVEY DATE-BY WHOM	LOCATION	
300a.	GOLDEN QUARTER	21 July 1678, William Stevens, Assigned to Edward Smith on the seaboard side near the head of Assategue. Possessed by Peter Camell	Poquadenorton	100
300a.	WINKFIELD,	13 Apr.1678, William Stevens. Assigned to Christopher Reynolds. Between the head of Pocomoke and Seaside. Possessed by John Cavenough	Poquadenorton	100
200a.	POPLAR HILL,	17 Sep.1671, John Richards, Assigned to John Devoraux on the south side Pocomoke about a mile back in the woods. Possessed by John Deveraux	Poquadenorton	100
300a.	LINEATH,	19 Apr.1679 William Stevens Assigned to John Price, on the seaside about 4 miles in the woods. Possessed by Thomas Morris	Poquadenorton	100
400a.	HAPPY ENTRANCE,	14 Sep.1678, William Stevens, Assigned to John White, on the seaside on the north side of St.Martins River. Possessed by Wrixham White	Poquadenorton	100
600a.	TAUNTON	14 Sep.1678, William Stevens, Assigned to Thomas Selby, on the north side of St.Martins and east side Muddy Creek. Possessed by- 300a. Nathaniel Ratcliffe 300a. Peter Burton	Poquadenorton	100
400a.	FISHING HARBOR,	14 Jul.1679, John White, Assigned Ambrose White, a little northward of the mouth of St.Martins River. Possessed by Wrixham White	Poquadenorton	100
200a.	SMITHS CHOICE,	14 Jul.1679, John White Assigned Ambrose White, on the north side of St. Martins River. Possessed by-100a. Rihcard Webb 100a. John Tull	Poquadenorton	100
500a.	CORAM	15 July 1679, John White Assigned to Samuel Cooper, on the west side of Dividing Creek at St. Martins. Appartains to Samuel Sanford in London	Poquadenorton	100
2000a.	CARMELL	14 Jun.1679, Col.William Stevens, In Sinepuxon on the northmost part of the neck. Possessed-500a. William Massey 500a. Alexander Massey 500a. William Faucett 500a. John Watts in Virginia, Nathaniel Cooper is by his right.	Poquadenorton	100
1400a.	NEIGHBOURHOOD,	16 Jun.1679, William Stevens, Assigned to William Walton. In Sinepuxon. Possessed by-700a. William Walton 700a. John Walton	Poquadenorton	100
400a.	SANDY WHARF,	30 July 1679, William Stevens, Assigned to Henry Morgan, near the head of the Pocomoke River. Possessed by William Whittington	Poquadenorton	100
300a.	AMEE DOWN,	16 July 1679, John White Assigned to John Smock and Robert Cade, near the head of Pocomoke. Possessed by William Round	Poquadenorton	100

| ACRES | TRACT | SURVEY DATE-BY WHOM | LOCATION |

300a. BECKFORD, 16 July 1679, John White   Poquadenorton 100
    Assigned to Aaron Bishop, on the road between
    Poquadenorton and Assateage. Possessed by same.

200a. SANDY POINT, 25 July 1679, William Turvill, Poquadenorton 100
    Assigned to Robert Cade, in a fork of Assateage.
    Possessed by Ephraim Heather, in right of Daniel
    Selby's orphans

800a. CROPTON   18 Jun 1679, William Stevens,   Poquadenorton 100
    Assigned to Samuel Powell, at the seaboard side of
    St. Martins. Possessed by David Hudson

450a. MOUNT PLEASANT, 28 Jun 1679, John Robins   Poquadenorton 100
    Assigned to Edward Wall and Charles Ratcliff. Near
    the head branch of Assateage. Possessed by-
    225a. Ebenezer Franklin in right of Edward Watts
    225a. John Evans

500a. CREEDWELL, 16 July(none) John White   Poquadenorton 100
    Assigned to John Smock and Robert Cade. On the west
    side Assateage. Apportains to Samuel Layfield

450a. HUSBANDS TORRENT, 15 Nov.1675, Robert Richardson, Poquadenorton
    Near Assateage River by a Crooked Creek. Apportains
    to Richard Hill's orphan but possessed by Henry Rich

400a. RIPPLE   27 Oct.1679, John King,   Poquadenorton 100
    Assigned to Edward Smith, near head of Assateage.
    Possessed by-100a. Presgrave Turvill
              300a. Peter Camell

250a. FLUDBURY, 18 Apr.1678, William Stevens,   Poquadenorton 100
    Assigned to Edward Smith, on the south side Pocomoke
    near the head. Possessed by William Rounds.

800a. WINCHESTER, 12 Dec 1678, George Hamblin,   Poquadenorton 100
    on the south side St.Martins River. Possessed by-
    400a. Presgrave Turvill
    400a. Francis Hamblin

2200a. GENZAR, resurv.4 Nov.1678, William Stevens, Poquadenorton 100
    Assigned Edward Wall and Charles Ratcliff, on the
    south side Sinepuxon Neck. Possessed by-
    800a. Edward Wall
    300a. Nathaniel Ratcliff in Accocomac
    500a. Eliau Ratcliff
    600a. Charles Ratcliff

150a. HILLIARDS DISCOVERY, 6 Aug.1679, John Godwyn, Poquadenorton 100
    Assigned to Walter Powell, on the north side of the
    head of St.Martins. Possessed by-75.a Walter Evans,
    75a. Hugh ingle

1050 BASSING   4 Mar 1679, John Godwyn   Poquadenorton 100
    on the seaboard side near Sinepuxon, Possessed by same

300a. SUPPLY   23 Mar.1680, William Stevens   Poquadenorton 100
    A little to the southward of St.Martins Creek.
    Possessed by Margaret Towers

450a. THE ROYAL OAK, 18 May 1680, William Stevens, Poquadenorton 100
    Assigned William Turvill, a neck of land a little
    wouthward of St.Martins River. Possessed by-225a.
    Margery Turvill, 225a. Presgrave Turvill escheated
    for want of heirs of Thomas Profitt in whom the
    right was.

ACRES	TRACT	SURVEY DATE-BY WHOM	LOCATION	
100a.	CHANCE	22 Mar.1680, William Stevens on the seaboard side in the woods from the St. Martins River. Possessed by John McManus in the right of Stukley and his heirs or in his wife's right	Poquadenorton	100
200a.	HILLIARDS MISTAKE,	22 Mar.1680, Wm. Stevens, To the northward of St.Martins River. Said to be possessed by David Hudson	Poquadenorton	100
250a.	CASTLEHILL,	15 Mar.1680,Wm. Stevens, Assigned to Joshua Leigh, on the south side of Pocomoke. Possessed by-125a. Willian Nelson, 125a. Samuel Ball in right of Wm.Laurence's orphans	Poquadenorton	100
300a.	CANNADEE,	2 May 1680, John Smock Assigned Nathaniel Junis, on the west side Mobjack Bay. Possessed by Charles Junis vide Benjamin Leafield account	Poquadenorton	100
150a.	STURBRIDGE,	20 Feb.1681, John Cropper, on the south side of the head of Pocomoke near Quaponqua. Possessed by William Pointer	Poquadenorton	100
200a.	HOGG QUARTER,	20 Feb 1667, John Cropper, Near the head of Pocomoke and Assateague. Noone possessed this land neirther is the land known. The heir is in Accocomac.	Poquadenorton	100
1000a.	MULBERRY GROVE,	26 Sep.1680, William Stevens, On the south side Pocomoke on the south side of a fresh water run. Possessed by- 600a. George Truitt 148a. William Rownd 167a. Abraham Heather 85a. John Godden	Poquadenorton	100
200a.	THE RESERVE,	6 Oct.1681,Matthew Scarborough, Assigned to John Bishop, at Poquadenorton. Apportains to the orphan of John Bishop now in possession	Poquadenorton	100
250a.	THE GOLDEN VALLEY,	10 Dec.1681,Richard Fassett, Assigned John Cropper. At the head of Pocomoke. Not Possessed nor claimed by any. The heirs lives in Accocomac Virginia	Poquadernorton	
500a.	JONES ADVENTURE,	1 Mar.1666, James Jones On the seaboard side not far from Poquadenorton Since granted to Andrew Jones. Possessed by Henry Hudson Sr.	Poquadenorton	100
200a.	POPLAR RIDGE,	2 Mar.1666, James Jones, On the seaboard side on a ridge where the indian road runs from Pocomoke to Assateague. Possessed by Henry Hudson Sr.	Poquadernoton	100
200a.	ST.PATRICKS HILL,	21 Mar.1670, Roger Patrick, Possessed by Daniel Patrick	Poquadenorton	100
500a.	WEYMOUTH,	13 Jun.1671, John Jazard. Possessed by William Richardson	Poquadenorton	100
500a.	WILTSHIRE,	13 Jun.1671,John Glass At the mouth of Poquadenorton. Possessed by- William Richardson	Poquadenorton	100

| ACRES | TRACT | SURVEY DATE-BY WHOM | LOCATION |

200a. RATCLIFFES ADVENTURE, 19 Mar. 1674, Charles Ratcliff.
On the northwest side Mobjack Bay. Poquadenorton 100
Possessed by the widow in the right of Osburns
orphans.

400a. MUSKETA POINT, 29 Nov. 1676, William Cord, Poquadenorton 100
On the seaboard side at Mattapany, at the mouth
of a small gut. Possessed by William Cord son and
heir to William

100a. RUMLEY MARSH, 30 Jun. 1676, Ambrose White, Poquadenorton 100
On the seaboard side where Mattapany and Assawoman
inlets head into the marshes. Possessed by Thomas
Powell

250a. HUNTINGTON, 30 July 1683, Assigned Robert Johnson. Poquad.100
Possessed by-175a. Thomas Pointer
175a. Michael Godden in the right of Nicholas Cornwells orphans

200a. CONVENIENCE, 29 May 1683, John Smock   Poquadenorton 100
Possessed by Henry Smock

200a. ST. MARTINS RIDGE, 29 May 1683, John Smock, Poquadenorton 100
Apportains to William Townsend

150a. POINT LOOKOUT, 6 Dec 1683, John Cropper.   Poquadenorton 100
John Godden owns the land and pays the rent

150a. BOSWORTH, 8 Oct. 1683, John Popplewell,   Poquadenorton 100
belongs to James Truitt

650a. EAGLE POINT, 24 Sep. 1683, Assign. Wm. Kennett, Poquadenorton 100
Possessed-250a. apportains to Martin Kennett
100a. William Bulger
300a. Edmond Cropper

200a. HOGGS NORTEN, 24 Sep. 1683, John Cropper,   Powuadenorton 100
The same entered before but this is the right
time of rent of the court.

200a. GIFT,   9 Oct. 1683, Assigned to William and Ann Wood.
Possessed by Martin Kennett   Poquadenorton 100

700a. SHAFTSBURY, 1 Oct. 1681, Edward Hammond   Poquadenorton 100
Lying in Quapianqua Neck. Possessed by Capt. Edward
Hammond.

400a. KELLY HILL, 25 May 1683, assigned Thomas Roberts, Poquadernorton 10
Possessed by-100a. John Boden
100a. John Maclany
200a. John Simpson

500a. MAYFIELDS, 3 Oct. 1683, Francis Jenkins   Poquadenorton 100
Possessed by William Faucett

500a. NEWINGTON GREEN, 4 Oct. 1683, Francis Jenkins, Poquadenorton 100
Possessed by-250a. William Kenny
250a. George Howard

150a. JESHIMON, 5 Oct. 1683, assigned Francis Jenkins, Poquadenorton 100
Possessed by Francis Jenkins

300a. HERRING QUARTER, 24 Dec. 1681, Assigned Martha and Mary Foster
The land not possessed by anyone or claimed or rent
ever paid. Said Martha and Mary lived in London

2900a. ROCHESTER, 10 Feb. 1682, John Godden,   Poquadenorton 100
Possessed by same.

ACRES	TRACT	SURVEY DATE-BY WHOM	LOCATION
150a.	MIDDLESEX, 4 Oct.1683, Francis Jenkins Possessed by Francis Jenkins		Poquadenorton 100
25a.	MILL ANGLE,20 Dec.1683,James Rownds, Possessed by Madam Mary Edgar vide John Hamton accts.		Poquadenorton 100
300a.	REDLAND, 17 Dec.1683, James Rownd Possessed by John Cropper		Poquadenorton 100
320a.	RATCLIFFES LATE DISCOVERY,27 Dec.1683, Charles Ratcliffe. Possessed by William Hadder in right of Richard Warren his heirs.		
80a.	ORKNEY	18 Dec.1683,Charles Ratcliffe Possessed by Charles Ratcliffe	Poquadenorton 100
400a.	NEW FAIRFIELD,29 Dec.1683, Thomas Powell Possessed by Thomas Purnell son of Thomas		Poquadenorton 100
53a.	THOMKINS MEADOW,15 Dec.1683, William Tomkins,Poquadenorton 100 Possessed by William Turvill		
500a.	HARRYGATE,15 Dec.1683,Edward Evans. Possessed by Richard Hudson		Poquadenorton 100
300a.	ANDOVER,16 Dec.1683, George Hamblin Possessed by Henry Hudson Jr.		Poquadenorton 100
200a.	NORTH FLEET,16 Dec.1683,Thomas Morris, Possessed by Warren Hadder		Poquadenorton 100
800a.	BUCKLAND, 9 Oct.1683,Col.Wm.Stevens Apportains to Co.Francis Jenkins, possessor		Poquadenorton 100
50a.	ARONS LOTT,21 May 1683.Assig. Aron Bishop, Poquadenorton 100 Possessed by Aron Bishop		
200a.	BRICKHILLHOE, 13 Dec.1683, Thomas Profitt, Poquadenorton 100 No heir or possessor, Must escheat to the propriety		
250a.	NORTHAMPTON, 17 Dec.1583, William Turvill, Poquadernorton 100 Possessed by the widow Turvill, belongs to her son John Turvill		
200a.	LUCAS'S CHOICE, 20 Dec.1684,William Bishop, Poquadenorton 100 Possessed in right of Thomas Lucas his orphans		
325a.	THE ADDITION, 29 Aug 1684,Richard Hill, Belongs to Richard Hill's orphans who is present with Thomas Morris		Poquadenorton 100
200a.	MOREHUSS, 18 Oct.1683,James Rownd. Possessed by Madam Mary Edgar		Poquadenorton
500a.	SOUTH BENEFIT,no date.James Round, Possessed by Mary Edgar vide John Harrison acct.		Poquadenorton 100
400a.	NORTH BENEFIT,13 Sep.1684, James Round, Possessed by Madam Mary Edgar		Poquadenorton 100
200a.	CAERVURTHEN,18 Sep.1684,Richard Harris Possessed by Thomas Purnell		Poquadenorton 100
200a.	SOUTHFLEET, 11 Dec.1683,Thomas Morris Possessed by Jeremiah Townsend.		Poquadenorton 100

| ACRES | TRACT | SURVEY DATE-BY WHOM | LOCATION |

300a. MOUNT HOPE, 20 Oct.1684, William Brown   Poquadenorton 100
 This land sold in Brown's lifetime to George
 Parker in Virginia but not allienated. No rent paid

110a. HOLLY HEAD, 7 July 1672, Samuel Powell,   Poquadenorton 100
 in right of Charles Fassetts orphans

350a. BOWNES CHOICE, 21 May 1683, assign.Wm. Brown, Poquadenorton 100
 In Quapainqua Neck. Possessed by Wm. Brown

600a. SPALDING, 27 May 1683, the remaining part of, Poquadenorton 100
 the land cut off by older survey. Possessed by
 100a. John Teage
 100a. Allivin Ross
 100a. Christian Henderson
 131a. Henry Hudson Jr.
 79a. Thomas Turvill

650a. UNITY   6 Oct.1683, assigned John White,   Poquadenorton 100
 Possessed-325a. William Messey
 325a. Francis Thorogood

200a. PINDERS NEGLECT, 18 May 1680, assig.Abraham Emmett.
 Possessed by John Patrick   Poquadenorton 100

500a. THOMAS'S COURT, 31 Oct(none), Thomas Godden, Poquadenorton 100
 In Nanticoke River. Patent voided. Rent not paid

400a. MEADFIELD, no date. Robert Dyne   Poquadenorton 100
 Land lies in Asquminesomson Town. Possessed by
 Indians.

500a. FRIENDSHIP, 27 Nov.1685, Thomas Jones,   Poquadenorton 100
 On the south side Nanticoke and Deep Creek.
 Possessed by Robert Catherwood for the orphans

250a. ADDITION 29 Nov.1685, Thomas Gordan   Poquadenorton 100
 Possessed by Thomas Gordon

300a. NOVA FRANCIS, 27 Nov.1685, Michael Disheroon, Poquadernortin 100
 belongs to William and Lewis Disheroon

500a. CONVENIENCY, 1 Apr.1686, Wm. Round.   Poquadenortin 100
 Possessed by same

200a. BACON QUARTER, 13 Nov.1585, Peter Parsons, Poquadenortin 100
 Possessed by George Bayley

300a. HEARTS CONTENT, 1 Nov.1685, David Harris,   Wicomico 100
 back in the woods from the Nanticoke. David
 Harris at the south now. Possessed, said to cut
 off by an older survey of Thomas Walker

500a. HOUNDS DITCH, 23 Nov.1685, John Webb.   Wicomico 100
 Possessed by John Bozeman

300a. WHITE CHAPPELL, 20 Nov.1685, Edward Wright, Wicomico 100
 Possessed by John Lamee

50a. STOOPING PINE, 7 Oct.1675, James Conner,   Wicomico 100
 knows not the land

500a. NEW SCOTTLAND, 27 Nov.1685, William Law,   Wicomico 100
 This land belongs to Wm. Lawes heir but the
 administrator refuses payment of the rent.

ACRES	TRACT	SURVEY DATE-BY WHOM	LOCATION
200a.	BACON QUARTER,	5 Apr.1686,Richard Cockshell, the person dead and no heir, therefore escheat	Wicomico 100
50a.	FLATTLANDS,	20 Nov.1685, know not such tr.	Wicomico 100
200a.	GOODNEIGHBOURHOOD,	24 Nov.1686, Possessed by John More vide James Obonton account	Wicomico 100
500a.	NEW IRELAND,	25 Nov.1685,Laurence Young, apportions to Laurence young orphan and heir under guardianship of Richard Russell	Wicomico 100
1200a.	CHOICE	5 Nov.1685,John Osborn in possession of Wm.Whittington who purchased	Wicomico 100
300a.	FRIENDS ASSISTANCE-	15 Nov.1685,Wm. Elgate, Possessed by Thomas Realph supposing to have been surveyed for William Loten.Elgate having no such land surveyed for him	Wicomico 100
150a.	FRIZELLS ENJOYMENT,	12 Nov.1685,John Frizell, Possessed by same	Wicomico 100
500a.	BROTHERS AGREEMENT,	25 Nov.1685,James Knox, belongs to Knox who denys payment of rent	Wicomico 100
150a.	CARPENTERS ENJOYMENT,	4 May 1686,John Brown, Possessed by Isaac ??Frenshan	Wicomico 100
400a.	KILKENY,	31 Mar1686, John Murphey, belongs to Thomas Murphy	Poquadenorton 100
200a.	FREDAGH,	24 Nov.1665,William Collins at deep creek on west side. William Collins long since run. No heir appears nor rent paid	Poquadenorton 100
109a.	ISLINGTON,	8 Feb.1685,Matthew Scarborough Possessed by same.	Poquadenorton 100
300a.	ENLARGEMENT,	18 Sep.1685,John Emmett Possessed -100a. Abraham Heathor, 200a. William Jarman	Poquadenorton 100
500a.	SAND DOWN,	17 Jan.1684,Assigned Simon Folken, belongs to same in Virginia who pays the rent	Poquadernorton 100
366a.	THE HEAD OF ST.ALURENCE NECK,	18 Sep.1684, Assigned Thomas Pointer,Possessed William Pointer	Poquadenorton 100
300a.	TREWETTS HARBOUR,	18 Sep.1684,George Trewett, Possessed by same	Poquadenorton 100
500a.	INCH	18 Sep.1684,Samuel Davis Possessed by John Faucett	Poquadenorton 100
130a.	FARMHILL,	10 Nov.1685, Thomas Purnell, Possessed by Thomas Purnell	Poquadenorton 100
100a.	BETTYS ENLARGEMENT,	20 Nov.1685, Lewis Beard, Possessed by Peter Doughty for Beards orphans	Poquadenorton 100
50a.	HENRYS ENJOYMENT,	19 Nov.1685, Henry Hayman, know not suchland, vide Phillip Covingtons account	Poquadenorton 100
100a.	CARLILE,	24 Nov.1686, Thomas Horseman, Possessed by Adrain Gordon	Wicomico 100

ACRES	TRACT	SURVEY DATE-BY WHOM	LOCATION

50a. LATE DISCOVERY-7 Nov.1686 Robert Collier, Wicomico 100
    possessed by Robert son of Robert Collier

200a. COOPHER HALL, 27 Nov.1685 William Marrutt, Wicomico 100
    possessed by John Cheesman

50a. MONMOUTH, 15 Nov.1685, Andrew Whittington, Wicomico 100
    not possessed nor rent ever paid.

none TAYLORS CHOICE, 7 Nov.1686, John Taylor, Wicomico 100
    on west side and near head of Naswangoe Creek, claimed by John Taylor of Annamessex, none possessed or rent paid

150a. CONTENTMENT, 3 May 1686, Thomas Dunam, Wicomico 100
    near Coy Folly. Possessed by Isaac Ironshan

50a. AMITY, 18 Nov.1685, Richard Peakes of Wicomico 100
    Great Money, on the north side possessed by Phillip Covington

50a. MEADOW 10 Nov.1685, Nathaniel Dougherty Wicomico 100
    know not the land nor possessed, long since dead. Possessed by William Matthews

100a. CLEAR OF CANNON SHOTT- no information

400a. CONVENIENCY, 24 Nov.1685, John Hewett Wicomico 100
    on south side Nanticoke above Broad Creek. This land hath been sold in Hewetts lifetime to John Ballinger but not conveyed. Lies unpossessed by any of the heirs claims and no rent paid.

500a. LIVERPOLL, 27 Nov.1685, Thomas Hester. Nanticoke 100
    This land I know not. The person dead or deceased the county long since. No heir appears.

400a. BRENT MARSH, 2 Apr.1686, John Miller and Baltimore 100
    Abraham Emett. Possessed by John Miller by Purchase from Emett. 100a. Possessed by Leonard Johnson and 200a. by John Miller

334a. FAIR MEADOW, 24 Apr.1685, James Rownd, Baltimore 100
    possessed by Madam Mary Edgar vide John Hamton Account

100a. BRANDFORD, 19 Oct.1685, Robert Cattlins. Baltimore 100
    Possessed by William Cattlin son of Robert & heir

100a. GILLEYS ADDITION, 21 Nov.1685, John Gilley Baltimore 100
    pretents elder survey cut this land off, refuses payment of rent

200a. INCH 10 Sep.1686, Alexander MaCollon, Baltimore 100
    from the water in Powaudernorton 100. Belongs to heirs of said Macullagh who lives at the Horekills

100a. FRIENDS ASSISTANCE, 3 May 1686, Richard Harris, Baltimore 100
    In the woods 2 miles from St.Martins. The right of the land lies in Christian Hemerson at the Horekills

ACRES	TRACT	SURVEY DATE-BY WHOM	LOCATION

100a. JUNIS ADDITION,4 May 1686,Nathaniel Junis Baltimore 100
on the seaboard side. In possession of
Charles Junis heir to Nathaniel

500a. COW QUARTER,14 Apr.1686, Thomas Fenwick, Baltimore 100
Possessed by John Smith

500a. FENWICKS CHOICE,12 Apr.1685,Assigned to Baltimore 100
John Barker, on seaboard side in the right of
of land in Thomas Fenwick, the patent being
made out in Fenwick's name before the assignment.
vide, Woodman Stockleys account

100a. CHANCE, no date. William Jingle Baltimore 100
in Nasswadux Neck. The person dead long since.
Land escheatable

200a. NEW WOOD HALL, 10 Nov.1686, Richard Farewell, Baltimore 100
on the north side Pocomoke. Possessed by Moses
Fenton

441a. MEANT MORE, 4 May 1686, William Stevens Baltimore 100
on seaboard side. Possessed by Henry Hudson Sr.

400a. FREEMANS CONTENTMENT, 30 Apr.1686,John Freeman,Baltimore 100
Possessed by Capt.John Franklin

100a. GOOD SUCESS, 28 Nov.1685,Alexander Thomas, Baltimore 100
Possessed-50a. James Russell
50a. John Brougher who married the coheiress
of Thomas

21a. DENWOODS INCLUSION, 6 Mar.1685,Levin Denwood, Baltimore 100??
Possessed by Arthur Denwood

300a. MARGARETS REST,5 Apr.1686,Peter Parker, Baltimore 100
on the seaboard side of St.Martins River.
Peter Parker did not seat this land but went away
to the south and said to be dead

500a. PARTNERS CONTENTION,2 Apr.1686,John Miller Baltimore 100
and Abraham Emmett. Possessed by John Miller alone

200a. DOGS DOWN BOTTOM,13 Nov.1685,Phenix Hall, Baltimore 100
possessed by said Fenix Hall

50a. CALLOWAYS ADDITION,18 Nov.1685,Peter Calloway, Baltimore 100
he pretents there is no such land. When survey
made he was away from home and no grounds found.
Refuses payment of rent

293a. CORNHILL 31 Mar.1686,Nicholas Cornwell, Baltimore 100
on seaboard side. Possessed by Michael Goddin
in right of Nicholas Cornwell's heirs.

100a. MATES ENJOYMENT,22 Oct.1685,John Culhoone, Annamessex 100
and John Ennis. Possessed by Jesse Eayres

50a. (no name) 18 Nov.1685,18 Nov.1685 Christopher -Nanticoke 100
Nutter. possessed, 25a. Charles Nutter
25a. Matthew Nutter

100a. BEACH AND PINE,3 Nov.1685,assigned John Annamessex 100
Dorman. Possessed by Richard Tull Jr. of
Annamessex

| ACRES | TRACT | SURVEY DATE-BY WHOM | LOCATION |

500a. SPITTLEFIELDS, 21 May 1683, assigned to Baltimore 100
    John Godden. Possessed by
    264a. Mr. Lamee
    235a. John Trouett

500a. COW PASTURE-14 Apr.1686, Col.Wm.Stevens Baltimore 100
    on Assawoman Sound or bay. Possessed by
    Samuel Layfield

300a. COXES CHOICE,16 Dec.1681,Cornelius Johnson. Baltimore 100
    I have made inquery of William Jones who held
    the rest of Cornelius Johnson's land who knows
    nothing of this land. Vide. John Frizzell Account

73a. NOBLES LOTT, 6 Mar.1685,Isaac Noble, Wicomico 100
    Possessed by Isaac Noble son and heir of Isaac.

300a. DENWOODS DEN, 16 Dec.1681, Levin Denwood, Wicomico 100
    near head of Rokiawakin. Possessed by-
    150a. Levin Denwood
    150a. James Hill

300a. GOOD SUCESS, 8 Apr.1686,assigned Capt.Henry Smith,Baltimore 10
    on the seaboard side Baltimore River. remains in
    the right of said smith who died intestate at
    the south. The heir a minor lives in Pennsylvania
    No rent ever paid.

500a. PLEASANT MEADOW, 7 Apr.1686, assigned Capt.Henry Smith.
    on the seaboard side. This the land as before
    lies on the south side Baltimore alias Indian
    River Baltimore 100

50a. WHITTYS LOTT, 28 Nov.1685, Richard Whitty, Wicomico 100
    on the north side of Manokin River. Possessed by
    William Turpin.

200a. TURNERS HALL, 15 Apr.1686, Richard Maclear. Baltimore 100
    on the seaboard side. Possessed by Thomas Morris

200a. WALTONS ADDITION, 22 Nov.1686, John Walton, Annamessex 100
    on the north side Pocomoke. Land sold by John
    Walton who is removed to Pennsylvania. Certificate
    not to be found on record. Rent unpaid.

500a. HIGH MEADOW,1 Apr.1680, assigned Capt.Henry Smith,Balitmore 10
    on the seaboard side, the right remains in said
    Smith's heirs. Minor lives in Pennsylvania, Rent
    unpaid.

100a. ENLARGEMENT, 20 Nov.1680, Thomas Davis, Bogerternortin 100
    on the north side Pocomoke. Davis long since
    dead. The land I know not.

256a. BETTYS REST, 4 May 1686, Edward Williams, Baltimore 100
    back from the seaboard side. Williams dead at
    the Horekills without heir. Vide, Isaac Ironside acct

150a. TIMBER GROVE, 9 June 1683,assigned William Noble.Pocomoke 100
    On the north side Pocomoke. Possessed Wm. Noble

300a. COX'S FORK, 16 Dec.1681, Thomas Cox. Wicomico 100
    at the head of Rokiawakin. Possessed by-
    150a. John Holder, 150a. John Disheroon

```
ACRES  TRACT      SURVEY DATE-BY WHOM                LOCATION
```
500a. WINTER PASTURE, 5 May 1686, Col.Wm.Stevens,Wicomico 100
       suppose it is Winter Quarter on Assateage
       Island or branches, by purchase.
       300a. claimed by Charles Taylor in Virginia by
             purchase
       100a. John Blake
       100a. Edward Green's heirs in England
200a. RETIREMENT,1 May 1686, Ellis Coleman.   Wicomico 100
       on seaboard side. Possessed by Robert Tizer
400a. NORTH WALES, 24 Nov.1685,Alexander Thomas, Wicomico 100
       lying on the south side of the Nanticoke.
       Possessed by-200a. John Bougher
       200a. James Russell who married the coheir of Thomas
150a. GLADSTEANS ADVENTURE,15 Jun 1682,John Gladstean,Wicomico 100
       on the south side Nanticoke, Possessed by same
500a. HOWARDS DESIRE, 13 Apr.1686, Col.Wm.Stevens.   Wicomico 100
       on the seaboard side. Possessed by Nathaniel
       Ratcliffe of Accocomac Virginia
200a. HAPPY ADDITION,17 Mar.1686, Roger Woolford,   Wicomico 100
       on the north side Manokin. Possessed by Mrs. Mary
       Woolford relic of Roger
200a. OAKHALL,16 Dec1686,John Deall,   Wicomico 100
       near the head of Pocomoke River. Possessed by
       Edward Shipham
300a. O'NORTONS LOTT, 9 May 1687 William O'Norton, Baltimore 100
       on the seaboard side. Possessed by John Fassett
150a. GLADSTEANS CHOICE, 2 Nov.1682 assigned Peter Elzey, on
       the north side of Nanticoke. Possessed by Richard
       Ashton
230a. NEWBURY, 16 Dec.1687, William Wooldhhave, Poquadenorton 100
       near seaboard side. Possessed by George Day and
       Walter Evans guardians to Wooldhave's orphan
400a. SCOTTISH PLOTT, 4 May 1687, Thomas Fenwick, Poquadenorton 100
       near seaboard side. Possessed by Hugh Tingle.
500a. DUMFRIZE,5 May 1687,Thomas Fenwick,   Poquadenorton 100
       on the seaboard side. Possessed by
       200a. Charles and Phillip Parker in Accoc. Va.
       200a. Hugh Tingle
       100a. Richard Woodcraft
250a. UPNER   28 Apr.1687, John Goddin,   Poquadenorton 100
       3 miles from the seaboard side. Possessed by same
240a. UNPLEASANT, 30 May 1687, Robert Avery   Poquadenorton 100
       John Freeman Sr. by assignment for Avery widow
       hath a patent for land in his own name.
284a. KILLKENY 1 Sep.1687, Daniel Selby   Poquadenorton 100
       back from the seaboard side. Possessed by
       Abraham Heather in right of Daniel Selby's orphan

| ACRES | TRACT | SURVEY DATE-BY WHOM | LOCATION |

200a. PATTY'S FOLLY, 20 Sep.1687, Richard Pattey, Poquadenorton 100
near seaboard side. Possessed by Jonas and
Joshua Woodman, vide William Ricketts account

200a. FORREST OF DEAR, 2 Sep.1687,John Storry, Poquadenorton 100
on the south side back from the Pocomoke RIver
Possessed by Benjamin Aydelotte

100a. MEDLEY, 21 Sep.1687,William Wooldhave, Poquadenorton 100
back from the seaboard side. Possessed by William
Richards

320a. CUMBERLAND,29 Apr.1687,William Wooldhave Poquadenorton 100
and Richard Hill. 2 miles from seaboard side.
Possessed by-140a. Christian Hermonsen at the
Horekills. 180a. George Day and Walter Evans for
William Wooldhaves orphans

190a. CARPENTERS FOLLY, no date. Thomas Huggett. Poquadenorton 100
possessed by no person, dead without heirs.

500a. SCARBOROUGHS ADVENTURE, 3 May 1687, Poquadenorton 100
on the seaboard side. Possessed by-
250a. John Barron at the Horekills
250a. Aaron Bishop

500a. MIDDLESEX, 3 May 1687,Matthew Scarborough, Poquadenorton 100
on the seaboard side. Possessed by David Hazard

234a. CADES ADDITION,20 Sep.1687, Robert Cade. Poquadenorton 100
on the seaboard side. Claimed by David Hudson

146a. THE CONCLUSION, 20 Apr.1687,Richard Hill, Poquadenorton 100
near the seaboard side. Thomas Morrice holds this
land as guardian to Richard Hill the heir.

160a. TEAGS CONTENT,2 May 1687, Robert Avery, Poquadenorton 100
back in the woods from the seaboard side. This
land was assigned over by the widow Avery to
John Freeman in whose name it was patented

207a. DONOHOES CHOICE,15 Feb.1687,Daniel Donohoe, Poquadenorton 100
Back in the woods from north side Pocomoke River.
claimed by William Millward in the right of his
wife's dower.

100a. MAJORS ADVENTURE, 6 Mar.1687,William Mason, Money 100
on the north side Manokin. Possessed by Thomas
Shaw, accounts Richard Whitty

50a. POLKS LOTT, 7 Mar.1687,Robert Polk, Money 100
on the north side Manokin.Possessed by widow
of Robert, Magdalen Pollock

300a. GLASCOW, 7 Mar.1687,David Brown Money 100
on the north side Manokin. Possessed by-
150a. Alexander Brown
75a. Ephraim Wilson
75a. Peter Dent

100a. POLKS FOLLY, 7 Mar.1687, Robert Polk, Money 100
on the north side Manokin. Possessed by widow
Magdalen Polk

ACRES	TRACT	SURVEY DATE-BY WHOM	LOCATION	

164a. CARYS CHANCE, 12 Mar.1687,Richard Carey   Money 100
       on the main branch of Great Money. Possessed
       by Richard Carey

120a. WOLFES DEN, 12 Mar.1687, Owen Macraugh,   Money 100
       on the north side Manokin. Possessed by
       the widow Mary Macraugh

100a. NICHOLSONS LOTT, 23 Mar.1687,Richard Nicholson, Money 100
       on the north side Cuttamachico River. Possessed
       by Richard Nicholson

200a. ELIZABETHS CHOICE, 23 Mar.1687,Manus Morris, Money 100
       on the west side Quantico, claimed by said
       Morris in Dorset County but now conveyed to
       John Parsons Jr.

150a. TOWER HILL, 23 Mar.1687, Manus Morris,   Money 100
       on the west side of Quantico, Assigned to
       John Nutter who is dead. No one possesses land
       nor rent paid, vide Alexander Carlisle account

100a. TURKEY RIDGE, 1687, Matthew Dorman   Money 100
       on the north side Manokin. Possessed by
       Mathew Dorman in Manokin 100. belongs to
       Charles Ballard

200a. BEAR RIDGE, 23 Mar.1687, Thomas Manlove, Money 100
       back in woods from Manokin. Possessed by
       Samuel Handy

100a. BEARS DEN, 23 Mar.1687, William Goldsmith, Money 100
       on the south side Manokin. Person dead in
       Pennsylvania. Posssssed by noone

200a. NEIGHBOURS GOODWILL,26 Mar.1688, James Bratten, Money 100
       on the north side Pocomoke River. Possessed by
       John More in Naswadux neck.

169a. COLCHESTER,26 Mar.1678, Peter Whaples,   Money 100
       part of land lyes within another survey. William
       Whaples the heir lives in the Horokills

232a. PORTERS DISCOVERY,25 Mar.1688, Hugh Porter, Money 100
       onthe north side Pocomoke River. Possessed by
       James Townsend

300a. HACHILA, 28 Mar.1688, Capt.David Brown.   Money 100
       on the north side Manokin. Possessed by
       Alexander Brown

300a. PINY HEAP, 1 Sep.1687, Francis Heap,   Money 100
       on the south side Manokin. Possessed by
       Charles Wharton

200a. THE GORE,6 Jan 1685, John Mellson   Nanticoke 100
       Possessed by Robert Watson

217 FARLOW WORTH, 25 Oct.1684, Richard Woodcroft, Poquadenorton 100
       near seaboard side. Possessed by same

215a. FARNHILL, July 1685, Christopher Reynolds, Poquadenorton 100
       back from seaside. Possessed by Corn.Ellis. Land
       lies in vide Benjamin Scolfields account.

| ACRES | TRACT | SURVEY DATE-BY WHOM | LOCATION |

160a. REFUGE 18 Oct. 1684, John Price   Mattapany 100
land claimed by Gabriell Waters in Virginia
no rent paid

500a. FAIR MEADOW, 21 Apr.1684, Col.Wm.Stevens   Poquadenorton 100
on seaboard side. This must be land assigned by
Charles Stevens to Capt. Henry Smith charged
before, Know no such land

450a. NUTTERS REST, 21 Apr.1684, Christopher Nutter, Nanticoke 100
in woods near head of north branch of the Nanticoke
River, land denied by Nutters sons

55a. BROWNS CHANCE, 27 Mar.1688, John Brown   Manokin 100
land devided by John Brown, supposed to go
to surroptitiuos survey made by I know not
whom. Presumed to be returned in a survey
of 80a. called Meadow with alterations.

366a. CEDAR NECK, 30 Apr.1688 Col.William Diggs Poquadernorton 100
on the seaboard side. Possessed by Mr. Edward Diggs
in Prince George County vide Henry Touchburys
Account

475a. DIGGS POINT, 30 Apr.1688, William Diggs   Baltimore 100
on seaboard side. Claimed and possessed by Edward
Diggs, as before

438a. FAIR MEADOW, 1 May 1688, assigned Wm.Whittington, Baltimore 100
on the south side of the Baltimore River. Possessed
by William Whittington

486a. SPRING FIELD, 1 May 1688, William Whittington, Baltimore 100
on the south side Baltimore River. Possessed same.

500a. SPRING BANK, 2 May 1688, Robert Doyne   Baltimore 100
on the south side Baltimore River. Belongs to coheirs of Robert Doyne and William Hutchinson in
Potomok

442a. FAIRFIELD, 2 May 1688, Robert Doyne   Baltimore 100
on the south side Baltimore River, belongs to coheirs of Robert Doyne and Wm. Hutchinson in
Potowmack

430a. COARDS LOTT, 27 Apr.1688, assigned Joseph Coard, Baltimore 100
on the seaboard side. possessed by Joseph Coard

443a. POWELLS LOTT, 2 May 1687, Walter Powell,   Baltimore 100
on the seaboard side. Possessed by-
343a. Charles Townsend for John in Accoc. Va.
100a. William Powell

200a. WINTER ...IGE, 2 July 1688, Thomas Hill   Annamessex 100
lying on the north side Annamessex, Possessed
by Thomas Tull

500a. EAST GATE, 28 Apr.1687, John Godden   Baltimore 100
on the seaboard side. Possessed by same

153a. SMITHFIELD, 2 Oct.1687, Richard Woodcraft Baltimore 100
back from seaboard side. Possessed by same

100a. HALLS PASTURE, 2 July 1688, Charles Hall   Annamessex 100
on the north side Annamessex River. Possessed
by widow Alice Hall

| ACRES TRACT | SURVEY DATE-BY WHOM | LOCATION |

176a. SHEWELLS ADDITION, 19 Sep.1687,Samuel Showell, Poquad.100
     on the seaboard side, Possessed by Charles
     Showell

100a. CROW LAND, 5 Oct.1687, Thomas Clifton.   Poquadenorton 100
     an island in Assateage Bay. Peter Watson
     Jr. married heir of Clifton

400a. LONG ISLAND,6 Oct.1687,John Pope   Poquadenorton 100
     In Assateage Bay. Possessed by-
     200a. Samuel Hopkins
     200a. John Pope

75a. PRICKLE COCKSHOLT-6 Jul 1686. George Collins,Nanticoke 100
     on the north side Wicomico River. Possessed by
     the widow Flewellyn, her husband Samuel purchased
     from George Collins

500a. NORTH PETHERTON, 27 May 1688, Matthew Scarborough. Poquad. 100
     on the seaboard side. Possessed by-
     250a. William Hall
     250a. John Shockley

75a. WOOLHOPE, 6 Jun 1688, George Collins   Nanticoke 100
     on the north side Wicomico River. Possessed by
     William Wainwright

100a. WOLFES QUARTER, 5 Jun 1688, William Wright,Wicomico 100
     on the north side Wicomico. Possessed by the
     widow of William Wright

45a. PENYWISE, 5 Jun 1688, William Wright   Wicomico 100
     on the south side Little Money. Possessed by
     the heir of Bloyce Wright

105a. WRIGHTS VENTURE, 5 Jun 1688, William Wright, Wicomico 100
     on the south side of Wicomico. Possessed by
     the widow of William Wright

200a. FRIENDS ASSISTANCE, 29 Jun 1685,Charles Pollard,Manokin 100
     near the main branch of the Manokin River.
     Possessed by Capt. Charles Pollard(Ballard)

500a. FRIENDS ASSISTANCE, 1687, Nathaniel Cropper, Wicomico 100
     Near Saint Bridge. The heir lives in Virginia
     named Sebastian Cropper. No rent paid

500a. FRIENDSHIP, 1 May 1688, Martin Curtis   Baltimore 100
     now possessed by William Dickson

500a. ROCHESTER, 2 May 1688, Henry Morgan   Baltimore 100
     on Baltimore River. Possessed by Michael
     Godden

251a. MORGANS CHOICE, 2 May 1688, Henry Morgan   Baltimre 100
     Possessed by Robert Johnson Sr.

500a. THE FRIENDS DISCOVERY, 27 Apr.1688, Walter Land,Baltimore 100
     Lying on Baltimore River. Land assigned to
     John Land to whom it apportains,by the name of
     FRIENDS KINDNESS

123a. MIDDLEMORE, 4 Oct.1687, John Pope   Baltimore 100
     An island in Assateage Bay. Possessed by same.

ACRES		SURVEY DATE-BY WHOM	LOCATION	
100a.	LOZANGE	4 June 1688 John Peter Frank The person who took up this land has run to Southward and noone ever seated or was in Possession. His wife declaims it.	Mattapony	100
300a.	WEAVERS CHOICE,	last day Feb.1688 Hope Taylor, on south side Pocomoke River, in Woods. Possessed by John Porter	Mattapony	100
500a.	LONDON DERRY,	2 May 1688 Walter Lane On the Baltimore River. Possessed by Leonard Johnson	Mattapony	100
50a.	ADDITION	5 June 1688 Benjamin Saucer Lying on the south side Little Money, Possessed by Benjamin Saucer	Mattapony	100
300a.	St. Martins Desart,	4 May 1688 Warren Hadder, lying back in the woods from Pocomoke Branch. Possessed by William Townsend	Mattapony	100
300a.	PEMBRIDGE,	John Bounds pat. 7 June 1688 On the south side Nanticoke. Possessed by William Bound	Nanticoke	100
500a.	GLASCOW	1 Oct.1687, Robert Perry out of a branch of St.Martins River. Certificate of land is not in the office, the warrent is since ordered. To be laid in another place and no grant returned	Mattapony	100
95a.	CONTENTION,	15 Aug 1688, Thomas Ralph On the north side Wicomico Creek. Po_sessed by Thomas Ralph	Wicomico	100
100a.	SMITHS HOPE,	resurveyed 11 May 1688 Capt. Henry Smith, on the north side Pocomoke Land since has been in suspence. The title in controversy. Several tracts being within the lines of bounds.	Wicomico	100
150a.	JAMES CHOICE,	24 May 1688 Richard Chambers, back in the woods near a branch of Wicomico Creek. Possessed by Richard Chambers	Wicomico	100
115a.	WOLFE SPITT RIDGE,	24 May 1688 Richard Chambers, Lying back in the woods from the head of the Wicomico. Possessed by Richard Chambers	Wicomico	100
160a.	THE DISCOVERY,	18 May 1688, James Weatherly, on the south side Nanticoke. Possessed by same.	Nanticoke	100
450a.	THE ADDITION,	18 May 1688 James Weatherly on the south side of Nanticoke. Possessed by same	Nanticoke	100
90a.	PREVENTION,	18 May 1688, James Weatherly on south side Nanticoke. Possessed by same	Nanticoke	100
100a.	JERICHO,	2 June 1688, Ambrose London on north side of the Annamessex. Possessed by Samuel Handy	Annamessex	100

ACRES	SURVEY DATE-BY WHOM	LOCATION
150a.	TICKFIELD, 22 May 1688, Edward Bennett On the south side Nanticoke on Quantico Creek. Possessed by John Tully	Nanticoke 100
300a.	FRIENDS DISCOVERY, 18 May 1688 James Weatherly, on south side Nanticoke Possessed by Henry Acworth	Nanticoke 100
9a.	RELPHS PREVENTION, 23 May 1688 Thomas Relph, On the north side Wicomico Creek. Possessed by the heirs of John Holland	Nanticoke 100
200a.	CHANCE, 17 May 1688 John Langford on the south side Nanticoke. Possessed by John Langford	Nanticoke 100
50a.	COW PASTURE, 16 Aug 1688, William Robinson on the south side Wicomico Possessed by Benjamin Cottman	Wicomico 100
500a.	CUCKOLDS DELIGHT, 25 May 1688, William Layton, Back from the south side Rokiawakin. Land belongs to Major Petyons heirs in Glocester Co. Virginia	Nanticoke 100
150a.	MOUNT PLEASANT, 24 May 1684, James Ingram Lying near the head of the main branch of the Wicomico River. Belongs to Abraham Ingram, heir at law of said James, vide Henry Williams account	Nanticoke 100
70a.	HENDERSONS CHANCE, 10 Sep.1688, John Henderson, Lying in south side Back Creek. The tract is 90acres. Possessed by James Wilk	Nanticoke 100
200a.	MILE END 22 May 1688, Edward Wright lying near the head of Barron Creek. Possessed 150a. John Lamee 150a. John Parramores widow	Nanticoke 100
300a.	CAMBRIDGE 24 May 1688 John Parker who fled out of the county. Paid neither for survey or patent. No Heir appears	Nanticoke 100
300a.	MORRISS LOTT,17 May 1688 Manasses Morris lying on the branches of Quantico. Possessed by Edward Rutledge	Nanticoke 100
295a.	DAYS BEGINNING, 15 May 1688, Edward Day back from the Nanticoke River. Belongs by right to Edward Day's heirs. The widow refuses payment of rent	Nanticoke 100
200a.	LIMSONE 5 Apr.1688 Abraham Emmett on the south side Pocomoke. Possessed by Martin Curtis	Pocomoke 100
100a.	PROMISE LAND, 2 June 1688 Thomas Wallston, In a neck between the Manokin and Annamessex Possessed by Hugh MacNeale	Manokin 100
150a.	JESHIMON 17 May 1688, William Ellgate on the north side Rokiawakin. Possessed by William Ellgate	Nanticoke 100

ACRES	SURVEY DATE-BY WHOM	LOCATION
300a.	MIDDLE NECK, 24 May 1688 William Brereton, lying near the head of Wicomico. Claimed by William Brereton heir.	Wicomico 100
420a.	ADDITION TO COLLINS ADVENTURE, 14 May 1688 Nehemiah Covington, at the head of the Rokiawakin. Possessed by Nehemiah Covington	Nanticoke 100
172a.	ALDERMANBURY, 14 May 1688 Thomas Cox on the south side of the Rokiawakin. Possessed by Thomas Cox	Nanticoke 100
200a.	ROODY, 4 June 1688 John Panter on the south side Little Money. Possessed by John Panter	Wicomico 100
200a.	FATSTERS QUARTER, 2 May 1688 William Curry near the branches of Wicomico. Possessed by James Spence for Isaac Booth	Wicomico 100
550a.	ALDERBURY, 14 May 1688 Thomas Cox on south side main branch of the Rokiawakin Possessed by Thomas Cox	Wicomico 100
246a.	COCKLAND 17 May 1688, Thomas Cox on one of the Barren Creeks branchs. Possessed by Peter Holloway	Wicomico 100
95a.	MERRILLS ADVENTURE,10 Aug 1688 William Merrill, on north side Pitts Creek. Possessed by William Merrill	Wicomico 100
200a.	BALLY BUGGER, 16 May 1688 John Caldwell on the north side of the head of Rokiawakin. Possessed by John Caldwell	Wicomico 100
850a.	LITTLE BOLTON, resurveyed 26 Oct.1688 Thomas Jones on the south side Annamessex Possessed by Robert Catherwood in the right of Thomas Jones' orphans	Pocomoke 100
200a.	DROWN COVE 25 Oct.1688 William Coleburn on the south side Annamessex. Possessed by the widow Coleburn	Pocomoke 100
150a.	LEATHERLAND,2 July 1688, George Benston, near Perryhawkin. Benston dead but hath heirs who is neither possessed nor claims by descent, and if not assigned to James Berry	Pocomoke 100
250a.	CALLD WHAT YOU PLEASE, 24 Oct.1688 Thomas Ball, on the east side main branch of Dividing Creek. Land surveyed for Fu_l. who died long since. His heirs declaims supposing his ancestor died in debt.	Pocomoke 100
50a.	FOSCOTT 2 Jan 1688, Henry Miles between mouth of Manokin and Annamessex River. Claimed by Samuel Miles heir to Henry.	Annamessex 100
100a.	GOSLINS LOTT, 28 Nov.1688, John Goslin on the north side Rowkiawakin. Possessed by John Goslin	Wicomico 100

ACRES	SURVEY DATE-BY WHOM	LOCATION
200a.	ST. GYLES 10 Sept.1688,William Giles between the Quantico and Rewastico Branchs possessed by William Wilson	Wicomico 100
100a.	NAPHILL 2 July 1688,George Benston near Perryhawkin. George Benston is dead and the land unseated or cutivated. The heir in minority.	Pocomoke 100
500a.	ACWORTH DELIGHT,5 Nov.1688 Richard Acworth on the south side Barren Creek. Possessed by Richard Acworth	Wicomico 100
200a.	BEWMARIS 3 June 1688 Thomas Morris five miles from the seaboard side claimed by Thomas Moris	Pocomoke 100
200a.	MARY'S CHOICE-1 Dec.1688, Thomas Humphreys on the south side of the Nanticoke. Possessed by Thomas Humphreys	Wicomico 100
200a.	HARTINGTON,20 Nov.1688 John Taylor who fled to Pennsylvania long since. Supposed to be dead. None possesses nor heir here.	Wicomico 100
600a.	FIRST LOTT, 7 May 1688, William Aylford It is doubted if the certificate for this land is on record. No. Patent. Alford left county long since. He left land of one Andrew Speers who deserted it long since and said the most part will be cut off by an older survey of John Covington.	Wicomico 100
73a.	LONG ACRE, 6 June 1688 John Godden On the seaboard side possessed by same.	Wicomico 100
200a.	CHANCE 5 May 1688 John Renshur on east side Little Creek. Possessed by same	Wicomico 100
300a.	NEWBURY, 27 Nov.1688 William Keen on south side Rokawaikin. Possessed by the widow Rebecca Price relict of Alexander Price to whom the right belonged.	Wicomico 100
36a.	WASHWATER (no date) assigned William Keen who desires the patent be vacacted. Cut off by anolder survey	Wicomico 100
150a.	MARLBOROUGH, 25 May 1688 Edward Wheeler back from the south side of Rokiawakin. Possessed by Peter Fitzgerald for the orphan of Edward Wheeler	Wicomico 100
200a.	HARRINGTON, 27 Nov.1688 William Keen said to belong to Peter Calloway if not cut off by an older survey	Wicomico 100
100a.	LANDRIDGE, 20 Nov.1688,John Taylor This person fled the county long since and dead at Pennsylvania. No hier appears, none possessed	Nanticoke 100

ACRES	SURVEY DATE-by WHOM	LOCATION
200a.	LITTLE BRITTIAN, 27 Nov.1688,John Hewett on head of Rewastico Branch. Possessed by Peter Calloway	Nanticoke 100
350a.	POORHALL 22 April 1689 James Atkinson back from the south side of Pocomoke River Possessed by James Atkinson	Pocomoke 100
150a.	KICKOTAN CHOICE, 24 Apr.1689 James Atkinson, about 2 miles from the south side Pocomoke River. Possessed byJames Atkinson	Pocomoke 100
200a.	WELCH FOLLY, 12 Dec 1688 John Broughton back in the woods from the south side of the Pocomoke. Possessed by John Broughton	Pocomoke 100
200a.	HILL GLASS, 29 Feb.1688 John Taylor claimed by Thomas Ironmonger in Virginia	Pocomoke 100
110a.	TAUNTON 31 Mar.1688 Walter Reed Jr. Possessed by same	Pocomoke100
180a.	ADAMS CHOICE, 1 Sep.1688 Sumner Adams. in a point between the Nanticoke and Wicomico. Possessed by same vide. Capt. John MacCloysters Account	Wicomico 100
745a.	COX'S DISCOVERY, 16 May 1688 Edward Day. back on Broad Creek Branchs. Belongs to the hiers of Edward Day but the widow refuses payment of rent	Mattapany 100
110a.	BARREN LOTT, 20 Nov.1688 James Henderson on the south side Pocomoke River. Possessed by Walter Taylor in right of James Hendersons orphans	Pocomoke 100
70a.	HAPHAZARD, 1 Jan. 1688 James Henderson back from the Pocomoke River on Poquadenorton Road.	Pocomoke 100
80a.	THE MEADOWS,14 Aug 1688 David Brown on the north side Manokin River. Possessed by Alexander Brown	Wicomico 100
80a.	LONG LOTT 30 May 1689 1John Faucett back from the south east side Pocomoke. Possessed by Thomas Morris	Mattapony 100
300a.	PARKERS ADVENTURE, 2 July 1688 John Parker back from the east side Pocomoke River. Land belongs to William Franklin. Possessed by John Dryden	Mattapony 100
100a.	ROSCOMMON 3 May 1689 Phillip Conway Sr. on the west side Morumsco Creek. Possessed by the widow Conway	Annamessex 100
100a.	DUNLAPS CHOICE, 1 Aug.1688 Ninian Dunlap belongs to William Benelson in Accoc. Co.Va.	Annamessex 100
300a.	ABERDEEN 22 Apr.1689 James Langstor claimed by James Langster son and heir of James. Lives in Virginia	Annamessex 100

ACRES	SURVEY DATE-BY WHOM	LOCATION

200a. THE ADVENTURE, 9 Dec.1688 John Renshur   Money 100
on the north side near the mouth of
Manokin River. Possessed by same

300a. BELFAST   4 May 1688 Woncey Maclaney   Annamessex 100
back in woods from Pocomoke River. Claimed
by Jacob Truett

260a. WALLBROOK, 4 May 1688 Edward Fowler   Annamessex 100
on little creek branch. Claimed by Thomas
Fowler heir of Edward

69a. LONGS PREVENTION, 3 May 1689 Samuel Long   Annamessex 100
on the west side Morumsco Creek. Possessed
by John Long, heir of Samuel

50a. FLATT CAP.18 Apr.1689 Thomas Jones   Annamessex 100
on the south side Annamessex. Possessed by
Robert Catherwood in right of Jones" orphan

123a. LONGS PURCHASE, 2 May 1689 Samuel Long   Annamessex 100
on the west side Morumsco Creek. Possessed
by John Long

200a. LITTLEWORTH, 1 Apr.1689 George Phebus   Manokin 100
on the north side Manokin. Possessed by same.

250a. PRESTEIN 28 Apr.1695 Thomas Pollet   Wicomico 100
back in the woods from Rokiawakin River.
Possessed by Thomas Pollet

200a. BEVERLEY, 13 May 1689, Edward Gold   Wicomico 100
in a fork of Barren Creek Branchs. Belongs
to orphans of Robert Downs. No Alienation
fine paid by Downs

200a. JENNERS LOTT 17 Apr.1689, John Jenner   Manokin 100
in Perryhawkin neck, now possessed with
the land Jenner hath an heir under the
guardianship of James Train who denys the rent

200a. SNOW HILL 23 May 1689 Nehemiah Covington   Nanticoke 100
back in the woods from the Rokiawakin River
Possessed by Nehemiah Covington

100a. POLEHAMBTON, 21 May 1689 John Hewett   Nanticoke 100
on the south arm of ROkiawakin. Disclaimed
by Hughes heirs that appear here at present

300a. LAND DOWN 1 May 1688 Angoll Richardson   Wicomico 100
on the south side Rokiawakin River. Possessed
by John Davis

500a. WILLSONS DISCOVERY, 1 Dec.1688 James Weatherly, Wicomico 100
on the south side Nanticoke. Possessed by James
Weatherly but now by James Hughes

200a. TROUBLESOME, 10 Nov.1688 John Richins   Nanticoke 100
near the head of Barren Creek. Possessed by
John Wheeler

500a. QUAIKESON NECK,1 Dec.1688 James Weatherly   Nanticoke 100
on the south side Nanticoke. Possessed by same

200a. BAGGSHOTT, 8 Dec.1688 for Henry Harman   Nanticoke 100
Henry Haman in Dorset Co. whether dead I know not
none Possessed. on the south side Nanticoke River.

ACRES		SURVEY DATE-BY WHOM	LOCATION
200a.	RAPHO	20 May 1689 William Alexander Jr. in a jork of the Southmost branches of Rokiawakin. Possessed by Wm. Alexander Jr.	Nanticoke 100
100a.	JERSEY	14 May 1689 Nicholas Toadvine back from the south side Rokiawakin Possessed by Nicholas Toadvine	Nanticoke 100
13a.	CONVENIENCE	10 May 1689 John Hewett on south side Nanticoke. Disclaimed by heirs. none possesses.	Nanticoke 100
200a.	NORTH WALES,	16 May 1689 John Hewett on south side Nanticoke. Disclaimed by heirs apparent and Capt. Evans who married the widow None in possession	Nanticoke 100
100a.	BEARS QUARTER,	25 May 1689 John Parsons back in the woods from the south side of teh Rokiawakin. Possessed by John Parsons	Nanticoke 100
400a.	ROTTERDAM,	Dec. 1688 Cornelius Johnson on the south side Nanticoke River. Cornelius Johnson in Dorset County (Whether dead with or without heirs I know not) land not possessed by anyone.	Nanticoke 100
200a.	TWITTERHAM,	8 Dec. 1688 Henry Herman on south side Nanticoke, the land with BAGGSHOTT as above. None possessed	Nanticoke 100
150a.	POORFIELDS,	11 Apr. 1689 James Ingram back from the south side Rokiawakin in the woods. The right in Abraham Ingram heir but not possessed by anyone.	Nanticoke 100
130a.	MOORFIELDS,	13 May 1689 James Ingram back in the woods from the south side of the Rokiawakin. Heir is Abraham Ingram but not possessed by anyone	Nanticoke 100
100a.	WHITE CHAPPELL GREEN	24 May 1689 Robert Crouch, back in woods from the south side Rokiawakin Possessed by Robert Crouch	Nanticoke 100
100a.	CROUCHES DESERT,	24 May 1689 Robert Crouch In the woods from the south side Rokiawakin River	Nanticoke 100
143a.	POINT PATIENCE	20 May 1689 William Ellgate on the west most side of main branch of the Rokiawakin River. Possessed by Andrew Cadwell	Nanticoke 100
380a.	CLONETT	10 Sep. 1688 John Caldwell on the north side Rokiawakin neck. Possessed by John Caldwell	Nanticoke 100
250a.	THE DESART	21 May 1689 John Caldwell on the north side Rokiawakin Neck. Possessed by John Caldwell	Nanticoke 100
140a.	RADBURN	3 Dec. 1688 Thomas Wilson on the south side Nanticoke. Possessed by same	Nanticoke 100

ACRES	SURVEY DATE-BY WHOM	LOCATION
62a.	DOWN'S CHOICE 11 May 1689 Robert Downs upon Quantico Creek. Possessed by John Kemphall	Nanticoke 100
70a.	ASKAUKIN 1 Oct.1689 Daniel Selby an island in Assateage sound or bay. Belongs to the heir of Parker Selby	Baltimore 100
400a.	HOLDFAST 1 Oct.1688 Richard Hall in Va, near Tundotank Town. Belongs to one Hall in Northumberland Co.Va. not possessed	Nanticoke 100
200a.	WILSONS LOTT 3 Dec.1688 Thomas Wilson on the south side Pokusin Branch. Possessed by Thomas Wilson	Nanticoke 100
150a.	GREEN MEADOW 1 Mar.1689 Jamers Givans back fromthe south side of the Nanticoke. Possessed by James Givans	Nanticoke 100
500a.	ORPHANS LOTT 13 May 1689 Gabriel Cooper in fork of Pemishan Branch on the south side of the Nanticoke. Possessed by Gabiel Cooper	Nanticoke 100
30a.	TREWETTS LOTT, 2 Oct.1689 John Trewett lying in Quaponqua Neck. Possessed by same	Nanticoke 100
200a.	PEACE 12 Nov.1689 John Richins. back from the south side Nanticoke. "Possessed by Jeremiah Barronclough	Nanticoke 100
150a.	ALLGATE 12 Nov.1688 Edward Wright in the woods from the main branch of Barren Creek. Possessed by James Larrmer	Nanticoke 100
250a.	NO TIMBER QUARTER,23 Jul 1689 Thomas Purnell, back from the south side Pocomoke.Possessed by John Purnell	Mattapony 100
300a.	CARLISLE 17 May 1689 Thomas Gorden on the south side Nanticoke River. Gorden denies this land yet in the certificate returned on the remained of a warrent of William Joseph's for 3000a.	Nanticoke 100
100a.	GORDONS DELIGHT 14 May 1689 Thomas Gordon at head of Tusekey Branch issuing out of Broad Creek. Held by said Gordon	Nanticoke 100
300a.	SCOTCH IRELAND, 9 Dec.1688 Edward Craige in fork of Deep Creek Branch. The owner lives in Sussex Co.Del. Not possessed	Nanticoke 100
100a.	WORCESTER 3 June 1689 John Jones back from the seaboard side. This land if claimed supposed to be within an ancient survey of Daniel Selby	Baltimore 100
130a.	TREWETTS PURCHASE, 1 May 1688 George Truett, back from the main branch of the Pocomoke. Possessed by George Truett	Mattapony 100
150a.	GRAYS IMPROVEMENT, 1 Oct.1689 Michael Gray. between the mouth of Manokin and Annamessex Possessed by Michael Gray	Manokin 100

ACRES		SURVEY DATE-BY WHOM	LOCATION	
150a.	WOODSLAND	1 Mar.1688 John Wood back from south side Rokiawalkin. Wood fled the county long since to Deleware Bay and dead No heir appears. land not possessed	Nanticoke	100
200a.	KIRKMINSTER	29 May 1689 Matthew Wallace Back from the south side Rokiawakin. Matthew Wallace deserted the county He lives in the woods at the head of Deleware Bay. Land not possessed	Wicomico	100
200a.	PENNY STREET	8 June 1689 Robert Pirrie Assinged William Henderson. Back in the woods from the seaboard side. Possessed by Robert Pirrie	Wicomico	100
500a.	SPRING QUARTER	1 Dec.1688 William Aylward. assinged William Robinson. Possessed by Robinson	Wicomico	100
135a.	LONG RIDGE	30 May 1689 Robert Cattlin. near the head of Morumsco dams. James Curtis claims this land	Annamessex	100
450a.	COVENTRY	31 May 1689 Hugh Porter on the south side Pocomoke River. Possessed by Thomas Pool	Pocomoke	100
27a.	CALDWELLS CHANCE,	10 July 1688 John Caldwell, onthe north side Rokiawakin River. Possessed by John Caldwell	Wicomico	100
360a.	RICKETTS CHANCE,	1 July 1689 William Ricketts, on the seaboard side, Possessed 150a. John Ricketts, 210a. William Ricketts	Baltimore	100
100a.	BAYNUMS PURCHASE,	1 Oct. 1687 George Baynum back from the seaboard side. Noone in possession nor know who claims the land unless Christopher Hermerson at the Horokills	Baltimore	100
150a.	LANES ADDITION,	11 June 1689 John Lane On the south side Pocomoke. John Lane claims this land who is now in the county	Annemessex	100
200a.	JONES' CAUTION,	29 May 1689 Walter Lane lying between Pocomoke Bay and Little Annamessex claimed by Walter Lane	Annamessex	100
170a.	PUZZLE,	3 Jun 1689 John Kirk back from Pocomoke Bay. Possessed by same.	Annamessex	100
230a.	JOAN'S HOLE,	3 Jun 1689 John Kirk on the north side Pocomoke Bay. Possessed by Thomas Davis	Annamessex	100
2700a.	FRIENDS ENDEAVOUR,	3 Oct.1689 William Joseph, hear the head of and on south side Nanticoke. William Joseph the heir denies payment. No one possesses	Nanticoke	100
420a.	SHEWELLS ADDITION	14 May 1689, Samuel Shewell, back from the seaboard side. Possessed by James Clogg	Baltimore	100

ACRES	SURVEY DATE-BY WHOM	LOCATION
200a.	GIVENS LAST CHOICE, 19 June 1689 Robert Givans, on the north side Deep Creek Branch. This vacated and right laid in another by order of his Lordship	Baltimore 100
200a.	ISLINGTON 13 May 1689 William Coard on the seaboard side. Possessed by John Smith	Balitmore 100
150a.	BAKERS FOLLY 10 June 1689 Isaac Baker on the south side Nanticoke. Isaac Baker died at Deleware Bay. No one possesses	Nanticoke 100
200a.	DUNGIVEAN, 19 June 1689 James Given on the south side Nanticoke about 2 miles above the Wading place. This vacated by order of his lordship. Lands in another Place.	Nanticoke 100
200a.	GORDONS LOTT, 9 June 1689 James Gordon 2½ miles above the Wading place over Deep Creek. This land held by William Broadwater in Accocomac Co. Virginia	Baltimore 100
200a.	NEVILLS FOLLY, 19 June 1689 James Neville on the south west side Deep Creek below the Wading place. Nevill fled to the southward long since. Not possessed	Baltimore 100
150a.	WINTER HARBOUR, 9 Aug. 1688 John Park in a neck between Pocmoke Bay and Annamessex possessed by John Perkins	Annamessex 100
57a.	ROACHS PRIVILEDGE, 1695 John Roach lying between Pocomoke Bay and Little Annamessex possessed by John Roach Sr.	Annamessex 100
300a.	IRELAND EYE, 1 Oct. 1688 Larence Young on the south side Nanticoke above Plumb Creek. Possessed by James Rawley	Nanticoke 100
200a.	HARDSHIFT, 13 May 1689 John Anderson on the south side Nanticoke. Possessed by Phillip Fleming who married the relict of William Phillips who had the right.	Nanticoke 100
130a.	PARKERS PEACE, 29 May 1689 Francis Martin at Watkins Point, the relict married William Brittingham in Virginia who claims the land in right of Francis Martin's orphans	Annamessex 100
200a.	CASTLE FINE, 10 June 1689 Phoenix Hall back inthe woods near the head of Ľokiawakin River. Possessed by Phoenix Hall	Nanticoke 100
48a.	HEPWORTH PASTURE, 10 June 1689 John Hepworth near Watkins Point. Possessed by Thomas Davis	Nanticoke 100
60a.	COW QUARTER, 6 Dec. 1688 George Phoebus on the north side Manokin. Possessed by James English if not sold to John Irvin	Wicomico 100

| ACRES | SURVEY DATE-BY WHOM | LOCATION |

50a. CORNWELLS ADDITION, 1 Oct.1687 Nicholas Cornwell, Baltimore 100 on the south most branch of St.Martins. Michael Godden the widow who holds the right of the orphans of Cornwell

500a. THOMPSONS PURCHASE, 4 May 1689 Christopher Baltimore 100 Thompson, on the south side Baltimore River Edmond Aires in Accoc. Va. claim this land

340a. BROTHERHOOD (no date.) for Joseph Robinson, Baltimore 100 John Parker or Phillip Parker, on the seaboard side. Claimed by Charles and Phillip Parker in Accoc. Co.Va.

450a. PLIMPTON 6 Mar.1689 Thomas Cox Nanticoke 100 on the south side of main branch of Rokiawakin River. Possessed by Thomas Cox

90a. WATCHETT, 20 May 1689 Walter Reed Baltimore 100 on Assawoman Sound. Seaside, claimed and belongs to George Parker of Mattapkin in Accoc. Co.Va.

450a. HALLS LOTT, 18 May 1689 William Hall Baltimore 100 on the seaboard side. Possessed by Wm.Hall

400a. SUMERFIELDS, 1 Apr.1688 assigned to William Baltimore 100 Whittington, on the south side near the head of Assawoman, alias Indian Creek. Belongs to William Whittington

100a. COOPERS PURCHASE, 4 Mar.1689 assigned to Baltimore 100 Richard Cooper, near Perrahawkin, The person long since dead. Never improved and no heir appears.

50a. DAVIE'S INLETT, 12 Jun 1689 Thomas Davis Annamessex 100 lying between Pocomoke Bay and Annamessex Possessed by same.

100a. AYLWARDS ADDITION, 4 Sep.1688 assigned William, Wicomico 100 Aylward, on north side main branch of Rokiawakin. Aylward long since left county. noone possesses the land. Supposed to go within an older survey of Thomas Walker

100a. ROTTEN QUARTER, 30 Nov.1688 assigned Francis Wicomico 100 Heap, on the southwest side Deep Branch. Francis Heap claims this land, saith the right is in an orphan girl of Jos.Lights who makes no claim or payment

200. GREEN PARK 13 Oct.1688 Summersett Dickerson, Annamessex 100 on the east most side Pocomoke Bay. Possessed by Peter Dickinson

350a. HOPEWELL 24 May 1688 Dennis Higgarty Wicomico 100 near head of a branch issuing out of Wicomico Creek and on a great savanah. The person fled out of the county since and nothing heard of him.

80a. WINTER HARBOUR, 22 Dec.1688 Capt.John King, Wicomico 100 lying in a neck between the Manokin and Annamessex, Possessed by Benjamin King

| ACRES | SURVEY DATE-by whom | LOCATION |

200a. LONDON DERRY, 5 Nov.1687 Adam Spence   Pocomoke 100
         lying on North East side Pocomoke
         Possessed by Adam Spence

400a. BASING STOKE, 5 Nov.1687 Simon Foskue   Pocomoke 100
         in Virginia, back from the Pocomoke.
         Claimed and rent paid by Simon Foskue in Accoc.Co.

100a. HOGG QUARTER, 25 Apr.1689 assigned William   Wicomico 100
         Alexander, back in the woods between
         the Manokin and Wicomico Rivers. Possessed
         by William Alexander Sr.

500a. PRICES CONCLUSION, 15 Nov.1694, Edward Price, Annamessex 100
         adjoining Yorkshire alias Smiths Island
         Possessed 100a. Samuel Horsey
                   400a. Thomas Ward

1200a. DIXONS LOTT, 14 Nov.1694 Thomas Dixon   Annamessex 100
         Lying between Little Annamessex and the
         sound to Nanticoke. Possessed by Capt.
         Thomas Dixon

150a. POOR QUARTER, 23 Mar.1689 Cornelius Anderson Wicomico 100
         Anderson fled the county long since. No
         heir appears

100a. KEEP POOR HALL, 13 Nov.1694 James Rowley,   Wicomico 100
         back in the woods from Little Money, claimed
         and rent paid by the same

150a. WHAT YOU PLEASE, 21 Mar.1694/5 Phillip Askew, Wicomico 100
         in Pasquandike Branch. Belongs to Phillip
         Askew son and heir to Phillip

120a. CHANCE   19 Mar.1694/5, Thomas Walker,   Wicomico 100
         between Little Creek and Little Money
         Possessed by Thomas Shaw

300a. LAYTONS RECOVERY, 22 Mar.1695 William Layton, Wicomico 100
         on the south side Rokiawakin. Possessed by
         James Breedy

50a. NONE SUCH 15 Nov.1694 Anthony Bell   Annamessex 100
         between Annamessex and Pocomoke Bay. Possessed
         by Anthony Bell

50a. LONG LOTT 19 Mar.1694, James Langrell   Annamessex 100
         about a mile from Little Money. Claimed
         by James Langrell

40a. FRUSTRATION, 16 Nov.1694 Francis Martin   Annamessex 100
         near Watkins Point. William Brittingham in
         Virginia claims the property as marrying the
         widow.

130a. TROUBLESOME 15 Nov.1694 Francis Martin   Annamessex 100
         lying between Pocomoke Bay and Annamessex.
         Possessed by William Brittingham as marrying
         the widow.

225 NOTHING WORTH, 10 Apr.1695 Frances Joyce   Annamessex 100
         back from the south side Pocomoke River.
         Possessed by Francis Joyce

ACRES		SURVEY DATE-by Whom	Location
140a.	CHANCE,	1695, Thomas Horsman on the south side Rokiawakin. Possessed by Richard Horseman heir to Thomas	Wicomico 100
100a.	GOLDEN QUARTER,	no date, William Wallace on the south side Rokiawakin back from the river. Claimed and rent paid by John Hall	Wicomico 100
100a.	GREAT NECK,	no date, assigned William Wallace, back from the south side Rokiawakin. Belongs to William Hayman	Wicomico 100
160a.	CLAYS ADVENTURE,	2 Mar.1694/5 John Clay Clay dead and no heir appears	Wicomico 100
350a.	KINGSAILE,	29 Apr.1694 Dennis Driskill back in the woods from the south side Rokiawakin. Possessed by said Dennis Driskill	Wicomico 100
180a.	MITCHELLS CHOICE,	17 Mar.1694 Thomas Potter, in a neck between Pocomoke Bay and Annamessex, Possessed by Thomas Potter	Annamessex 100
125a.	LONGRIDGE,	22 Apr.1695, Jos.Stanford back in the woods from the Wicomico. Stanford dead and no one possesses	Wicomico 100
250a.	BOZMANS ADDITION,	1 Mar.1694 John Bozman on the north side Manokin. Possessed by same.	Wicomico 100
225a.	KIRKMINSTER	15 May 1694 assigned Thomas Davis, between Pocomoke Bay and Annamessex. Possessed of said Davis	Annamessex 100
200a.	HUNGRAY QUARTER,	20 Nov.1694 John Frissell on the east side of a branch of Rokiawakin. Possessed in right of Frisell	Wicomico 100
100a.	DIXONS KINDNESS,	16 Nov.1694, George High lying between Annamessex and Pocomoke. Possessed by Thomas Prior	Annamessex 100
100a.	SUNKEN GROUND,	16 Nov.1694 George High back from Pocomoke Bay. Possessed by George Hey	Annamessex 100
125a.	HAPHAZARD	22 Apr.1695 William Curry back in woods. Possessed by William Curry, belongs to Thomas Phillips	Wicomico 100
225a.	DISCOVERY,	28 May 1685 John Outen at Condaqua. Possessed by John Outen	Annamessex 100
400a.	WICKENOUGHS NECK	13 May 1695, John Parker in Askomonocouson Neck. Possessed by same.	Wicomico 100
200a.	RATTCLIFFE,	20 May 1695 Nathaniel Ratcliffe on the north side Turkey Branch Creek on the seaboard side. Possessed by Nathaniel Ratcliffe of Accocomac Co. Virginia	Pocomoke 100
100a.	RAMBLING POINT,	20 Nov.1694 Phillip Conway, being at the west most point of Morumsco Creek. Possessed by Phillip's widow	Pocomoke 100

| ACRES | SURVEY DATE-by whom | location |

200a. MIDDLE NECK, 17 Apr.1695, William Curry   Wicomico 100
        back from the south side Rokiawakin. Possessed
        by William Curry

200a. HEARN QUARTER, 23 Apr.1695 John Christopher   Wicomico 100

110a. WORTHLESS, 28 Nov.1694, William Matthews   Annamessex 100
        between Pocomoke and Morumsco Creek.
        Possessed by William Matthews

50a. MEADOW   21 Nov.1694, William Matthews   Annamessex 100
        on the north ease side Morumsco Creek. Possessed
        by William Matthews

116a. TURKEY HALL, 20 Apr.1695 Phillip Askew   Wicomico 100
        back in the woods from Wicomico Creek.
        Possessed by Phillip Askew

100a. BRITTAIN, 15 Apr.1695 Michael Disharoon   Wicomico 100
        1 mile from the south side Rokiawakin. Possessed
        by Michael son to Michael Disharoon

100a. HOUNSLON?- 22 Apr.1695 William Yaulding   Wicomico 100
        who is dead. no heir appears nor anyone possessed

210a. ROXBOROUGH 22 Apr.1695 Roger Phillips   Wicomico 100
        back from the head of Wicomico Creek. Possessed
        105a. Thomas Phillips who pays rent for his
            sister who hath the right
        105a. Richard Phillips in his sisters right

100a. MAGDALENES CHOICE, 16 Apr.1695 John Jenner   Wicomico 100
        back in the woods from the south side of the
        Rokiawakin. Possessed by Thomas Highway

400a. FORKEDNECK, 15 Apr.1695 John Jenner   Wicomico 100
        about 2 miles from Fundotank, Claimed by
        the heirs of John Jenner under the guardianship
        of her brother James Train

150a. OUTENS ADDITION, 28 May 1695 John Outen,   Annamessex 100
        on the westmost side Morumsco. Possessed
        by John Outen

450a. GOLDS DELIGHT, 1695 Edward Gold   Nanticoke 100
        back from the south side Nanticoke River.
        Possessed by Edward Gold

450a. GILES LOTT 11 June 1695 William Gyles Jr.   Nanticoke 100
        back from seaside of Nanticoke. Possessed
        by William Giles Sr.

100a. PRICES PURCHASE 3 June 1695, Alexander Price   Nanticoke 100
        in a fork of Barren Creek alias Pocoson Branch
        Widow Rebecca Price possesses

200a. WALLACES ADVENTURE 19 Mar.1694 James Wallace, Nanticoke 100
        lying in the woods from the branches of
        Rokiawakin. Possessed by George Smith

200a. BELLS FIRST CHOICE, 16 Jun 1695 John Bell   Nanticoke 100
        back from the north side Rokiawakin River.
        Bell removed to the southward. William Keen
        assumed to pay the rent.

ACRES-Tract	SURVEY DATE-BY WHOM	LOCATION
150a. CROSS	16 June 1695, John Ricketts lying back in the woods from the south side of the Nanticoke, Possessed by John Ricketts	Nanticoke 100
100a. MILL LOTT	3 June 1695 Lambrook Thomas on the north side Rokiawakin. Possessed by Lambrook Thomas	Nanticoke 100
30a. FRIENDS DISCOVERY,	4 June 1695, Roger Burkum upon the Quantico near branch claimed by Adam Heath	Nanticoke 100
85a. STEVENSON	16 June 1695 Stephen Tully on west side of Quantico Branch. Possessed by Stephen Tully	Nanticoke 100
500a. BEYOND EXPECTATION	29 Apr.1695 assigned to John Duncan, near seaboard side. Possessed by Capt. Edward Hammond	Balitmore 100
25a. BOSTON GREEN	10 June 1695, Isaac Boston on east side Morumsco Creek. Possessed by Adrain Marshall	Annamessex 100
25a. PHILLIPS ADDITION,	17 Apr.1695 Roger Phillips on the south side Rokiawakin River. Possessed by Richard Phillips son of Roger	Nanticoke 100
125a. GREENFIELD	20 Feb 1694/5 Sampson Wheatley at Quandaqua. Possessed by Sampson Wheatley	Annamessex 100
100a. ADAMS PURCHASE,	1695 Phillip Adams on the west side near Morumsco Creek. Possessed by Thomas Adams	Annamessex 100
100a. HAPHAZARD,	1697 Jeffrey Minshull on the west side near mouth of Morumsco Ck. Claimed and possessed by Helena relict of Minshull	Annamessex 100
300a. no name	1695, John Kellum in Ascomona Conson Neck, land actually possessed by Indians	Annamessex 100
260a. EMMETTS DISCOVERY,	1 Nov.1695 Stephen Costin on the seaboard side near St.Martins 160a. possessed by Stephen Deere 100a. Peter Benton	Baltimore 100
150a. CADE CONTRIVANCE,	13 July 1695, Daniel Selby about 3 miles from the seaboard side. Possessed by Ephraim Heather in right of Daniel Selby's orphan.	Baltimore 100
100a. WOODCROFT,	no date, Richard Woodcraft on seaboard side. This land cut off by an older survey of Wrixam White	Baltimore 100
150a. SCANDEROON,	1 May 1695, Charles Ratcliffe on the seaboard side. Possessed by Nathaniel Ratcliffe.	Baltimore 100
112a. POWELLS RECOVERY,	27 May 1695, Walter Powell on the seaboard side. Possessed by Capt.Edward Powell	Baltimore 100

| ACRES | TRACT | SURVEY DATE-BY WHOM | LOCATION |

300a. PARTNERS DESIRE, 9 June 1696, Edward Green   Pocomoke 100
 on south east side Pocomoke River.
 No one possessed. Green dead and heir in England

350a. TENDERDALL 31 May 1695, John Tarr   Bogerternorten 100
 on south side Pocomoke River on Calkers
 Creek. Possessed in right of Tarr's heir
 under the guardianship of Johnson Hill

100a. MEADOW, 1695, Robert Cattlin   Annamessex 100
 on the south side near the mouth of the
 Manokin River. Claimed by William Cattlin
 heir to Robert. Land but 50a.

130a. NONE SUCH 1 Nov.1695, Henry Hudson Jr.   Annamessex 100
 back from the seaboard side. Possessed by same.

200a. ADVENTURE 8 Nov.1695, James Curtis   Annamessex 100
 on the south side near the mouth of Manokin
 Possessed by James Curtis

425a. NEW INVENTION, Nov.1695, William Faucet   Annamessex 100
 on the south side near the mouth of the
 Manokin River. Possessed by Samuel Handy

250a. MATTUX INCLOSURE, 10 Nov.1695, Lazarus Mattux, Annamessex 100
 on the south side Manokin River, near the mouth.
 Possessed by Lazarus Mattux

200a. MARISH GROUND, 20 Nov.1695, Richard Davis   Annamessex 100
 on the south side Manokin River, near the mouth.
 66 2/3a. to John Davis son of Richard
 133 1/3a. William Davis the other son

88a. VAILE OF MISERY, 4 Apr.1696 John Roach Jr.   Annamessex 100
 on the north side Annamessex River. Possessed
 by John Roach Jr.

840a. FLATT LAND, 1 June 1696 Thomas Everonden   Annamessex 100
 lying between the Manokin and Annamessex.
 Possessed by Richard Waters

375a. PARTNERS DESIRE 10 Oct.1679 Richard and John, Annamessex 100
 Waters and Charles Hall, on the north side
 near the mouth of the Annamessex River. Possessed
 144a. John Roach Jr.
 231a. John Waters

725a. CHEAP PRICE, 3 Aug.1696 resurveyed for   Annamessex 100
 William Planner on the south side of the
 Annamessex River. Possessed by Wm. Planner the
 son and heir.

116a. FRIENDS KINDNESS, 1 June 1696 assigned to   Annamessex 100
 Richard Waters, on the north side of the
 Annamessex. Possessed by Richard Waters.

500a. WEST RECOVERY 16 July 1696, Thomas West   Baltimore 100
 on the south side of the Baltimore River.
 On seaboard side. Possessed by Thomas West.

| ACRES | TRACT | SURVEY DATE-BY WHOM | LOCATION |

100a. WILLIAMS ADVENTURE, 9 June 1696 Michael Williams, Annamessex 100
a mile from the south side Annamessex River.
No one possesses belongs to the heir of Michael
Williams

240a. TIMOTHYS CHOICE, 16 July 1696 Timothy Harvy, Baltimore 100
about 3 miles on the south side Baltimore
River. Possessed by the widow of Timothy

300a. STOCKLEYS ADVENTURE, 25 May 1696, Samuel Hopkins Sr. Baltimore 10
two miles from the south side of the Baltimore
River. Possessed by Nathaniel Hopkins

175a. HANDYS CHOICE, 4 June 1694, Samuel Handy   Annamessex 100
between the Manokin and Annamessex Rivers.
Possessed by Samuel Handy

300a. JONES'S MEADOW, 1 July 1696 Samuel Jones   Annamessex 100
at Dam Quarter. Possessed by Samuel Jones

500a. EVERDENS LOTT, Thomas Everdon 16 July 1689   Annamessex 100
on the south side Annamessex River. Belongs to
the same who lives in Dorset County

250a. BRADSHAWS PURCHASE, 1 Sept.1688 William Bradshaw, Annamessex 100
on the south side Pocomoke River. Bradshaw
fled to Deleware Bay and dead. coheirs disclaim,
said it was sold to Robert Hutchinson and John
Rolls in Accocomac but not alienated

150a. THE GREEN MEADOW, 1 Mar.1688 James Givan   Nanticoke 100
on the south side of the Nanticoke River, at
the head of a branch of Broad Creek called
Pursoaky Branch. Possessed by James Givan

170a. GLADSTEANS INDUSTRY, 18 June 1689, John Pantor Nanticoke 100
on the south side of the Nanticoke River 2 miles
from Broad Creek. Possessed by John Pantor

200a. SOUTH WALES 16 May 1689 John Hewitt   Nanticoke 100
on the south side of the Nanticoke and eastmost
side of Broad Creek. Disclaimed by the heirs
apparent and Ca. Evans who married Hewitts widow.

150a. GIVEANS LOTT, 1 Mar.1688 Robert Givean   Nanticoke 100
on the south side of the Nanticoke River near
Tussucky Branch. Possessed by Robert Givean vide
Laurence Conner account

100a. COVYS PURCHASE, 1 Mar.1688 Richard Covy   Annamessex 100
near Perryhawkin, near the south most side of
a branch of Dividing Creek. The land is COOPERS
PURCHASE

400a. HOLD FAST, 30 Oct.1688 Richard Hull   Nanticoke 100
on the south side of the Rokiawakin Ck. 1 mile
south of Tundotank Indian Town. Belongs to
Richard Hull in Northumberland Co. Virginia

500a. QUIANKESON NECK, 1 Dec.1688 James Weatherly   Nanticoke 100
on the south side Nanticoke River. near Indian
Quiankeson houses. Possessed by James Weatherly

ACRES	TRACT	SURVEY DATE-BY WHOM	LOCATION
500a.	WILLSONS DISCOVERY,	1 Dec.1688 James Weatherly, on the south side Nanticoke River, on west side Beaver Dam Creek. Held by James Weatherly	Nanticoke 100
300a.	LITTLE GOSHEN,	23 Apr. 1684 George Layfield 8 miles form the north east branch of the Nanticoke River. Apportains to Samuel Layfield heir to George	Nanticoke 100
800a.	SALEM,	25 Apr.1684 George Layfield on the north east branch of the Nanticoke River. same as before.	Nanticoke 100
500a.	GREAT GOSHEN,	23 Apr.1684, George Layfield 8 miles from the northeast branch of the Nanticoke River. Same as before	Nanticoke 100
300a.	BASHAN	24 Apr.1684, George Layfield 6 miles from the north east branch of the Nanticoke River towards the head of Smith's neck. Apportains to Samuel Layfield heir to George	Nanticoke 100
540a.	FRUITFULL PLAIN,	24 Apr.1684 George Layfield, 4 miles from the north east branch of the Nanticoke River in Smiths Neck. Apportains to Samuel heir to George	Nanticoke 100
200a.	WHITE CHAPPELL	24 May 1689 Robert Crouch on the south side Rokiawakin River, near the road leading to Tundotank Indian Town. Possessed by Robert Crouch	Nanticoke 100
86a.	CHERRY GARDEN	15 May 1695, William Noble on the north side of the Pocomoke River. Possessed by William Noble	Annamessex 100
364a.	GOERGES ADVENTURE	16 Nov.1688 George Betts on the north side of the Manokin River in Askankin Neck. Possessed by George Betts	Wicomico 100
50a.	PETERBOROUGH	1 Oct.1688 Nicholas Cornwall 3 miles from the main branch of the Pocomoke River on the east side St.Martins River. Possessed by John Cornwall	Wicomico 100
160a.	CLAYS ADVENTURE	2 March 1694 John Clay 1 mile from Tundotank Indian Town	Wicomico 100
90a.	WOLFS QUARTER,	24 Dec.1701, John Watts in Va. being pt. of an Island in Assateage Sound. Possessed by John Watts.	Mattapony 100
600a.	no name	24 Dec.1671 George Parker in Va. on the east side Ascomonoconson Neck. This land lies within the Indian lines of Asomonaconson Town. Claimed by said Parker	Mattapony 100
425a.	AYLWARDS FIRST LOTT,	17 May 1688 Wm.Aylward near head on the north side ROkiawakin. Aylward long since left the province. The land then possessed by Andrew Speer who deserted. Part of this land is supposed to be cut off by an older survey of John Covingtons	Nanticoke 100

ACRES	TRACT	SURVEY DATE-BY WHOM	LOCATION
100a.	BARREN NECK	23 Oct.1695 Edmund Hoggins on the south side of the Nanticoke and eastmost side of Wetepkewant Creek. Possessed by same	Nanticoke 100
200a.	WILSONS MISTAKE,	1 Nov.1688 James Weatherly on the south side Nanticoke River and south side of Barren Creek. Possessed by Richard Russell	Nanticoke 100
300a.	CHANCE,	1 Nov.1688 James Weatherly on the south side of the Nanticoke. Possessed by John Gilly	Nanticoke 100
140a.	LAYTONS CONVENIENCE,	1 Mar.1679 Henry Layton, near Dam Quarter. Possessed by George Hutchins who married Layton's widow	Annamessex 100
100a.	CHESNUT RIDGE	5 Nov.1696 James Henderson on the south side Pocomoke River. Possessed by James Henderson	Annamessex 100
100a.	REEDS CONTRIVANCE	23 Nov.1682 Walter Reed on the south side Pocomoke River. Possessed by John Aydelott	Annamessex 100
125a	WEAVERS PORTION,	5 Dec.1698 Richard Penock lying toward the head of Ascomononconson Neck. Possessed by Richard Penock	Annamessex 100
200a.	APES HOLE	8 Oct.1698 Thomas Jones being a piece of escheat land. Possessed by William Jenkins by the appointment of Robert Catherwood guardian of Jones's orphans	Annamessex 100
100a.	GILLYS ADVENTURE,	16 Dec.1682 William Merrill, on the north side of the Rokiawakin River. Land was assigned to John Gilly and possessor refuses to pay rent pretending it is cut off by Thomas Walkers lines	Wicomico 100
45a.	FRIENDS ADVICE	1 Apr.1699 William Waller on the south side of Little Money. Possessed by William Waller	Money 100
150a.	HORSEYS FANCY	15 May 1699 Stephen Horsey between the Annamessex River and Pocomoke Bay. Possessed by Stephen Horsey	Annamessex 100
250a.	FORLORN HOPE,	20 Feb.1695 Edward Green on the north side of the Pocomoke River. Green dead, know no such land being surveyed in the Revolution by one Barkstead not withstanding the date of the certificate. The heir in Liverpool Eng.	Annamessex 100
85a.	FATHER AND SONS DESIRE,	18 Nov.1699 John White and, Richard Wallace. Near Dam Quarter, Possessed by same	Annamessex 100
150a.	TURNERS CHOICE,	8 Jan 1699 Samuel Turner on the west side Vasecanquo Creek. Possessed by Samuel Turner	Annamessex 100
125a.	NEWFOUNDLAND,	16 Nov.1699 Francis Roberts near Dam Quarter. Possessed by the widow Roberts	Annamessex 100

ACRES	TRACT	SURVEY DATE-BY WHOM	LOCATION	
200a.	WEATHERLYS CONVIENCY, 6 Nov.1699 James Weatherly, on the south side of the Nanticoke. Possessed by James Weatherly		Nanticoke	100
460a.	COVINGTONS MEADOW, 1 Dec.1699 Phillip Covingington, on the north side of Gr.Money Creek. Possessed by same.		Money	100
360a.	CHANCE	5 Nov.1695 Thomas Purnell, near a corner tree of Smiths Chance. Possessed by Thomas Purnell	Poquadenorton	100
1000a.	COXES PERFORMANCE 16 Oct.1696 John Windsor in a fork of branches of Broad Creek. Possessed by John Windsor		Poquadernorton	100
200a.	DONNINGALL, 17 Oct. 1696 Andrew Speer Possessed by Andrew Speer		Poquadenorton	100
100a.	AGHEU LOWE, 21 Oct.1696 James McWilliams on the south side of the Nanticoke. Possessed by James Givans		Nanticoke	100
300a.	PARTNERS DESIRE, 9 June 1696 Edward Green On the south side of the Pocomoke River. Green dead and land not possessed. Heir in England		Annamessex	100
137a.	ANYTHING 21 Oct. 1696 James Dashiell on the south side Nanticoke River. Possessed by James Dashiell		Nanticoke	100
50a.	WOOLFORDS VENTURE, 14 Oct.1696 Roger Woolford on the north side Manokin River. Possessed by Mary Woolford relict of Roger		Manokin	100
200a.	SAMUELLS LOTT, 23 Oct.1696 Richard Samuels on a neck between the Nanticoke and Wicomico River. Possessed by Richard Samuels		Wicomico	100
50a.	MILKMORE 23 Oct.1696 Samuel Flewellyn on the north side near the mouth of the Wicomico River. Possessed by widow Flewellyn		Wicomico	100
75a.	FRONT OF LOCUST HAMMOCK, 11 Oct.1697 John Pollikey, near a place cllled Dam Quarter. Possessed by John Marvell		Wic.	100
50a.	CLEAR OF CANNON SHOTT, 22 Oct.1696 Samuel Flewellyn, 4 miles from the south side Nanticoke. Possessed by the widow Flewellyn		Wicomico	100
64a.	MEADOWLAND, 21 Nov.1697 John Roach in a neck between the Annamessex River and Pocomoke Bay. Claimed by John Roach		Pocomoke	100
300a.	HOGSDON 30 May 1696 Samuel Truett in Ascomonoconson Neck. George Truitt owns this land		Mattapany	100
400a.	PARKERS ADVENTURE 16 Oct.1698 Edward Green on the west side of the Pocomoke River. Heirs in England. Supposed land lies in Indian Town		Mattapany	100

ACRES	TRACT	SURVEY DATE-BY WHOM	LOCATION	
400a.	ARMENIA	15 Aug 1698, John Parker on the north west side of the Pocomoke. Lies in the lines of Indian Town	Mattapany	100
135a.	MATHEWS ADVENTURE,	no date, William Matthews on the north side of the Pocomoke River. Possessed by William Matthews	Annamessex	100
600a.	no name	29 Sep.1698 Benjamin and John Aydelotte, on the east side of Ascomonoconson Neck. Possessed by Robert and William Davis	Mattapany	100
400a.	MISERABLE	QUARTER, 9 Oct.1698 John Clark on the east most side of the main branch of the St.Martins River. Possessed by John Clark	Mattapany	100
40a.	CLONMELL	1 Oct.1696 Pierce Bray on the northwest side Pocomoke River. Possessed by Pierce Bray	Annamessex	100
500a.	VINES NECK,	15 Oct.1679 Samuel Hopkins on the south side of Indian Alias Baltimore River Possessed by Andrew Derrickson	Baltimore	100
50a.	FLUELYNS	PURCHASE 23 Oct.1696 Samuel Fleulyn 4 miles from the south side of the Nanticoke. Possessed by the widow Fleulyn	Nanticoke	100
400a.	SWEETWEED	HALL, 23 Oct.1696 John McLavor near Nanticoke point. John McClester owns land	Nanticoke	100
100a.	CANNONS	PEACE 14 Feb.1699 Stephen Cannon on the south side of the Nanticoke and west side of Wetepkewant Creek. Peter Body possesses	Nanticoke	100
223a.	COLLINS	ADDITION 22 May 1700 Samuel Collins on the north side Pocomoke. Possessed by same.	Annamessex	100
100a.	HORSE	HUMMOCK 24 May 1700 James Curtis on the south side near the mouth of the Manokin River. Possessed by James Curtis	Annamessex	100
150a.	CONVENIENCY	5 May 1688 John Emmett patented for William Round, on the southeast side of the Pocomoke River. Possessed by same.	Annamessex	100
200a.	ALEXANDERS	DESIRE,1 Oct.1696 Wm.Planner on the eastmost side, 2 miles from the Pocomoke River. Land assigned to Alexander Macullough and Possessed by Charles Godfree	Annamessex	100
300a.	BABLE	15 Oct.1698 Samuel Hopkins on the south side of the Baltimore River. Possessed by Andrew Dickenson	Baltimore	100
33a.	RECOVERY	24 Dec.1701 Benjamin Schoolfield on the south side of the Pocomoke River. Adj. land of Mr.Schoolfields called Desert. Possessed by Richard Lamberton vide Banjamin Schoolfield account.	Annamessex	100
200a.	LOGGMORE	1 May 1701 Clement Giles. in the woods from the seaboard side near land of John Freeman Jr. Orphans land under guardianship of Robert Johnson	Baltimore	100

ACRES	TRACT	SURVEY DATE-BY WHOM	LOCATION

50a. GRAYS LOTT 7 Dec.1701 James Gray   Annamessex 100
            about 2 miles from the south side of the Annamessex
            River. Claimed by James Gray

250a. GRAYS LOTT 31 Dec.1701 James Gray   Annamessex 100
            on the south side near the mouth of the Annamessex
            River. Possessed by James Gray

1000a. BALTIMORE GIFT, 10 Oct.1702 Wm.Whittington Sr. Baltimore 100
            pt. of Assateage Island on the seaboard side
            Possessed by William Whittington

100a. ANYTHING 15 May 1702 Robert Caldwell   Wicomico 100
            between the Rokiawakin and Manokin River.
            Possessed by Robert Caldwell

50a. ADDITION 8 Apr.1703 Philip Ascue. On the south side, 2
            miles from the Rokiawakin River.   Wicomico 100
            Possessed by Phillip Ascue

50a. BEARS HOLE 4 May 1703 Peter Benton   Pocomoke 100
            on the north side Pocomoke River, 1 mile
            from Dividing Creek. Possessed by Peter Benton

50a. SAPLING RIDGE 15 Oct.1703 Peter Benton   Pocomoke 100
            4 miles from the north side of the Pocomoke River
            2 miles from the west side Dividing Creek.
            Possessed by Peter Benton

250a. TIMBER LOTT 15 Mar.1702/3 Walter Taylor   Pocomoke 100
            2 miles on the north side Pocomoke River.
            Possessed by Walter Taylor. Quo. if not TAYLORS
            LOTT

200a. POINT MARSH 8 Dec.1703 John MacLester   Wicomico 100
            onthe north side between Wicomico and Nanticoke
            Possessed by John MacLester

300a. CONVENIENCE 30 Nov.1703 John Aydelott   Pocomoke 100
            on the south side Pocomoke River, 2 miles from
            the river. Possessed by John Aydelott

700a. FAIR MEADOW 15 Dec.1703 John McLester   Wicomico 100
            near the mouth on the north west side of the
            Pocomoke River. Possessed by same.

390a. MATTAPANY 18 Sep.1701, George Parker   Mattapany 100
            on seaboard side on the north side Herring Creek.
            Found to be but 300a.. Possessed by Ste.
            Warrington in right of said parker

100a. THE OUTLETT 22 Sep.1701 John White   Annamessex 100
            in Dam Quarter. Possessed by John White

100a. GOSHEN 16 Aug 1701 John Cottingham   Annamessex 100
            near Pocomoke Bay. Possessed by John Cottingham

200a. ADDITION 5 Dec.1701 John Smith   Annamessex 100
            near seaboardside near the dividing line of Maryland
            and Virginia on the north side Swanscutt Creek.
            James Smith lives in Accocomac, owns and possesses

| ACRES | TRACT | SURVEY DATE-BY WHOM | LOCATION |

95a. FRIENDS ACCEPTANCE,13 Aug 1701 Richard Wallace, Annamessex 100
 In Dam Quarter. adj.Francis Roberts. Possessed
 by Richard Wallace

25a. POINT NEXT THE WORST, 18 Aug.1701 John Collins, Annamessex 100
 in Pocomoke Bay at Johnsons Creek. Possessed
 by John Collins

100a. MOSES'S LOTT 18 Sep.1701 Moses Owens   Annamessex 100
 near Pocomoke Bay in Annamessex Neck near
 land of Phillip Conner. Possessed by Moses Owens

60a. WINDSORS PREVENTION 28 Oct.1701 Thomas Roe, Annamessex 100
 on Devils Island adj. land of John Windser.
 Possessed by Francis Craydon

160a. PURGATORY 28 Oct.1701 Thomas Roe   Annamessex 100
 on Devils Island,land found to be 130a.
 Possessed by Francis Gradon

160a. DEAR LOTT 11 Sep.1701 John Dear   Manokin 100
 Possessed by Archibald Smith but he denies
 rent so John Dear must pay in who the right
 is possessed

188a, STEVENS MEADOW 30 Sep 1701 William Stevens Manokin 100
 between Annamessex and Manokin in Jericho Neck
 Possessed by Samuel Handy

1225a. SHIELLS FOLLY,no date, James and Thomas Dashiell on-Wico.100
 the north side Wicomico River. Found to be 1350a.

109a. FATHERS CARE 8 May 1702 Hermer Herinorson   Manokin 100
 on seaboard side near Spalding. No one possessed
 purchaser a minor with his father in Sussex
 Territory of Pennsylvania

112a. TOWERS ADDITION 7 May 1702 Margaret Towers   Mattapany 100
 on the seaboard side and west side of main
 Road from St.Martins. Possessed by same

525a. DESART   13 June 1702 special Warrent   Annamessex 100
 Thomas Walston. Near Jericho between Manokin
 and Annamessex River, orignial grant was 400a.

400a. THE MISTAKE 8 May1702 Matthew Jones   Annamessex 100
 on the south side at mouth of Annamessex River.
 Possessed by Robert Catherwood for Jones' orphans

150a. SLAUGHTER RIDGE 4 May 1702 Thomas Powell   Mattapony 100
 on seaboard side. 2 miles from St. Martins
 Claimes by same

100a. COOPERS MISTAKE 1 Oct.1695 Samuel Flewellin Wicomico 100
 assigned to Thomas Larramore between the Wicomico
 and Nanticoke.Possessed by Thomas Larramore.
 Now Possessed by widow Fleullin in her childs right.

200a. HOPEWELL 13 Sep 1702,Roger Woodcroft   Annamessex 100
 on the south side Deep Branch 2 miles from
 seaboard. Richard Woodcroft owns

180a. NORTONS LOTT 25 Mar.1703 John Norton   Mattapony 100
 on the north side St.Martins River. Possessed
 by John Norton

ACRES	TRACT	SURVEY DATE-BY WHOM	LOCATION	
100a.	BATCHELLORS CHOICE, no date. John Wilson. John Wilson, on the south side Nanticoke and west most side Barren Creek. Possessed by same.		Nanticoke	100
50a.	WILLSONS LOTT, no date, John Wilson on ths south side Nanticoke River. West side Barren Creek. Possessed by same.		Nanticoke	100
50a.	DOUGHTYS PRIVILEDGE, no date. Peter Doughty between the Nanticoke and Wicomico Rivers Possessed by Peter Doughty		Nanticoke	100
150a.	CUMBERLAND, 12 Oct.1705 John Waters on north side Annamessex adj. tr. WATERS RIVER		Annamessex	100
100a.	RIGGINS CONTENT 2 Sep 1704 John Riggin on west side Nasiango Creek. Possessed by same.		Annamessex	100
100a.	POYK 1 May 1704 John Biriam, in Asomonconson Neck on the east side Massiango Creek. claimed by John Biriams		Annamessex	100
100a.	NOD 6 Sep.1704 John Harris on the west side bounds Nassiango Creek. Claimed by John Harris		Annamessex	100
75a.	CURTIS'S LOTT 15 May 1704, James Curtis 2 miles from north side Annamessex. Possessed by James Curtis		Annamessex	100
80a.	SAMPIRE 15 May 1704 James Curtis on the south side near mouth of Manokin River. Possessed by James Curtis		Annamessex	100
200a.	PARTNERS AGREEMENT 1 Dec.1701 Furbeg Rugg and Charles Cottingham. Possessed by the widow of Furbey Rugg and Charles Cottingham		Annamessex	100
325a.	THE REFUSED 5 May 1703 Peter Dent on the west side Nasiango Creek, on north side of the Ppcomoke River. Assigned to William Whittingham who possesses		Annamessex	100
180a.	COVINGTONS COMFORT 6 May 1706 Nehemiah Covington, on the north side Money Creek, west side Poplar Neck. The land in dispute, taken up in bounds of a tract belonging to Phillip Covington		Money	100
50a.	FORCE PUTT 9 Oct.1700, Peter Doughty on the west side Wicomico River, east side of Broad Creek. Possessed by Peter Doughty		Wicomico	100
38a.	WILSONS LOTT 15 Aug.1704 John Wilson on the main branch of Blackwater, on the south side Nanticoke River. Possessed by John Wilson		Nanticoke	100
100a.	ADDITION 27 Sep.1704 Robert Givan possessed by same		Nanticoke	100
200a.	CALDWELLS LOTT, 15 Sep.1704 Robert Caldwell on the south side Nanticoke River. on north side Rowastico Glade. Possessed by Robert Caldwell		Nanticoke	100
70a.	HAPHAZZARD 7 Dec.1698 John Cullens in Annamessex Neck near Prices Cowpen Branch Possessed by John Cullens		Annamessex	100

| ACRES | TRACT | SURVEY DATE-BY WHOM | LOCATION |

150a. CUMBERLAND 12 April 1705, William Laws   Bogertenortin 100
in Ascomononoconson Neck, 4 miles north
of Indian Town. Claimed by William Laws

480a. EVERYS POLICY 25 Sep.1704 William Elgate, includes 300a.
on north side Rokiawakin River. Possessed by
William Elgate   Nanticoke 100

75a. SMALL LOTT 16 Nov.1705 Honour Small   Pocomoke 100
on the south side Pocomoke River adj. tract
Hendersons Choice, Possessed by Honour Small

100a. BASHAW 26 Nov. 1705 Andrew Bashaw   Pocomoke 100
on the westmost side Nassango Creek. Possessed
by Andrew Bashaw

260a. PASTURAGE 20 Oct 1705 James Macmorrie   Wicomico 100
and William Wainright, on the north side
Wicomico River. Claimed by the same.

200a. ROYALL OAK, no date. Part thereof being   Pocomoke 100
escheated for want of heirs of Thomas Profit
and resurveyed by special warrent for Charles
Ratcliff. Possessed by Presgrave Turville

100a. COME BY CHANCE, 4 Apr.1706 Samuel Davis   Pocomoke 100
on the west side Dividing Creek in Perryhawkin
Neck. Possessed by Samuel Davis

50a. FATHERS CARE 18 Mar.1705 John Conner   Pocomoke 100
in Annamessex Neck on Pocomoke Bay possessed
by the widow Conner in her son's right

75a. HOPEWELL 15 Mar.1705 William Faucett   Manokin 100
in the marshes on the south side and near
the mouth of the Manokin River. Claimed by same.

100a. DAVIDS DESTINY 1 Apr.1706 David Dryden   Pocomoke 100
back in the woods from the north west side
of the Pocomoke River. Possessed by David Dryden

40a. MARYS ADVENTURE 29 Sep.1705 Widow Mary Macraugh Manokin 100
on the north side of the main branch of the
Manokin River. Possessed by Mary Macraugh

40a. UNEXPECTED 27 Sep.1705 Arthur Denwood   Manokin 100
1½miles from the north side of the main branch
of the Manokin River. Possessed by Arthur Denwood

95a. HOGGYARD 16 May 1704 Thomas Beauchamp   Manokin 100
on the south most side of Morumsco Dam branch.
Claimed by Thomas Beauchamp

300a. STONERIDGE no date, laid out by special warrent Manokin 100
for Levin Denwood including 50a. from former
survey for the same called STONRIDGE which survey
was erroneous. Lying between the Money and Manokin
Claimed by Levin Denwood

70a. ADVENTURE 5 May 1706 Richard Crockett   Manokin 100
in a fork made by Crocketts Creek. Possessed by
the widow Lowe

ACRES	TRACT	SURVEY DATE-BY WHOM	LOCATION

274a. LONG DELAY 20 Mar.1705 Ephraim Pollock   Manokin 100
   possessed by William Pollock to whom it was
   assigned

70a. JOSEPHS LOTT 19 Apr.1706 Benjamin Wales   Manokin 100
   Possessed by Benjamin Wales

70a. COVINGTONS FOLLY 6 May 1706 Samuel Covington   Manokin 100
   Possessed by Samuel Covington

125a. LONG ACRE 22 July 1706 Capt.John Franklin   Balitmore 100
   back in the woods from the seaboard side
   near Coys Folly. Claimed by John Franklin

250a. FREEMANS LOTT 7 Aug 1706 John Freeman Jr.   Baltimore 100
   2 miles form the south side of the St.Martins
   River on seaboard side. Possessed by John
   Bowden in said Freeman's right

125a. PROVIDENCE 2 Aug 1706 William Massey   Baltimore 100
   2 miles from the seaboard side near Horse Bridge
   and road leading to Senepuxon Neck. Possessed
   by William Massey

400a. GLINEATH 23 July 1663 Jenkins Price   Pocomoke 100
   in Pocomoke River on the westmost side.
   Resurveyed for and in the name of Col.William
   Stevens. Is now 850a. called THE ENTRANCE vide
   rent rolls for the possessors

700a. JOLLEYS DELIGHT 20 July 1663 James Jolly   Pocomoke 100
   on Pocomoke River on eastmost side. Cut off by
   the dividional line of Virginia and Maryland

250a. LITTLE BOLTON, 1663 Alexander Draper   Annamessex 100
   in Annemessex River on southmost side of Mark
   Creek. Resurveyed for 850a. and in the name
   of Thomas Jones. Now belongs to his orphan
   vide rent roll.

300a. THE CONTENTION alias DICKSTON, 5 Sep.1663   Manokin 100
   Edward Dixon on Annamessex River in fork
   called DICKSTON, resurved by special warrent
   and called THE CONTENTION. No such land,must
   be included in a latter survey

300a. JOHNSTON 5 Sep.1663 George Johnson   Annamessex 100
   on the south most side of the Annamessex. The
   heir in England. Thomas Everdon was last possessor.

600a. SKIPPERS PLANTATION 20 Sep.1663 Matthew Armstrong, Annamessex 100
   on the north side of the Annamessex River. No such
   land in this county. Land Armstrong held is now
   possessed by Samuel Handy and James Curtis, vide
   rent roll. Must be same land but agrees not in
   quantity

500a. CROUCHS CHOICE 20 Jan 1664 Ambrose Crouch   Manokin 100
   on the south side Manokin River. No such land
   in this county

1000a. WICOMICO 12 Mar.1663 Henry Sewell Esqu.   Pocomoke 100
   in Pocomoke River on the south side. This cut off
   by the divisional line between Va. and Md.

| ACRES | TRACT | SURVEY DATE-BY WHOM | LOCATION |

500a. **PUNGATESSEX** 3 Mar 1663 Jenkins Price — Pocomoke 100
on Pocomoke River on south side. This land
might be cut off by divisional line between
Maryland and Virginia

250a. **COLD HARBOUR** 6 Mar.1663 German Gillett — Pocomoke 100
in Pocomoke River on the south side. This
land included in former survey, may be cut off
as before

200a. **JAMES GROVE** 13 Mar.1663 Percival Reed — Pocomoke 100
in Pocomoke River on south side. This land cut
off as before.

100a. **ELLEYRS ISLAND** 13 Mar.1663 Henry Ellery — Pocomoke 100
on the south side of the Pocomoke River. Land
cut off as before

600a. **HACKWORTH CHARITY** 16 Mar.1663 Richard Acworth, Manokin 100
on the north side Manokin River. This land
is not the quantity, being altered by former
resurvey. Must be the same held by Arthur
Denwood

450a. **DAVIS'S CHOICE** 20 Mar.1663 Thomas Davis — Manokin 100
on Back Creek the south side. resurveyed for
600a. Possessed
150a. Capt.Henry Smith
330a. John Fisher
120a. widow Jane Wilson

300a. **CATTLYNS LOTT** 9 Apr.1664 Robert Cattlyn — Manokin 100
on thenorthbranch of the Annamessex River.
Land included in later resurvey of HARTFORD
BROAD OAK

600a. **TAYLORS CHOICE** 9 Mar.1663 Walter Taylor — Manokin 100
onthe north side Manokin River. No such land
known must be included in later survey

300a. **DAVIS'S LOTT** 5 Mar.1663 Richard Davis — Manokin 100
on the south side Back Creek of the Manokin River
Possessed by Ephraim Wilson

1000a. **NASWORTHYS CHOICE** 10 Mar.1663 George Nasworthy, Manokin 100
on the south side Manokin River. Resurveyed by
CapT. Henry Smith and possessed by John Tunstall
and several others being found but 700a. called
SMITHS RECOVERY being all patented of THOMPSONS
PURCHASE

300a. **KINGS CHOICE** 6 Mar.1663 John King — Manokin 100
on the south side Manokin River. No such land
found

200a. **UNDOE** 2 Apr.1664 Stephen Horsey — Annamessex 100
Included in later resurvey and held by Thomas Davis
for 300a.

150a. **WALES ISLAND** 26 Aug 1665 George Wale — Pocomoke 100
on south side Pocomoke River. No such land known
Must be cut off by Virginia Line.

| ACRES | TRACT | SURVEY DATE-BY WHOM | LOCATION |

1500a. REVELLS GROVE 1 Oct.1665 Randall Revell   Annamessex 100
on the north side of the Pocomoke River. This
land assigned to Col.Edward Carter of Nansemond
in Virginia and patented in Carters name. Lies
in Ascomonoconson Indian town if to be found

300a. WHTIEFIELD 2 May 1665 William Whitefield   Annamessex 100
on the south side of the Pocomoke River. No
such land or person known

250a. STAPELFORDS NECK 2 Nov.1665 Raymond Stapleford, Annamessex 100
on the north side Pocomoke River, No such land
or person known

150a. TOWNSENDS NECK, 5 Nov.1665 John Townsend   Annamessex 100
on the north side Pocomoke River, East side
Morumsco Creek. Possessed by Peter Kersey

200a. PRICES HOPE 13 Feb 1663 Edward Price   Annamessex 100
in Annamessex, No such land known

200a. PRICES VINEYARD 14 Feb 1663 James Price   Annamessex100
possessed by Thomas Ward in right of the heiress

150a. IRISH GROVE 10 Nov.1665 Morris Liston   Pocomoke 100
on the north side Pocomoke River, on west side
Morumsco Creek. Possessed by Sampson Wheatly,
Thomas Mattocks and Phillip Conner

150a. HORSEY DOWN 30 Mar.1680 Stephen Horsey   Annamessex 100
on the east sideof a dam between Morumsco and
Annamessex, Possessed by Stephen Horsey and
Anthony Bell

200a. BEAR POINT 26 Feb 1663 Cornelius Ward   Annamessex 100
no such land known

150a. BLOYCES HOPE 1 Mar.1666 Thomas Bloyce   Money 100
on the east side Back Creek of Little Money
Possessed by Thomas Shaw vide rent rolls.

50a. CLARKS MARSH 12 Mar.1666 John Clark   Wicomico 100
on the west side Wicomico River, No such land known

150a. CURTIS'S IMPROVEMENT 8 June 1667 William Stevens, Pocomoke 100
on the north side Pocomoke River, west side Dividing
Creek. Assigned Daniel Curtis. No such land,must
be included in some resurvey

100a. HILLYARDS ADVENTURE 2 Apr.1667 John Hillard   Pocomoke 100
on the east side Morumsco. Assigned John Ellis
possessed by William Matthews

50a. LONDONS ADVISEMENT 3 June 1667 William Furniss, Annamessex 100
in a neck of land called Desart between the
Annamessex and Manokin. Assigned George Johnson.
The heir lives in England, Thomas Everondon possesses

600a. CHANCE   24 Feb 1666 Richard Preston   Pocomoke 100
on the north side Pocomoke, west side Dividing Creek.
Assigned William Furniss. This land included in
later survey and held by the other title.

10a. THE LAST CHOICE 6 Sep. 1667 Ambrose London   Annamessex 100
on neck of land between Annamessex and Manokin Rivers.
in a ridge next to the east side Middle Creek. Possessed
by Samuel Handy.

100a.

| ACRES | TRACT | SURVEY DATE-BY WHOM | LOCATION |

300a. BARKIN 5 June 1667 William Smith   Pocomoke 100
on the north side Pocomoke River in Dividing
Creek. Included in some later survey

300a. AMERICA 7 June 1667 James Henderson   Pocomoke 100
on north side Pocomoke River, East side Dividing
Creek. Included in later survey called MOORFIELDS
possessed by Joseph Gray

100a. BARSHEBA 7 June 1667 John Ellis   Pocomoke 100
on the north side Pocomoke River in Dividing
Creek. No such land

100a. BETHSAIDA 5 June 1667 William Stevens   Pocomoke 100
on the north side Pocomoke River, east side
Dividing Creek. Assigned to John Ellis. No such land.

550a. NOBLE QUARTER 3 July 1668 Nicholas Rice   Wicomico 100
on the north side Wicomico River. Possessed by
Capt. Nicholas Evans

150a. DISCOVERY 2 May 1668 William Cheseman   Annamessex 100
at head of the Annamessex River. Thomas Everndon
last possessed. The heir lives in England

200a. FURNIS'S ADVENTURE 3 Dec 1666 William Furnis, Annamessex 100
in a neck of land called Desart between Manokin
and Annamessex. No such land, included in later
survey

50a. LOCUST RIDGE alias HUMMOCK, 3 Feb 1666   Annamessex 100
William Furniss, on the south side Manokin River
near the moth therof in Furnis's creek. Possessed
by John Marvile

600a. A FRIENDS CHOICE,10 Sep.1667 William Waters Pocomoke 100
on the north side Poco;oke River, west side
Dividing Creek. Must be included in later survey.

1200a. A FRIENDS CHOICE, 3 Mar 1666 Richard Preston of Putuxent.
on the south side Pocomoke River over against a
place called Askomonconson. Assigned George Johnson.
Included in a patent of 900a. ROCHESTER. Possessed
by John Godden

1200a. ADVENTURE 3 Mar 1666, Richard Preston   Pocomoke 100
on the south side Pocomoke River. Assigned to
George Johnson. Included as above. Possessed by
John Godden

800a. HOG QUARTER 18 Sep.1668 John Anderson   Pocomoke 100
on the south side Pocomoke River. Possessed lately
by Samuel Layfield

900a. LONGFIELD GENEZER,5 Sep.1668 William Stevens, Mattapony 100
on the seaboard side at the southmost part of a
neck called Synepuxon alias Jenipoxon. Resurveyed
and found to be a considerable quantity more and
held by the name GENEZER

200a. CONVENIENCE 20 Aug 1668 William Stevens   Pocomoke 100
on the south side Pocomoke River. No such land.
must be included in later survey of 1300a. being
mostly cypress swamp of the same name.

| ACRES | TRACT | SURVEY DATE-BY WHOM | LOCATION |

300a. IGNOBLE QUARTER 14 Sep.1668 Thomas Shield   Wicomico 100
on the north side Wicomico River. Possessed
by Thomas Shield his son. 150a. by John Shields,
32a. Thomas Dashiell, 158a. Thomas Shield

600a. BRISCO'S LOTT 1 Dec.1668 Arthur Brisco of Ann Arundel Co.
on the north side Wicomico River. No such land,

500a. THOMPSONS PURCHASE, 20 Dec 1668 William Stevens, Manokin 100
on the south side Manokin River. No such land.
Must be included in the later survey made for
Capt.Henry Smith, this and NASWORTHYS CHOICE was
but 700a. and now called SMITHS RECOVERY

200a. MIGHT A HAD MORE, 26 Nov.1669 James Jones   Wicomico 100
on the north side Wicomico River. No such land found

200a. DOE BETTER,1 July 1669 Thomas Gillis   Wicomico 100
on the south side Cuttomoctice River. no land found

300a. HILLARDS CHOICE 6 June 1667 Richard Stevens Pocomoke 100
on north side Pocomoke River in Dividing Creek
in Nascoatoe Neck. Assigned William Stevens. No
such land.

736a. PHARSALIA alias LITTLETONS DELIGHT, 6 Apr.1666, Mattapony 100
Southy Littleton, on the north side Swansecutt
Creek, on seaboard side. Land resurveyed for a
greater quantity

200a. WARWICK   10 Apr.1671 George Eves   Pocomoke 100
on the north side of the Pocomoke in
Naswatuck Neck. resurveyed for 400a. Possessed
by Rowland Bivan

100a. SCOTTS LOTT 16 Sep.1672, William Scott   Pocomoke 100
on the south side of the Pocomoke River about
2 miles in the woods from the now dwelling house
of Robert Houlston. Possessed by Robert Houlston

1200 ALMODINGTON 4 Dec 1671 Arnold Elzey   Manokin 100
on the north side of the Manokin River. Possessed
by Arnold Elzey. rent paid for but 1000a.

300a. DANBURY   4 Feb 1672 Samuel Jackson   Wicomico 100
on the north side of the Rokiawakin River near
Cottingham Creek.

500a. FRIENDSHIP 6 Aug 1673 John Walker   Baltimore 100
on the seaboard side near Deleware Bay, 4 miles
from the Whorekills Creek, east side Rehobeth
Bay. Out of this county (now Deleware)

300a. AVERYS CHOICE 6 Aug.1673 John Avery   Baltimore 100
on the seaboard side near Deleware Bay. Same as above.

200a. OAK HALL 18 Dec 1673, Henry Smith   Pocomoke 100
on the north side Pocomoke River, Land not known

100a. CHARLES'S CHOICE 10 Mar.1674/5 Charles Ratcliffe, on the
seaboard side. No such land by this title.

96a. MITCHELLS LOTT alias DEAR LOTT, 30 Sep. 1674 Wicomico 100
William Elgate,on north side Cuttimachtico River.
Possessed by same.

ACRES	TRACT	SURVEY DATE-BY WHOM	LOCATION	

2000a. MOUNT EPHRAIM 6 May 1671 Robert Richardson, Bogerternortin 100
at Poquadernorton at seaboard side. First
surveyed in Virginia, right now called Mt.Ephraim

700a. SMITHS CHOICE 2 Mar.1674 Edward Smith   Bogertenortin 100
on the north east side of Robert Richardsons
land. Resurveyed by Benjamin Schoolfield
by the name of SMITHS FIRST CHOICE

1050a. ROBINSONS INHERITANCE 1 Mar.1675 Richard   Bogertenortin 100
Robinson, on seaboard side bounded by Hearn Creek.
Held by Richard Robinson

1500a. PARRAMOURS DOUBLE PURCHASE 14 Nov.1674   Bogeternortin 100
John Parramour, lying between Parramours Creek
alias Weetuxion. On the east side. resurveyed.

550a. PURNELLS LOTT 1 Mar.1675 Thomas Purnell   Bogertenortin 100
on seaboard side. Possessed by John Purnell

200a. HASFORTS PURCHASE 8 Nov.1675 George Hasfort Pocomoke 100
near the Pocomoke River on west side Morumsco Ck.
William Brittain died possessed and escheats
to his lordship for want of heirs.

500a. RECOVERY 8 Dec.1675 Major Thomas Brereton   Nanticoke 100
on the east side Nanticoke River, south side of
Quantico Creek. Possessed by George Dashiell

50a. LITTLEWORTH 15 Sep.1676 William Stevens   Pocomoke 100
on the northside Morumsco, on east side Planners
Creek. Assigned to Thomas Cottingham. Possessed
by the widow Rugg in her son's right

500a. FIRST CHOICE 2 Jan 1676 William Stevens   Nanticoke 100
on the south side of the Nanticoke River, near
the main branch of Rowastico Creek. Assigned
to William Manlove. Possessed 250a. Charles
Williams, 250a. George Hutchins

300a. MAIDEN LOTT 4 May 1677 William Stevens   Nanticoke 100
on the south side of the Nanticoke River, south
side of Barren Creek. Assigned to Elizabeth
Williams. Possessed by John Gilly

300a. SCOTLAND 12 July 1677 William Stevens   Annamessex 100
on the north side of Pocomoke Bay, 3 miles from
Watkins Point. Assigned to William Scott. Possessed
by William Scott

150a. KINGSALE 12 Oct.1677 Josias Seaward   Annamessex 100
on the north side Pocomoke Bay. Possessed by
Matthew Parker at the Whorekills

2800a. ARRACOCO 19 Nov.1679 Randall Revell   Manokin 100
the surplus land adj. to DOUBLE PURCHASE,
included in a resurvey made by Randall Revell
called DOUBLE PURCHASE

700a. NEWPORT PAGNELL 22 July William Stevens   Mattapony 100
on the seaboard side, north side Assateage River
Possessed-350a. John Watts in Virginia,
350a. Laurence Ryley in right of his wife

ACRES	TRACT	SURVEY DATE-BY WHOM	LOCATION

1000a. SUFFOLK 11 June 1679 William Morris   Pocomoke 100
on the north side of the Pocomoke River, on south
west side Dividing Creek. Part cut off by older
Survey
464a. belongs to Mr. Heith
200a. John Tull
75a. Tripshaws orphans. The older survey COLEMANS
ADVENTURE possessed by Richard Tull

600a. JONE'S CHOICE 6 Sep.1675 Samuel Jones   Bogertenortin 100
on the seaboard side, 3 miles back in the woods
Possessed 300a. Samuel Hopkins by the name of
NUNS GREEN
150a. Nathaniel Hopkins
150a. Matthew Scarborough

600a. WING 19 July 1678 William Stevens   Pocomoke 100
on the north side of the Pocomoke River in a
neck called Ascomonoconson. Assigned to Joseph
Gray and James Gray. Possessed by John Kellum Sr.

250a. FIRST CHOICE 17 June 1679 William Stevens Annamessex 100
on the south side of Bever Dam at head of the
Annamessex River. Assigned Robert Cattlyn
75a. possessed by Joseph Benston, the rest cut
off by an older survey vide William Cattling's
account

500a. RECOVERY 8 Dec 1676 Thomas Brereton   Nanticoke 100
on the east side of the Nanticoke River, south
side Quantico Creek. Resurveyed 1679. same quantity

200a. WORTON 13 July 1679 John Brown   Pocomoke 100
on the north side of the Pocomoke River. Assigned
to Robert Smith, Possessed by Robert Smith

100a. HOGRIDGE 1 May 1680 Daniel Hast   Pocomoke 100
on the northside of the Pocomoke River, north
side Morumsco Creek. Assigned to George Wilson.
Possessed by William and George Wilson

100a. MARSH HOOK 15 Dec.1679 James Weatherly   Nanticoke 100
by the creeks of Rewastico and Manumquak.
Possesssed by Charles Nutter for Piper's orphans

250a. MILE END 20 May 1680 William Stevens   Wicomico 100
in a fork of the Wicomico River. assigned to
William Brereton. Possessed by Benjamin Brereton
the heir.

150a. STEPNEY 4 Apr.1681 William Stevens   Pocomoke 100
on the north side of the Pocomoke River between
said river and Morumsco Creek. Assigned Richard
Lewis. No such land or person known

150a. COVINGTON alias SASAFRAS NECK 5 Apr.1681 Money 100
William Stevens on the north side Manny River.
Assigned to John Covington. Possessed by Phillip
Covington

1100a. CASAWAY 2 Apr.1680 William Stevens   Nanticoke 100
near head of Rokiawakin River between branches of
the Nanticoke and Rokiawakin. Assigned to Thomas
and Susan Walker

ACRES	TRACT	SURVEY DATE-BY WHOM	LOCATION

50a. SAUCERS LOTT 1 Oct 1681 John Austin   Manokin 100
on the north side of the Manokin River, in
a fork of Broad Creek. Possessed by Benjamin
Saucer

300a. WHITEMARSH DELIGHT 20 Mar.1681 John Lyon   Nanticoke 100
on the east side Nanticoke River, south side of
Rewastico Creek. Possessed by James and Robert
Givan

1100a. DOUBLE PURCHASE 25 Mar.1680 James Henderson   Pocomoke 100
three tracts of land into 1 tract on the south
side of the Pocomoke River. Possessed by the
heirs of Henderson but by the 1st grant

500a. BOSTON TOWN 30 Mar.1682 William Planner   Annamessex 100
on the south side of the Annamessex between Crane
Creek and Redcap Creek. Possessed by William
Planner the heir

500a. MOORFIELDS 5 Apr.1682 Henry Smith   Pocomoke 100
part of several parcels on the north side of
the Pocomoke River east side Dividing Creek in
Naswattux Neck

230a. RICH RIDGE 3 June 1682 William Stevens   Nanticoke 100
near the nead of the Nanticoke River. Assigned
to Christopher Nutter. Possessed by same

288a. RECOVERY 23 Nov.1681 John Tarr   Nanticoke 100
on the east side of the Nanticoke River, south
side of Wetipkin Creek. Possessed by Peter Calloway
and George Andrews. Calloway the survivor denys
this land. Supposed to be included in other survey

900a. FAIRFIELD 2 Feb 1682 Thomas Pemberton   Wicomico 100
in a fork of the Wicomico River. Possessed by
William Whittington Jr.

100a. ROWLEY HILL 28 May 1683 William Stevens   Pocomoke 100
on the south side of Dividing Creek. Assigned to
Abraham Heath. Possessed by Anthony Moor

50a. ISLAND MARSH 9 Feb 1683 William Brereton   Wicomico 100
on the north side of the head of the Wicomico River
Possessed by John Frizell

150a. GOLDEN QUARTER 31 May 1681 William Stevens   Manokin 100
on the north side of the main branch of the Manokin
River, a mile from the Wadding place. Assigned
to John Goldsmith. Possessed by the relic of John

100a. RIGGENS MINE 7 June 1683 William Stevens   Annamessex 100
on the south side of Morumsco Creek. Assigned to
Teague Riggin. Possessed by Ambrose Riggin

100a. SMITHFIELD 8 July 1682 Randall Revell   Wicomico 100
from the head of the Wicomico River at Tamaroons
Ridge. Assigned James Ingram. Possessed by Roger
Phillips

50a. COW QUARTER 5 June 1683 William Stevens   Manokin 100
on the south side Manokin above the mouth of
Teague Creek. Assigned John King. Possessed by
James Curtis.

ACRES	TRACT	SURVEY DATE-BY WHOM	LOCATION
150a.	MORRIS ADVISEMENT	5 Oct.1683 William Stevens, on the north side of the Pocomoke River at Whitemarsh Branch, near Dividing Creek. Assigned Francis Jenkins. Possessed by Edward Harper	Pocomoke 100
175a.	MIDDLE PLANTATION	12 May 1683 William Stevens, on the north side Dividing Creek on north side of the Pocomoke River. Assigned William Harper. Possessed by Edward Harper in right of his child	Pocomoke 100
700a.	CHASBURY	1 Oct 1681 Edward Hammond on the south side of the Pocomoke River in Quapanquoh Neck. Possessed by Hammond by the name of SHAFTSBURY	Pocomoke 100
400a.	CHOCKLEYS PURCHASE	18 May 1682 William Stevens, on the north side of the Pocomoke River, east side of Dividing Creek. Assigned Richard Chockley. Possessed by Richard Shockley by the name of SHOCKLEYS PURCHASE	Pocomoke 100
100a.	DAM QUARTER	23 May 1683 William Stevens in Annamessex. Neck of land assigned to Thomas Dixon. Possessed by same	Annamessex 100
100a.	ADDITION	16 May 1683 William Stevens on the north side of the Manokin River. Assigned to Owen Macraugh. Possessed by the widow Mary	Manokin 100
50a.	POWELLS ADDITION	2 Apr.1683 William Stevens on the north side of the Pocomoke River between Asquntica and Pomunge. Assigned Walter Powell. Possessed by William Powell	Pocomoke 100
200a.	COCKLAND	14 Feb.1682 Richard Jefferson at the head of Rokiawakin River. Possessed by the heir of Jefferson	Wicomico 100
300a.	LONG HILL	10 May 1683 William Stevens on the south side of the Nanticoke River, north side of Wetepkin Creek. Assigned James Dashiell. Possessed by his widow	Nanticoke 100
100a.	WINDSOR	13 June 1683 William Stevens on the south side of the Wicomico River. Possessed by George Goddard	Wicomico 100
50a.	WALES	22 May 1683 William Stevens on the east side Nanticoke River, north side of Rewastico Creek. Assigned to John Lyon who died in Dorset Co. The right is found to be possessed by William Marrut in Dorset Co.	Nanticoke 100
300a.	FORKED NECK	2 Oct.1683 William Stevens on the east side of the head of Nanticoke. Assigned to Francis Jenkins. Possessed by John Crouch	Nanticoke 100
300a.	HOPEWELL	15 Nov.1683 William Furnis on the south side Manokin River. Assigned James Berry. Possessed by James Berry	Manokin 100

ACRES	TRACT	SURVEY DATE-BY WHOM	LOCATION
150a.	BUCK LODGE	6 May 1683 William Stevens	Pocomoke 100

on the north side Pocomoke River, south side of Morumsco Creek. Assigned to Edward Doaks. Possessed by Edward Dikes

600a. NEW HOLLAND 13 May 1685 Cornelius Johnson　Wicomico 100
    6 miles up from the south east branch of the Wicomico River. Nicholas Tylor bought and removed to South Carolina and died. Noone possesses, vide John McCarty account

144a. HAPPY ENJOYMENT 29 Apr.1684 Alexander Thomas, Nanticoke 100
    in Nanticoke River, in Quantico Creek. Thomas in his life pretended to hold no such land

500a. FRIENDSHIP 1 May 1688 Martin Curtis　Baltimore 100
    on the seaboard side, south side of Indian alias Baltimore River. Possessed by William Godden

150a. COLCHESTER 27 Mar.1688 Peter Whaples　Mattapony 100
    on the seaboard side of the Pocomoke River on the west side Assawango Creek. Most part cut off by older survey called CHOICE. The heir removed

100a. WILLIAMS HOPE, resurveyed 11 May 1688　Pocomoke 100
    Henry Smith on the north side Pocomoke River

100a. TAUNTON 30 Mar.1688 Thomas Jones,　Mattapony 100
    on the south side Pocomoke River, 1 mile form Mattapony landing. Assigned Walter Reed. Possessed by Walter Reed

200a. LANES CAUTION 29 May 1689 Walter Lane　Annamessex 100
    between Pocomoke and Annamessex called APES HOLE near Watkins point. Possessed by Walter Lane

500a. LINANKES ON NECK 1 Dec.1688 James Weatherly Nanticoke 100
    on the south side near the Nanticoke River in Quiankeson Neck. Possessed by James Weatherly

430a. SOUTH PETHERTON 27 May 1688 Matthew Scarborough, Mattapany 100
    near seaboard side. Possessed by Walter Evans

250a. no name 14 Aug 1688 David Brown　Manokin 100
    on the north side of the Manokin River. Possessed by Alexander Brown the heir.

200a. BAG SHOTT BUTTON 8 Zec.1688 Henry Harmanson Nanticoke 100
    on the south side of the Nanticoke River 2 miles above Broad Creek. In the right of Henry Harman of Dorset County.

300a. KELLUMS CHOICE 29 May 1695 John Kellum　Pocomoke 100
    on the northwest side of the Pocomoke River in Ascomonoconson Neck. Possessed by the Indians.

300a. HOCKLEYS ADVENTURE 16 July 1696 Samuel Hopkins, Baltimore 100
    5 miles from the seaboard side, 2 miles from the south side of the Baltimore River, now SHOCKLEYS ADVENTURE, possessed by Nathaniel Hopkins

ACRES	TRACT	SURVEY DATE-by whom	LOCATION

550a. ALDERBURY, 14 May 1688 Thomas Cox   Wicomico 100
on the south side of the main
branch of the Rokiawakin River. Possessed
by Thomas Cox

100a. WOLFS DENN, 5 Dec 1698 John Trewett   Boggrtenorton 100
at head of Ascomonoconson Neck. Possessed
by John Trewett

100a. DESIRE   6 Dec.1698 Jeremiah Townsend   Bogerternorton 100
4 miles from the seaboard side. Possessed
by Jeremiah Townsend

120a. HENDERSONS CONVENIENCY, 1 Mar.1696   Pocomoke 100
John Henderson. on the south side of
the Pocomoke River. Possessed by same

1000a. KILLGLAN 22 Apr.1699 Ephraim Wilson   Money 100
on the south side of the Maonkin River.
Possessed by Ephraim Wilson

100a. LITTLEWORTH, 5 Dec.1701 Benjamin Summers   Annamessex 100
in Little Annamessex River. Possessed by same

165a. FLOWERFIELD 8 Oct.1701 Robert Givan   Nanticoke 100
on the south side Nanticoke River, on south
side Rewastico Branch. Possessed by same

100a. OWENS LOTT 18 Sep.1701 Moses Owen   Annamessex 100
near the Pocomoke Bay in Condonqua Neck.
Possessed by same

100a. ANGLESEY 8 Dec.1701 Thomas Davis   Annamessex 100
on the northeast side Pocomoke Bay. Possessed
by same.

300a. KAERSEYS INDUSTRY 17 Dec.1701 Robert Kaersey, Annamessex 100
on the east side Morumsco Creek. Possessed
by Peter Kaersey

60a. SHIELS MEADOW 4 Dec.1701 1 John Shields   Wicomico 100
a parcel of marsh on the north side of
the Wicomico River. Possessed by John Shields

50a. WOLF TRAP RIDGE 2 Dec. 1701 James Dashiell   Nanticoke 100
on the south side of the Nanticoke River, ½m.
from the westmost side of Wetepkowant Creek.
Possessed by James Dashiell

525a. LONG ACRE 9 Dec 1701 Cornelius Ward   Annamessex 100
between Gr.Annamessex and Little Annamessex
Possessed by Same

35a. BARNETT   20 Dec.1701 James English   Manokin 100
about 2 miles from the north side of the
Manokin River. Possessed by John Erwin

35a. BARNETT   20 Dec.1701 Richard Barns   Annamessex 100
on the neck between Annamessex and Pocomoke
Bay. Possessed by same

100a. COW QUARTER 10 Dec.1701 James English   Money 100
2 miles from the north side of the Manokin
River. Possessed by John Erwin

80a. CONVENIENCE 13 Dec.1701 Richard Waters   Manokin 100
on the north side Annamessex River. Poss. same.

ACRES	TRACT	SURVEY DATE-BY WHOM	LOCATION
500a.	PLAIN HARBOUR,	18 Dec.1701 Isaac Horsey, and Nathaniel Horsey, between the sound and Pocomoke Bay and Cedar Straights. Possessed 250a. Isaac Horsey, 250a. Nathaniel Horsey	Manokin 100
50a.	ST GERMAINS,	8 Oct. 1700 Peter Doughty on the north side of the Wicomico River. Possessed by Peter Doughty	Wicomico 100
200a.	BALLYHACK	8 Nov.1700 Robert Poalk at the mouth of the west side of a creek issuing out of Many Bay called Pigeonouse Ck. Possessed by Robert Pollock	Manokin 100
100a.	CLONMELL	20 Sep 1700 Ephraim Poalk between Manokin Branch and Pigeonhouse Little Creek. Possessed by same	Manokin 100
250a.	BARREN QUARTER	15 Sep 1700 Edward Wright on the north side of a creek issuing out of the south side of the Nanticoke River called Barren Creek. Possessed by same.	Nanticoke 100
250a.	ANNAMESSEX (Marsh)	31 Dec.1701 James Gray near the mouth of the south side of the Annamessex River. Possessed by same	Annamessex 100
1034a.	NEW HAVEN	10 Dec.1705 Thomas Everenton who assigned to William Whittington, on the north side of the Rokiawakin River, in a fork of same Meadow Branch, near landing where the Caldwells Cart	Wicomico 100
300a.	KILLGLASS	23 Sep.1700 Edward Green assigned on the seaboard side near a road leading to Senepuxon at the corner of a tract surveyed for John White dec'd called BUCKINGHAM	Bogertenortin 100
100a.	BEVANS CHANCE	28 Feb.1704 William Bevans on the north west side Nassango Creek, on the north side of Forrest Branch	Pocomoke 100
50a.	ADDITION	8 Apr.1703 Phillip Askew on the south side Wicomico River, south west side of Cowasick Creek.	Wicomico 100
200a.	FRIENDS GOODWILL	8 April 1703 John and Lewis Disharoon, on the south side of east branch of the Wicomico and Rokiawakin Rivers between the fork and Long Bridge	Wicomico 100
23a.	CHANCE	2 May 1705 Alexander Brown on the south side of the Manokin River.	Manokin 100
600a.	WHICKENOUGH	11 Dec.1701 George Parker on the east side Ascomononconson Neck near the head of Tims Branch	Bogertenortin 100
75a.	PURGATORY	28 Oct.1701 Thomas ROe part of an Inland called Devills.	Manokin 100
200a.	LACHISH (alias Hunting Quarter,)	15 Sep.1705, William Taylard on AnnArundel Co. assigned to John Stockley of Som.Co. On seaboard side at Cedar Neck Creek.	Bog.100?

ACRES	TRACT	SURVEY DATE-BY WHOM	LOCATION	
250a.	COMMONS	12 Aug.1704 James Givan on the south side Rewastico Branch between Rewastico and Quantico being the 2nd. ground of a parcel of land called KINGSTON	Wicomico	100
100a.	CHANCE	25 May 1705 Joseph Gray on the west side Pocomoke River, west side Dividing Creek, on edge of a cypress swamp near the corner of Court House land	Pocomoke	100
150a.	SLAUGHTER RIDGE,	4 May 1702 Thomas Powell 5 miles from the seaboard side, at a ridge near St.Martins River called Church Branch	Bog.	100
100a.	PARKERS DENYALL	15 Aug.1705 William Taylard, of AnnArundel Co. assigned Hugh Tingle. on the seaboard side, pt of Rumbling Marsh, at a cove issuing out of Assawoman Bay, west side of a sandy ridge that runs thru Rummey Marsh	Baltimore	100
500a.	MORRICES PURCHASE	1 Aug 1705 Wm. Taylard of AnnArundel Co. assigned to Samuel Morris on the seaboard side, on west side of Patys Creek out of the Baltimore River	Baltimore	100
200a.	RYLEYS PORTION,	22 Sep.1699 James Trewett on the east most side of Ascomonaconson Neck on the north side of a branch of the Pocomoke River, dividing it from a tract formerly surveyed for John Truett	Mattapony	100
80a.	SAMPIRE	15 May 1704 James Curtis on the south side near the mouth of the Manokin River, northward of Teagues Creek issuring out of the Manokin River at a corner of Cow Quarter	Manokin	100
100a.	COME BY CHANCE	4 Apr.1706 Samuel Davis on the west side of a branch of Dividing Creek near Perryhawkin	Pocomoke	100
125a.	LONG ACRE	22 July 1706,John Franklin 4 miles from the seaboard side near Coys Folly on the south side Millytone Swamp	Bog.	100?
50a.	FATHERS CARE	1 Mar 1705 John Conner on the north side of and near Pocomoke Bay	Annamessex	100
260a.	PASTURAGE	20 Oct.1705 James MacMorris & William Wainright, on the south side of the Wicomico River at a Great Gutt	Wicomico	100
100a.	BASHAN	26 Nov.1705 Andrew Bashan on the west side Nassango Creek, issuing out of the Pocomoke River.	Pocomoke	100
274a.	LONG DELAY	26 Mar.1705 Ephraim Polk in Dame Quarter on west side Balls Creek.	Manokin	100
300a.	WHITTINGTONS CHANCE,	26 June 1706 Wm.Whittington, on the north side of the Rokiawakin River at 1st bounder of a tract surveyed for Thomas Holbrook	Wicomico	100

ACRES	TRACT	SURVEY DATE-BY WHOM	LOCATION
200a.	JAMES MEADOW	1 June 1705 James Polk in Dames Quarter, on northeast side of Williams Creek. Borders on FORLORN HOPE	Manokin 100
220a.	EDWARDS LOTT	29 Mar 1705 Ann Roberts on bayside, north side of Williams Creek and Dames Quarter Bay, at corner of land surveyed for Francis Roberts	Manokin 100
40a.	MARYS ADVENTURE	29 Sep 1705 Mary Magraugh in Manokin at a corner of IMPROVEMENT	Wicomico 100
75a.	HOPEWELL	15 May 1705 William Faucett on the south side of the Manokin River	Manokin 100
70a.	ADVENTURE	7 May 1706 Richard Crockett on the south side of Shiels Creek. Bounds LITTLE MONMOUTH	Wicomico 100
200a.	SYLAS'S PURCHASE	10 Apr.1706 Sylus Chapman on the east side of the Pocomoke River	Pocomoke 100
27a.	MARVELLS CHANCE	2 Apr.1705 John Marvell byside in Dame Quarter, bounds land surveyed for Francis Roberts	Manokin 100
40a.	UNEXPECTED	27 Sep 1705 Arthur Denwood 1 mile from the Manokin River	Wicomico 100
600a.	LARGEY	2 Oct.1706 James Givan on the south side of the Nanticoke River at the head of Beaver Dam Creek	Nanticoke 100
22a.	SPITTLE	4 Nov.1706 Abraham Heath on the east side of the Manokin River, 1 mile from the Wading Place	Manokin 100
100a.	WILSONS DISCOVERY	31 Mar 1707 Ephraim Wilson, near the south side of the mouth os the Manokin River, near Dames Quarter	Manokin 100
200a.	AYDELOTTS IGNORANCE	2 Aug.1707 Benjamin Aydelotte, On Indian River (alias Baltimore) issuing out of Rehobeth Bay, on west side of Payless Creek. Bounds tract of Samuel Morris called CUMBERLAND	Bogertenortin 100
100a.	BATCHELLORS CHOICE	1 Aug 1704 John Wilson on the south east side of the Nanticoke River halfway between Rewastico and Barren Creeks.	Nanticoke 100
140a.	CHARLIES ADVENTURE	28 Mar 1705 Charles Williams, on the south side of the Wicomico River at Dames Quarter, at a corner of land surveyed for Francis Roberts	Manokin 100
500a.	ASSATEAGUE	8 Oct. 1706 Capt.John Franklin on seaside, at a gut issuing out of Assateague Sound near William Faucetts hummocks	Bogternortin 100
250a.	FREEMANS LOTT	8 Aug.1706 John Freeman 2 miles from the St.Martins River on the seaboard side and north side Murpheys Branch. Bounds tract of Clement Gyles	Bogtenortin 100

ACRES	TRACT	SURVEY DATE-BY WHOM	LOCATION

125a. PROVIDENCE 2 Aug.1706 William Massey   Mattapony 100
   on seaboard side, west most side of Senepuxon

50a. SMALL LOTT, 15 Nov.1705 Honor Small   Mattapony 100?
   on the south most side of the Pocomoke River

600a. EXCHANGE 20 July 1696 John Franklin   Mattapony 100
   on the seaboard side, west side of a branch of
   the Assateague River

450a. BALD BEACH 8 Oct.1706 Richard Holland, William
   Walton, William Turville   Baltimore 100

280a. GREENLAND 2 Jun1707 Charles Nicholson   Pocomoke 100
   on the east side Nassango Creek at Charles Branch

200a. CORK 2 Apr.1707 Pierce Bray   Pocomoke 100
   on the west side of the Pocomoke River

300a. STONIDGE 18 Nov.1704 Levin Denwood   Money 100
   in Money Creek in woods.

310a. SNEADS PURCHACE 5 Nov.1709 Wm.Whittington   Baltimore 100
   assigned Robert Snead, in Baltimore River
   issuing out of Rehobeth bay on seaside

95a. HOGYARD 16 May 1704 Thomas Beauchamp   Pocomoke 100
   4 miles from the north side of the Pocomoke
   River, south side of Mourmsco Dam

500a. PINEY POINT 1 Dec.1702 John Norton assinged   Baltimore 100
   to John Parker, on the seaboard side, south
   side of the Baltimore River, west side of
   Pateys Creek

150a. ROBINSONS PURCHASE 6 Oct.1706 Wm.Robinson   Baltimore 100
   on seaboard side, north side Assawoman Ck.
   at corner of tract surveyed for Wm.Ricketts

70a. JOSEPHS LOTT 19 Apr.1706 Benjamin Wales   Wicomico 100
   in Wicomico River, 2 miles from the west side
   on a branch of Jones Creek at corner of tract
   DORCESTER

200a. CUMBERLAND 15 Sep.1705 Wm.Taylard of AnnArundel   Balt.100
   County assigned to Samuel Morris. on the seaboard
   side at a creek issuing out of the Baltimore River

100a. FANCY 2 Oct.1707 Benjamin Aydelotte   Baltimore 100
   at seaboard side and south side of the Indian
   River, 2 miles from Duck Creek

150a. FORREST 4 Oct.1707 Benjamin Aydelotte   Baltmore 100
   at seaboard side of the south side of Indian
   River, east side of a branch of Duck Creek.

150a. DUCKHEAD 2 Oct.1707 Benjamin Aydelotte   Baltimore 100
   at seaboard side, south side Indian River, at
   the mouth of Duck Creek.

200a. GOULDING MINE, 28 Sep.1706 John Shockley   Pocomoke 100
   on north sideof a branch of Dividing Creek,
   near land of Francis Jenkins

200a. WHAT YOU WILL, 10 Nov.1707 Phillip Hinning?   Nanticoke 100
   on the east side of the Nanticoke River.

| ACRES | TRACT | SURVEY DATE-BY WHOM | LOCATION |

300a. GLASCOE 30 May 1706 Thomas Gordon Nanticoke 100
 on the south side of the Nanticoke River
 the south side of Broad Creek

175a. THE CELLAR 4 Mar 1708/9 Richard Woodcraft Bogeternortin 100
 on the seaboard side, southmost side of a gutt
 issuing out of Assateague Bay. Against THE COLLAR

1300a. SHIELLS FOLLY 20 Sep 1700 Thomas and James Wicomico 100
 Dashiell. North side of the Wicomico River.

250a. WINTER RANGE 10 Oct.1706 Laurance Ryley Bogetenortin 100
 on the seaboard side being out of Assateague

150a. LOCUST RIDGE 13 Mar.1709 John Dennis Pocomoke 100
 on the southeast side of the Pocomoke River.
 Bounds TRAILS CHANCE of Wm. Traile

150a. RICH SWAMP 26 Mar.1711 Joseph Maclester Wicomico 100
 and Elizabeth his wife. At Wettipquin

170a. PENTLAND HILLS 25 Mar.1709 Robert Perry Baltimore 100?
 at the seaboard side, bounds tract of Richard
 Woodcraft

190a. BALLY BUGIN 1 May 1688 John Caldwell Nanticoke 100
 patented 10 Aug.1713 on north side at head
 of the Rokiawakin River.

85a. COME BY CHANCE 31 July 1713 John Disheroon Wicomico 100
 patented 10 Dec.1713 on south side of the
 Wicomico River, 4 miles from John Roach's fence

100a. REEDS FOLLY 14 Sep.1713 John Reed Nanticoke 100
 in Davis Neck

548a. LONG ACRE 31 July 1713 John Roach Jr. Annamessex 100
 patented 10 Dec.1713 on the south side
 of the Pocomoke River.

270a. FRIENDS CONTENT, resurveyed 22 Sep.1701 Money 100?
 patented 2 Sep.1713 John White and Richard
 Wallace being escheated to his lordship,
 formerly called FRIENDS CHOICE and belonging
 to Thomas Jarrott dec'd, near Money Bay and
 west side of Williams Creek.

68a. WILSONS FINDING 31 July 1713 Alexander Carlisle, Manokin 100
 patented 1 Dec.1713 and assigned Robert Wilson
 at Pocosions Place, 4 miles from the head of
 the Manokin River.

100a. ADDITION 9 Sep.1713 Alexander Carlisle Wicomico 100
 on the north side of a branch of Quantico
 patented 10 Dec.1713

none FERNHILL Formerly surveyed 10 Nov.1685 Mattapony 100?
 for Thomas Purnell by whom no patent was
 issued until Jan 1713. Patent issued to Thomas
 Purnell and his son and devisee. see liber
 DSnoB f.138 pat. 21 Jan 1713

30a. FRIENDS ADVICE 12 Sep 1713 Alexander Carlisle, Wicomico 100
 patented 10 Dec.1713 on the north side of Little
 Creek out of the south side of Broad Creek

| ACRES | TRACT | SURVEY DATE-BY WHOM | LOCATION |

50a. HENRYS ADDITION 31 July 1713 John Henry   Pocomoke 100
on the north side of the Pocomoke River.
Patented 10 Dec.1713

1000a. ASKEKSKY 18 Jan 1711 Col.Wm.Whittington   Baltimore 100
assigned to Woacomocomis the Indian Queen.
Robins the interpreter and ambassador, and
Robins his son. On the south side of Indian
River at Baltimore River. Patented by the
Indians 2 July 1174

217a. FARLOW WORTH (no date)Richard Wooder   unknown
vide the record of 1684 Liber DSnoB-f381

200a. HOPEWELL 30 Sep 1700 Edward Green   Wic.100?
on seaboard side on Deep Branch of Broad Ck.
Bounds tract of Robert Cade. Assigned by
Francis Jenkins adm. of said Green. Richard
Woodcraft to whom it was patented 2 July 1714

400a. LONG ISLAND 10 Dec.1713. Pat. issued in common   Bog.100?
to Samuel Hopkins,John Pope on the seaboard
side originally laid out for John Pope
dec'd father to said John, vide land
record of 1687

180a. HOGS NORTEN 25 Mar.1703 John Norton   Balt.100?
whose father William Norton formerly took
up lands as adm. to father. On the seaboard
side on north side of St.Martins River.
Patented 2 Sep 1713

206a. SASSAFRAS NECK 2 Oct.1706 Phillip Covington   Wicomico 100
on the north side of the Maney River, at mouth
of King's Gutt. Patented 2 Sep 1714

200a. ADKINS FANCY 28 May 1707 WIlliam Coleburn   Annamessex 100
in Annamesses and on south side of Coleburns
Creek. Pat. 2 Sep 1714

125a. TOWERS PASTURE 25 Mar 1709 Margaret Towers   Balt.100?
on seaside, on southn side of a gut running along
the beach. Patented 2 Sep 1714

110a. SAND BEACH 1 Mar.1713 Benjamin Aydelotte   Baltimore 100?
on the seaboard side on the north side of a
gutt leading out of Assateague Sound running
to the beach. Pat. 2 Sep 1714

200a. SPENCES LOTT 20 Oct.1708 Adam Spence,   Bogetenortin 100
on seaside, near the mouth of a gut issuing
out of Assateague Sound, on north side of Horse
Island Pat. 16 Dec.1714

200a. ADAMS FALL 15 Dec.1710 Wm. Whittington   Bog.100
assigned Thomas Purnell, on seaboard side.
Bounds land on the beach surveyed for John
Franklin. Patented 15 Dec.1714

200a. HUDSONS PURCHASE 15 Sep.1710 Col.Wm.Whittington Bog.100
on seaboard side. at a gut out of Assateague
Sound. Surveyed for Richard Woodcroft. This is
assigned by Whittington to Henry Hudson, to
whom the patented is issued 26 Nov.1714

| ACRES | TRACT | SURVEY DATE-BY WHOM | LOCATION |

200a. TAYLORS CHOICE, originally laid out　　　Wicomico 100
　　　　for James Bound who assigned to
　　　　John Taylor to whom the patent was issued,
　　　　vide, original certificate in records of
　　　　1686 Lib DS noB F142

160a. BEAR QUARTER 24 Sep.1713 George Howard　　Baltimore 100
　　　　2 miles from the south side of the Baltimore
　　　　River near a beaver Dam. Pat. 2 Oct.1714

190a. MIDDLEMORE, 10 Mar.1713 Wm.Whittington　　Pocomoke 100
　　　　2 miles from the southeast side of the Pocomoke
　　　　River, south side of Colemans Branch. Patented
　　　　21 Oct.1714

134a. PURCHASE 15 Oct.1706 John Caldwell　　Wicomico 100
　　　　on north side of the main branch of the
　　　　Rokiawakin River, bounds tract MAIDENHEAD
　　　　Patented 20 April 1715

158a. HOBBS CHOICE 10 Dec.1713 William Waples　　Baltimore 100
　　　　in the woods back from the Indian River.
　　　　Patented 10 Dec.1714

340a. CHANCE 2 Dec.1714 William Burton　　Baltimore 100
　　　　on the east side of Indian River, a little
　　　　below Cove bridge. Patented 10 Dec.1714

66a. DAVIDS LOTT, 13 Aug.1714 David Hazzard　　Baltimore 100
　　　　on the seaboard side. Pat. 10 Dec.1714

75a. DANIELLS LUCK 28 Dec.1713 Daniel Wharton　　Baltimore 100
　　　　on the south side of Indian River, west side of
　　　　Viners Branch. Patented 10 Dec.1715

200a. RICH RIDGE 2 Oct.1713 Robert Givan　　Wicomico 100
　　　　assigned to Robert Gilley. Pat. 10 Dec.1715

64a. GOOD LUCK 3 Nov. 1714 Lazarus Kenny　　Baltimore 100
　　　　on the south side of Indian River, west side
　　　　of Beaver Dam Branch. Assigned by Lazarus
　　　　Kenny to Stephen Kenny. Pat. 20 April 1715

100a. GOOD HOPE 20 Oct. 1713 Morris Morris　　Wicomico 100
　　　　on the south side of Broad Creek. Patented
　　　　20 April 1715

100a. STUGGS PURCHASE 15 Oct.1706 Thomas Stuggs　　Baltimore 100?
　　　　patented 10 Dec.1714

100a. COVINGTONS ADVENTURE 10 Nov.1707 Phillip　　Money 100
　　　　Covington, on the east side of Money Creek.
　　　　Patented 10 Dec.1714

100a. QUIET ENTRANCE 9 Sep.1713 Andrew Caldwell　　Wicomico 100
　　　　on the north side of the Wicomico River.
　　　　Bounds Thomas Covington. Pat. 10 Dec.1714

195a. DULSERFE 15 Apr.1714 Alexander Adams　　Nanticoke 100
　　　　on the south side of the Nanticoke River. North
　　　　west side of Deep Creek. Patented 20 Apr.1715

78a. TURTLE SWAMP 13 Aug.1714 Daniel Wharton　　Balt.100?
　　　　near the head of Herring Br. Pat.10 Dec.1713

| ACRES | TRACT | SURVEY DATE-BY WHOM | LOCATION |

100a. LON'S PURCHASE 3 Nov.1714 William Lon   Baltimore 100
      on the west side of Beaver Dam Branch out
      of Indian River above CowBridge Pat.20 Apr.1715

100a. DANIELS FIRST CHOICE 3 Dec 1713 (no name)   Balt.100?
      on the south side of Patesis Creek.
      Pat. 10 Dec.1714

100a.(no name) 3 Nov.1714 Lazarus Kenny   Baltimore 100
      on the north side of Beaver Dam Branch, out of
      Indian River. Pat. 10 Dec.1714

150a. WOODMANS FOLLY 1 Mar.1713 1 Mar.1713   Baltimore 100
      Col.William Whittington. On seaside at head
      of Cedar Neck Creek issuing out of Rehobeth Bay
      Patented 10 Dec.1714

160a. FOLLY 2 Dec 1714 William Burton   Baltimore 100
      on the south side of Indian River. South side
      of Shiles Branch

56a. PURCHASE   13 Aug 1714 Mark Cannady   Baltimore 100
      on the seaboard side by Beaver Dam Branch

200a. LUCK   2 Feb.1714 William Pepper   Baltimore 100
      on the south side of Indian River, north
      side of Shiles Branch. Pat.10 Apr.1715

265a. TROUBLE   26 Nov.1714 William Burton   Baltimore 100
      on the south side of the Baltimore River
      west side of Indian Town Branch near end
      of Indians land Pat. 10 Dec.1714

40a. GOOD LUCK 14 May 1714 John Pearson   Wicomico 100
      on the east side of the main branch of
      Wicomico Creek. Pat. 10 Dec.1715

760a. CEDAR NECK 18 Nov.1713 Col.Wm.Whittington   Baltimore 100
      formerly in 2 tracts, Surveyed for Col.
      Diggs and FENWICKS CHOICE surveyed for Thomas
      Fenwick on the seaboard side, south side of
      Rehobeth Bay Patented 10 Dec.1714

1300a.ASSATEAGUE BEACH 29 Feb.1711 Wm. Whittington, Baltimore 100
      near Assateague Bay. Pat. 10 April 1716

150a. GOOD HOPE 23 Dec.1715 Simon Kolick   Baltimore 100
      bounds tract of Edm.d Butler. Patented 10 Sep.1716

200a. KENNYS LOTT 23 Dec.1715 Lazarus Kenny   Baltimore 100
      near Tussuckey Branch of Baltimore River
      Patented 10 Sep.1716

100a. LITTLE NECK 11 Oct.1715 Mark Webb   Bogetemortin 100
      on the south west side of St.Martins River
      Patented 10 Sep 1716

100a. HOGRIDGE 24 Dec.1715 William Burton   Baltimore 100
      on the south side of Indian Branch of the
      Baltimore River, opposite Indian Town.
      Pat. 10 Sep 1716

150a. JOHNSONS LOTT 12 Oct.1715 Benjamin Johnson Baltimore 100
      at Herring Creek. Pat. 10 Sep.1716

ACRES	TRACT	SURVEY DATE-BY WHOM	LOCATION

15a.. CHANCE 20 June 17 15 Charles Wharton Pocomoke 100
on the west side of William Nobles pasture
Pat. 10 Sep 1716

75a. BARRONFIELD 10 Oct.1713 Alexander Adams Wicomico 100
pat. 20 Sep 1716

117a. COX'S FOLLY 20 Dec.1715 Thomas Cox Wic.100?
on the south side of the main branch of
Broad Creek. Pat. 10 Sep 1715

563a. PLUMTON SALTASH 15 Dec.1715 Thomas Cox Sr. Wicomico 100
on the south side of the main branch of the
Rokiawakin River. Pat. 10 Sep 1716

100a. NEW DUBLIN 29 Dec.1715 Matthew Hosea Nanticoke 100
on Cypress Branch in Great Neck. Pat.10 Sep 1716

100a. STRAIGHTS MOUTH 28 Sep 1713 Joseph Derrickson, Balt. 100
bounds Mary Derexson Jr's land. Pat.10 Sep.1716

70a. COVINGTONS FOLLY 6 May 1706 Samuel Covington Wicomico 100
on the west side of a path to Nehemiah
Covington's land and William Harris's. Pat.
10 Sep 1716

100a. FREEMANS CHANCE 28 Sep.1713 William Freeman, Baltimore 100
between the head of Herring Branch and Vine's
Branch pat. 10 Sep 1716

560a. COMELY CHANCE 22 Mar.1707 Adam Heath Wicomico 100
near Cottinghams Creek. Pat. 10 Sep.1716

150a. FOLLY 10 Sep 1713 William Pepper Baltimore 100
pat. 10 Sep 1716

150a. EXCHANGE 28 Sep.1713 Mary Derickson Baltimore 100
in a fork of Daneek Harbour. Pat.10 Sep.1716

150a. WHARTONS ADVENTURE 28 Sep 1713 John Wharton Baltimore 100
on the south side of Pattis's Creek. Pat.
10 Sep 1716

320a. GOOD LUCK 18 Oct.1715 Archibald Smith Manokin 100
assigned to Robert King. South end of a small
island on north side of the Manokin River.
patented 10 Sep.1716

100a. GIDEONS LUCK 25 Aug.1715 John Caldwell Pocomoke 100
assigned to Solomon Tillman. On the south side
of Equintinah Branch. Pat. 10 Sep 1716

50a. GIDEONS LUCK 20 Aug.1715 John Caldwell Pocomoke 100
assigned to Gideon Tillman, on north side
Noble Branch. Pat. 10 Sep 1716

150a. CHANCE 1 May 1707 John Evans Wicomico 100
at a tract called LITTLE MONMOUTH. Patented
10 Sep.1716

275a. MOIETY OF ROYAL OAKE, Charles Ratcliffe Bogeternortin 100
on a south branch of Turvils Creek. Pat.
28 May 1717

50a. TAURTUM 14 Apr.1714 Adam Heath Pocomoke 100
assigned to Edward Martin, on Pocomoke River
against a causway. Pat. 20 Apr.1717

ACRES	TRACT	SURVEY DATE-BY WHOM	LOCATION	

386a. COMELY CHANCE, 22 Feb.1716 Robert Caldwell, Baltimore 100?
on the seaboard side, near the mouth
of a creek out of the north side of Rehobeth
Bay. Patented 20 Apr.1717

63a. GOOD LUCK, 28 Aug.1706, John Caldwell   Nanticoke 100
assigned to James Caldwell. on the North
side of Roastice Clsoe. Pat.25 Apr.1713

50a. JOHNS LOTT, 20 June 1715 John Caldwell   Baltimore 100
who has not assigned to John Bradford. On the
east side of St.Martins Desart. Pat.25 Apr.1717

50a. RICH RIDGE, 10 May 1715 John Caldwell   Baltimore 100
assigned to Edward Clark. Bounds Bear Harbour
Patented 25 Apr.1717

100a. LAWES SECOND CHOICE, 25 Feb.1714 William Lawes, Pocomoke 100
on the west most side of Nassiango Creek.
Patented 25 Arpil 1717

150a. FRIGS ADVENTURE, 20 Dec.1715 Henry Friggs Baltimore 100?
on the north side of The main branch of Broad
Creek. Patented 10 Sep.1716

229a. THRUMCAPPS FIELD, resurveyed by John Mills, Pocomoke 100
formerly 250a. Pat. 23 Apr.1717

248a. MATTAPONY MARSH, resurveyed 8 Oct.1714 John Purnell, Matt.100
formerly two tracts viz. Mattapony Marsh and
Georges Marsh, on Mattapony Creek. Patented
23 Apr.1717

100a. CLARKS LOTT, 20 June 1715 John Caldwell   Baltimore 100
assigned to Edward Clark. North west side of
Great Bever Dam. Patented 25 Apr.1717

100a. PHILLIPS PRIVILEDGE, 23 Sep.1714 Phillip Quinton, Pocomoke 100
on the north side of Turkey Cock Trap Branch
Patented 25 Apr. 1717

100a. SAFETY 10 Sep.1713 William Pepper   Baltimore 100
on the north side of Pattys Creek. Pat.25 Apr.1717

50a. COW MARSH 2 Oct.1713 Somerset Dickenson   Baltimore 100
patented 25 Apr.1717

126a. PINEY ISLAND 25 Sep.1714 John Purnell   Mattapony 100
on south east of a tract surveyed for Daniel
Selby called BANTRY. Pat.25 April 1717

100a. FOLLY 20 Nov.1176 John Caldwell   Baltimore 100
assigned to Jonathan Clark. On the west side
of the head of St. Martins River. Pat.25 Apr.1717

150a. GOOD HOPES 23 Dec.1715 Symon Kollock   Baltimore 100
on the south side from the head of the Indian
River. Bounds tract surveyed for William Pepper
where Edmond Butler lives

100a. HOPINGTONS ADVENTURE, 13 May 1715 John   Natricoke 100
Hopington. On the northwest fork of the
Nanticoke River. Bounds MARSHY HOPE

610a. CEDAR GROVE, resurveyed for Phillip Selby Mattapony 100
on seaboard side. Bounds land of Daniel Selby

| ACRES | TRACT | SURVEY DATE-BY WHOM | LOCATION |

100a. PEPPERS DELIGHT, 24 Dec.1714 Wm.Pepper   Baltimore 100
      on the seaboard side from the head of the
      Indian River near a great savanah

100a CHANCE   10 Oct.1715 Thomas Quillan   Baltimore 100
      on the seaboard side, north east of the river
      opposity to Rice Clarks house

50a. WILSONS FOLLY, 25 Apr.1715 William Wilson   Manokin 100

150a. YOUNGS PURCHASE 25 May 1717 William Young   Nanticoke 100
      On the east side of the Nanticoke River, north
      side of Barren Creek. East corner of Richard
      Huffingtons cornfield. Possessed by Edward
      Killam

200a. CARLAVEROCK 13 Jan 1720 Robert Martin   Bogeternortin 100
      On the north side of the Pocomoke River in
      Askomaconson Indian Town opposite to Snow Hill
      and 10 perches from the west side of Snow Hill
      landing

248a. LONG MEADOW 25 May 1709 John Tunstall   Manokin 100
      near the mouth os the north west fork of Fishing
      Creek.

750a. AQUANGO 25 Apr.1717 William Whittington   Pocomoke 100
      on the west side of the Pocomoke River near the
      head. south most end of Aquango Marsh

234a. EASTWOOD 2 Oct.1710 Alexander Adams   Wicomico 100?

55a. JOHNS FOLLY, 19 July 1713 James Bonjer   Pocomoke 100?
      On the north side of Friggs Branch at the
      mouth of Mirey Branch

116a. SATISFACTION, 25 Apr.1714 George Dashiell   Wicomico 100
      on the west most bounder of a tract belonging
      to Phillip Covington

60a. TOWNSENDS CHOICE 21 Sep.1721 Elizabeth Townsend, Pocomoke 100

100a. PATRICKS LOTT 14 Oct.1721 John Patrick   Bogerternorten 100
      On the seaboard side, on east most side of
      tract PINDALLS NEGLECT

50a. FORCE PUTT 15 Aur 1718 Alexander Carlisle   Wicomico 100
      near Robert Crouchs and south east side of the
      Wicomico River, south side of the main branch
      of MyLords Creek.

50a. POOR CHOICE 10 June 1718 James King   Wicomico 100
      on the east side of the road to Broad Creek
      from the head of the Wicomico River

50a. PASTURAGE 8 Sep.1719 John Lomay   Nanticoke 100
      on the south most side of the Nanticoke River,
      1 mile above Barren Creek mouth against the
      lower end of Vienna

40a. HOGS NECK 22 Sep.1721 Elizabeth Townsend   Pocomoke 100
      on the south side of Brushey Savanah

ACRES	TRACT	SURVEY DATE-BY WHOM	LOCATION
133a.	RACHELLS LOTT,	13 Oct.1721 Rachel Powell on the seaboard side, north east of tract Covingin	Pocomoke 100?
100a.	GEORGES PURCHASE,	30 Jan 1721 George Benston,	Pocomoke 100?
40a.	HICCORY LEVELL,	5 Sep.1718 William Twiford	Nanticoke 100
500a.	DULL FOLLY	19 Aug.1721 John Murray near a path leading to Snow Hill Landing	Bogerternorten 100
77a.	DERRY	2 Feb.1721 John Gray	Manokin 100
118a.	PATRICKS FOLLY	2 Feb.1721 John Gray on the east side of a small road from Perrahawkin to Wicomico	Manokin 100
100a.	MULLINS FIELD	24 May 1721 John Roach on the south side of the Wicomico River.	Wicomico 100
100a.	CORDRYS BEGINNING	4 June 1721 John Cordray bounds other tract of John Cordrey's	Wicomico 100
560a.	COME BY CHANCE	2 Apr.1721 Adam Hatch on the north side of the Wicomico River, south side of the main branch of Cottingham Creek	Wicomico 100
50a.	MEADOW	3 June 1721 Richard Wallace bounds a tract of said Wallace called FRIENDS ACCEPTANCE	Nanticoke 100?
200a.	FELLOWSHIP	16 Sep.1720 Robert and Samuel Owen, in a fork of the Nanticoke River, at the lower end of FLINDS NECK	Nanticoke 100
110a.	GRAYS ADVENTURE,	13 June 1721 William Gray on the south side of the road leading from Manokin Bridge thru the Pocasans to the court House	Manokin 100
200a.	OAK GROVE	8 June 1721 Daniel McLester	Nanticoke 100
50a.	CAMP NECK	9 July 1720 James Boucher in a fork of the main branch of Broad Creek	Nanticoke 100
160a.	COW QUARTER	6 June 1721 Thomas Maddux	Annamessex 100
250a.	WHAT YOU WILL,	4 Oct.1688 William Donahoe	Pocomoke 100
20a.	UNITY	22 July 1720 John Fleming	Pocomoke 100
200a.	CASTLE HILL	12 Sep.1720 James Deals	unknown
50a.	FATMANS FOLLY	9 Nov.1718 John Reed on the south most side of the Nanticoke River, south side of the main branch of Broad Creek, north branch of little creek dividing it from tract DAYS NECK	Nanticoke 100
100a.	BRIDGETS LOTT,	9 Dec.1719 Bridget Kirk on the west side of Paocomoke Bay near land belonging to John Gunby	Pocomoke 100
100a.	WHARTONS FOLLY	1 Dec.1719 Charles Wharton on the north side of the Pocomoke River, north west of Stevens Branch	Pocomoke 100
100a.	LODSGATE HILL	17 Nov.1719 Jos. Lingley on the south side of Broad Creek at Tarkill Branch	Baltimore 100?

| ACRES | TRACT | SURVEY DATE-BY WHOM | LOCATION |

100a. BELLS PURCHASE 30 Sep.1719 Anthony Bell   Annamessex 100
 on the seaboard side between Pocomoke Bay and
 the Annamessex River.

50a. COBBS PURCHASE 30 Oct.1719 John Cobb   Baltimore 100
 on the seaboard side, east side Deep Branch

50a. SWINE HARBOUR 23 July 1720 Teague Donohoe   Pocomoke 100
 on the north side of the Pocomoke River, North
 side of Dividing Creek and lower Bever Dam.Creek

50a. WINTER QUARTER 20 Apr.1720 George Benston   Pocomoke 100
 in Jenkins Neck, north side of the main branch
 of Dividing Creek issuing out of the Pocomoke River

50a. CHADWICKS ADVENTURE 15 July 1720 James Chadwick, Wicomico 100
 on the south side of the Wicomico River

138a. TILLMANS CARE 11 Aug.1720 Gideon Tillman   Pocomoke 100
 on the north side of the Pocomoke River, west side
 of a tract of Lazarus Maddux called NEWTON

70a. MARLOS PRIVILEDGE 25 Mar.1720 William Marlo   Pocomoke 100
 on the south side of the Pocomoke River, north
 side of Pitts Creek, near land of Charles
 Ramsey, south side of Dums swamp

500a. TIMPLE HALL 27 May 1720 Robert Wood   Baltimore 100
 on the seaboard side, south side St.Martins River,
 east side of Bruch Branch

100a. DORMENTS CHANCE 5 Sep.1720 Matthew Dorment   Wicomico 100
 on the south side of the Wicomico River, south
 side of Grodon Branch issuing out of
 the eastern fork of the Wicomico River

100a. KELLEN 28 May 1720 John Gilliland   Baltimore 100
 on the seaboard side between tract of William
 Collins and tract of Robert Wood

30a. HOOP RIDGE 25 Mar.1720 William Mearle   Pocomoke 100
 on the south side of the Pocomoke River, north
 side of Piles Creek, north side of tract LITTLE
 TOWN, north line of LLOYDS GROVE, belongs to
 Charles Ramsey

80a. HOG HARBOUR 22 July 1720 John Fleming   Pocomoke 100
 on the north side of the Pocomoke River, east
 side of Dividing Creek

100a. MEADOW 15 Feb.1720 John Gunby   Pocomoke 100
 on the north side of Pocomoke Bay in Kirks Neck
 at the mouth of Plivers Creek

10a. PINEY ISLAND 28 Nov.1717 Robert King   Manokin 100
 on the north side of Manokin River

100a. CHAPMANS CHOICE 18 Aug.1721 Edward Chapman   Pocomoke 100?
 on west side of tr. CHAPMANS ADVENTURE belonging
 to Silas Chapman

100a. HOGG PALACE 27 July 1715, Thomas Jones   Nanticoke 100
 on east side of Broad Creek of Nanticoke

| ACRES | TRACT | SURVEY DATE-BY WHOM | LOCATION |

150a. CHANCE 26 Jan 1715 Thomas Jones   Nanticoke 100
      on the north side of Deep Creek

100a. PAINTERS DEN 12 May 1707 Archibald Smith   Manokin 100

136a. THE THREE BROTHERS 15 Mar.1718 Capt.John Rider, Wicomico 100
      on east side of Cypress Swamp, 1 mile from the
      north side of Barren Creek.

200a. HILLS VENTURE 10 Sep.1721 David Hazard   Baltimore 100
      on the south side of Indian River, seaboard side

220a. HOPE STILL, 2 Dec.1722 Mary Hampton and   Annamessex 100
      patented to Southy Whittington on Little
      Annamessex River

2a.   SNOW HILL LANDING 21 June 1722 John Caldwell   Mattapony 100
      Patented to Southy Whittington on north
      side of the Pocomoke River

350a. INCREASE 3 Sep.1723 Robert Weir   Annamessex 100
      on the north side of the Pocomoke River

50a. WHAT YOU PLEASE 9 Sep.1788 Wm.Calloway   Nanticoke 100
      on the south east side of the Nanticoke River

100a. ROUND POOR 9 Sep.1718 John Huffington   Nanticoke 100
      on the south east side of the Nanticoke River

50a. PURCHASE 12 June 1720 James Parmour   Nanticoke 100
      on the south east side Nantiicoke River

50a. GRAVELLY HILL 10 Dec 1721 John Cottman   Wicomico 100
      on the north side of Wicomico Bay

20a. CHANCE   25 Nov.1721 John Reid   Nanticoke 100
      on the south side of the Nanticoke River

200a. STRIFE   9 Aug.1718 Abraham Ingram   Nanticoke 100
      on the south side of the main branch of the
      Nanticoke River

100a. GOSHEN   20 Oct.1721 Samuel and Robert Owens, Nanticoke 100
      on the east side of main branch of Nanticoke River

50a. BETTY MARGERY 20 Dec.1717 Robert Hasting   Wicomico 100
      on the southmost branch of Little Creek

50a. WILLETTS DISCOVERY 3 Nov.1721 Wm.Whittington   Pocomoke 100
      patented to Ambrose Willett on south side of
      the Pocomoke River

65a. HOLDERS CHANCE 25 Oct.1714 John Holder   Baltimore 100
      on county road to Cypress Bridge

50a. OLD CASTLE 20 Sep 1713 Wm. Hackman   Nanticoke 100
      on the south side of the Nanticoke River

60a. PASTURAGE 20 Oct.1715 James Train   Nanticoke 100
      on the east side of the Nanticoke River

30a. ADDITION 10 Sep.1722 James Train   Nanticoke 100
      on the south side of the Nanticoke River

100a. DENNIS'S ADDITION 26 Jan 1721 John Caldwell   Wicomico 100
      patented to Dennis Driscoll, on east side of
      Cypress Swamp

| ACRES TRACT | SURVEY DATE-BY WHOM | LOCATION |

9a. POINT MARSH 9 Sep.1720 Richard Crockett   Wicomico 100
   on the north side of the Wicomico River

200a. SHANTAVANNAH 25 Apr.1722 James Givan   Nanticoke 100
   on the south side of the Nanticoke River

45a. PASTURAGE 25 Nov.1721 Jacob Messex   Nanticoke 100
   on the south side of the Nanticoke River

100a. PLEASANT GREEN 14 Oct.1721 Richard Ellingsworth,Nanticoke 100
   on the east side of Whorekill Road

50a. CATEYS FOLLY 10 June 1718 John Smith   Nanticoke 100
   patented to John Calloway on east isdeof the
   head of Little Creek

500a. THE AGREEMENT 15 Dec.1717 William Bozman   Mattapony 100?
   on the seaboard side

200a. BEYOND EXPECTATION 10 Aug.1721 Samuel Davis Bogeternorten ?
   on seaboard side in Newport Neck

300a. RYANS CHANCE 18 Nov.1715 John Caldwell   Pocomoke 100
   patented to Robert Martin on the north west
   side of the Pocomoke River

556a. CONTENTION resurveyed 15 June 1724   Wicomico 100
   by Alexander Lockey on the Wicomico River

100a. NINE PIN BRANCH NECK 22 Sep.1714   Pocomoke 100
   Robert Martin on south most side of Pocomoke River

11a. DESART 12 Mar.1724 Robert Martin   Pocomoke 100

100a. CHANCE 16 Mar.1724 Christopher Glass   Mattapony 100
   on east side Cankors Creek

300a. HAZZARDS CHANCE 27 Sep.1723 David Hazzard   Baltimore 100
   on seaboard side

300a. BARBADOS 21 Nov.1722 Robert King   Manokin 100
   On Devills Island

713a. ADDITION 2 Mar.1724 Joseph McClester   Wicomico 100
   on the south side of Quantico Creek

100a. PARESH 17 Jan 1715 Thomas Jones   Wicomico 100
   patented to Thomas Walker, at head of a
   branch of Barren Creek.

100a. CALLAWAYS INVENTION 29 Jan 1715 Thomas Jones,Baltimore 100
   patented Peter Callaway, on north east side
   of Little Creek.

64a. WILLIAMS ADVENTURE 22 Dec.1723 Wm.Owens   Manokin 100
   at Shipwrights branch

200a. GREENLAND 18 Mar.1724 Matthew Rain   Bogerternorten 100
   on the south side of tr.ROYLEYS PERCON

100a. TOWER HILL 9 Sep.1718 Edward Kellum   Nanticoke 100
   on the south side of the main branch of Plain Ck.

100a. PEASLEYS LIKING 20 Dec.1714 Abraham Ingram Nanticoke 100
   in Gravelly Branch

ACRES	TRACT	SURVEY DATE-BY WHOM	LOCATION	
50a.	INGRAMS LOTT	6 Apr.1722 Jacob Ingram	Nanticoke	100

on the north side of Deep Creek Branch

100a.	AQUINTICA SAVANAH	18 June 1722 John Bevans	Pocomoke	100

near John Kellams

100a.	DRESSEYS QUARTER	28 Sep.1723 John Messey	Baltimore	100

on the seaboard side

200a.	HOLLANDS DISCOVERY	15 Oct.1723 Richard Holland,	Baltimore	100

on the seaboard side at Newington Green

50a.	THE STONES	26 June 1722 Charles Tindell	Naniticoke	100?

on the north side of the main branch of Deep Ck.

50a.	ASSEKECTOMS NECK	26 June 1722 Samuel Tindall	Nanticoke	100?

in a fork of the main branch of Deep Creek

30a.	CONTENT	21 Sep 1721 Joseph Timmonds	Pocomoke	100

on the east side of main branch of Pocomoke River

100a.	KINGSDALE	10 Jan 1721 James Nicholson	Pocomoke	100

near King Daniells Branch

25a.	ADDITION TO LIMRICK	19 Aug.1721 Edmond	Pocomoke	100

Dickenson, on west side of land LIMRICK

160a.	HAZARD	28 Sept.1721 John King	Manokin	100

on the south side of the Manokin River

50a.	BENJ. ADVICE	28 Sep.1721 John King	Manokin	100

on the south side of Kings branch

138a.	CONCLUSION	20 Apr.1720 John Caldwell	Manokin	100

patented Robert Wilson

87a.	NEARNS ADDITION	27 Aug.1720 John Caldwell	Pocomoke	100

patented to Robert Nearn on west side of the Pocomoke River.

50a.	COW HARBOUR	26 Jan 1721 John Caldwell	Wicomico	100

patented to Moses Driskell

50a.	HOPEWELL	16 Mar 1721 John Caldwell	Pocomoke	100

patented to Sarah Davis between the Pocomoke and Annamessex River

150a.	DAVIS'S NECK	2 Mar.1772 Samuel Davis	Wicomico	100

on the Wicomico River.

100a.	TOWER HILL	5 Aug.1720 James Perry	Baltimore	100?

on north side of Beaver Dam Branch

180a.	GOOD LUCK	26 May 1720 Benjamin Wales	Nanticoke	100

on east side main branch of Nanticoke River

50a.	CHANCE	22 Oct.1722 John Wooten	Nanticoke	100
100a.	INCLOSED	22 Oct.1722 Edward Wooten	Nanticoke	100

on west side of Cypress Branch

36a.	LOTT	25 Mar.1724 John Roach	Annamessex	100

near tract JOHNSONS LOTT

100a.	FLATTLAND	26 Mar.1724 Joseph Houston	Pocomoke	100

in neck Askomonaconson Indian Town

75a.	ADDITION	12 Mar.1723 John Houston	Pocomoke	100

on west side of tr. LAUGHTON

ACRES TRACT	SURVEY DATE-BY WHOM	LOCATION
50a. HOGG QUARTER	22 Apr.1724 James Taylor on the south side of Woolfspitt Swamp	Bogerternorten 100
75a. SMITHS POLICY	9 Mar.1723 Isaac Stutt bounds tract Deer Quarter	Manokin 100
50a. CHANCE	28 Apr.1724 John Kellum at corner of Dickersons Folly	Nanticoke 100?
200a. ADVENTURE	5 May 1724 John Linch on north side of swamp on seaboard side	Baltimore 100
100a. LANES CHANCE	2 Apr.1724 Robert Watson on the seaboard side	Mattapony 100
250a. LANES SURVEY	1 Apr.1724 Peter Claywell on the seaboard side	Mattapony 100
100a. FRIENDS KINDNESS	13 Mar.1723 Richard Chambers, on east side of a creek of Manokin	Manokin 100
50a. REFUGE	12 July 1722 Richard Carey near land of John McGraughs	Manokin 100
100a. BLUFF HAMMOCKS	26 Feb.1723 James Strawbridge, at south end of BLUFF HAMOCK	Annamessex 100
50a. CHANCE	25 Jan 1722 George Tull on north side of Freemans Branch	Pocomoke 100
50a. SOMMERSETT	8 Aug.1723 John Jones and Thomas Dashiell at head of tr.HOB NOB	Wicomico 100
100a. MARSH GROUND	12 Nov.1723 Christopher Nutter on north side of the mouth of Quantico Creek	Nanticoke 100
100a. MO'NEN	20 Oct.1721 William Polk on east side of a branch of the Nanticoke	Nanticoke 100
100a. DINIGALL	20 Oct.1721 William Polk on east side of a branch of the Nanticoke	Nanticoke 100
100a. RAMAS	20 Oct.1721 William Polk on east side of a main branch of the Nanticoke	Nanticoke 100
115a. WOOLFSPIT RIDGE	25 Feb.1723 John Murray on the west side of Woolfspitt Swamp	Bogeternorten 100
85a. ADDITION	26 Feb.1723 John Murray near trach surveyed for Ambrose White	Bogeternorten 100
16a. BENJAMINS GOOD SUCESS	8 Sep.1723 Benjamin Eason, at mouth,of east side of Nanticoke River	Nanticoke 100
34a. EASOMS CHANCE	8 Sep.1723 Benjamin Easom on south side of the Nanticoke River.	Nanticoke 100
50a. GOLDEN QUARTER	27 Dec.1715 Thomas Jones on north east side of Little Creek out of the Nanticoke River.	Nanticoke 100
100a. OXFORD	2 May 1682 John White on south side of the Wicomico River's mouth at Dam Quarter. Possessed by John White	Manokin 100
100a. THE HOPE	2 May 1682 John White between Manokin and Wicomico Rivers, Possessed by John White	Manokin 100

| ACRES | TRACT | SURVEY DATE-BY WHOM | LOCATION |

50a. NEWPORT PAGNELL 20 Feb.1679 John King   Money 100
     assigned John Panther on the south side
     of Money Creek. Possessed by John Panther

300a. ABINGTON 10 May 1683 assigned to Thomas Hobbs,Wicomico 100
     Possessed by Joh Hobbs son of Thomas

100a. TILBURY 1683,Robert Sterling   Manokin 100
     surveyed for Roger Sherly,now possessed by
     Ephraim Wilson

100a. FORLORN HOPE(no date)surv. for Augustin Stanford,Manokin 100
     Possessed by widow of Robert Pollock by the
     name of Pollocks Lott

100a. ROBERTS RECOVERY 10 Sep.1682 assigned Francis   Manokin 100
     Roberts.Possessed by the widow Ann Roberts relec.

150a. JESHIMON 10 Sep.1682 Francis Roberts   Manokin 100
     possessed by Ann the relict of Francis Roberts

50a. LOCUST HUMMOCKS 10 Sep.1682 John Polky   Annamessex 100
     Poss. Francis Cradon in right of the relict
     Polky and orphans

200a. WINTER QUARTER 6 Aug.1679 Thomas Godwin   Baltimore 100
     assigned Walter Powell, on the north side of St.
     Martins and south side of Herring Ck. Possessed
     by Charles Townsend in right of John Powell in Va.

350a. VERNAM DEAN 22 Mar.1680 Wm. Stevens   Baltimore 100
     on the south side of the head of main branch of
     the St.Martins. Possessed by Thomas Mumford.

150a. OLIVERS PORTION 5 Aug.1679 John Godwin   Baltimore 100
     assigned Walter Powell, at head of St.Martins
     Possessed by Hen. Scholfield

150a. FRIENDS GUIFT 5 Aug.1679 John Godwin   Baltimore 100
     Assigned Walter Powell on the north side of
     St.Martins. Possessed by James Gray

600a. CARARDEE 2 May 1680 William Ennis   Bogerternorten 100
     Near Poquadenorton on west side Mobjack Bay, north
     side Dividing Ck. Poss. by Cor. Ennis

100a. SILVER STREET 3 May 1680 William Woodhave   Mattapony 100
     on seaboard side at Assateague. Poss. by Christian
     Horinorson at the Whorekills

500a. BLETCHINGHAST 20 May 1680,Wm.Stevens   Bogerternorten 100
     assigned James Round, on seaboard side. Possessed
     by Madam Mary Edgar

400a. YORKSHIRE 2 May 1680 Wm.Stevens   Bogeternorten 100
     assigned Edward Howard, on seaboard side. Possessed
     300a. Abraham Heather, 100a. Henry Smock

100a. FISHING HARBOUR 23 Mar 1680 Col.Wm.Stevens   Baltimore 100
     as Island at mouth of St.Martins.Poss.by Thomas
     Fenwick at Sussex Co. Horekill

250a. GREENS CHANCE 7 July 1667 William Green   Pocomoke 100
     on north side Pocomoke River,on east side Dividing
     Creek. Assigned Thomas Miller, Assessed by Joseph
     Gray

INDEX

ABBOTT, Nathaniel-46
ACFORD, Thomas-53-54
ACWORTH, Henry-73
   Richard-23-24-41-42-43-44-49-75-99
   Thomas-42-43-46-48-53
ADAMS, Alexander-15-16-20-115-117-119
   Jacob-32
   Phillip-6-32-35-86
   Sumner-13-76
   Thomas-6-32-35-40-86
AIRES-AYRES, Edmund-82
AILWORTH-AYLWORTH-
   John-43-45
   widow-45
AINSWORTH, Wm.-52
ALEXANDER, Wm.-17-19-78-83
ALLEN, Richard-31
ALLERTON, James-10
ANDERSON, Cornelius-19-20-83
   John-34-36-81-101
   Joseph-51
   William-34
ANDREWS, George-9-105
   John-29
ARMSTRONG, Matthew-3-98
ASHTON, Richard-67
ASKEW-ASCUE-Phillip-14-18-42-46-83-85-94-109
ATKINSON, James-76
AVERY-John-14-102
   Robert-67-68
AUSTIN-John-105
   Joshua,-10
AYDELOTTE-John-52-90-93-94
   Benjamin-68-93-112-114
AYLFORD, Wm.-75
AYLWARD, Wm.-90-82-89
BAILY-BAYLEY-George-13-62
BALL, Thomas-9-10-30-74
   Samuel-59
BALLARD, Charles-12-13-23-69-71
BALLY, Richard-34
BALLINGER, John-64
BAKER, Isaac-81

BASHAN, Andrew-97-110
BASEY, Nathaniel-51
BAYNUM, George-51-80
BARNABY, James-22
BARNES-BARNS, Wm.-53
   Richard-4-108
BANASTER, Wm.-6
BARTLETT, Pascoe-15-21
BARKER, John-65
BARRON, John-68
BARRENCLAUGH,
   Jeremiah-79
BEARD, Lewis-46-63
BEAUCHAMP, Edward-37
   Dogett-37
   Thomas-1-2-112-97
BENELSON, Wm.,-76
BENNETT, Edward-44-47-73
   Richard-31-13
   William,-42
BELL-John-85
   Anthony-47-83-100-121
BERER, Phillip-22
BERRY, James-74-106
BENTON, Peter-86-94
BENSTON, Peter-35-36
   George-74-75-120-121
   Joseph-104
BETTS, George-11-9-28-33-46-89
BERRY-James-28
   William-28
BEVANS-BIVEN-
   John-124
   Rowland-33-37-102
   William-109
BIRIAM-96
BISHOP, Aaron-58-61-68
   Henry-32-54-55-56
   John-54-59
   William-61
BLADES, Robert-33
BLOYD, Thomas-9-11
BLOYES, Thomas-18-100
BLAKE, Joel-29
   John-67
BODEN, John-60

BONJER, James-119
BOCKBURN, Benja.-33
BODY, Peter-93
   (see Douty)
BOOK, Richard-11
BOOTH, Isaac-74
   John-17-21
BOSMAN, BOZMAN
   John-25-34-62-22-84
   Wm.-12-34-123-9-22
BOSTON-Esau-34
   Henry-1-2
   Isaac-86
BOUGHER-BOUCHER-BROUGHER, John, 42-46-65-67
   Robert-51
   James-120
BOUNDS, James-115
   John-42-72-26
   William-72
BOWDEN, John-98
BOYCE, Thomas-10
   William-2
BRADFORD, John-118
BRADSHAW, Wm.-38-88
BRATTEN, James-54-69
BRAY, Pierce-30-93-112
BREEDY, James-81
BRERETON, Ann-20
   Thomas-46-103-104
   Wm., 15-19-21-74-105
BRISCO, Arthur-102
BRITTAIN, Wm., 103
BRITTINGHAM, Wm.-6-7-34-40-81-83-33-38
   John-40
BROADWATER, Wm.-81
BRIDGES, Joseph-24
BROUGHTON, John-33-76
BROWN, Alexander-22-24-25-68-69-76-107-109
   John-23-24-37-46-63-70-104
   Sidney-43
   William-62
BURKUM, Lucy-46
BULLGER, Wm.-60
BURTON, Benj.-56
   Peter-57
   William-115-116
BUTLER, Edmond-116-118
CADE, Robert-57-58-68-114
CALDWELL, Andrew-78-115
   James-118
   John-16-74-78-80-113-115-117-118-122 cont.

CALDWELL,John-123-124
  Robert-94-96-118
CALLOWAY,John-123
  Peter-65-75-76-105
    123
  William-122
CAMELL,Peter-57-58
CANNON,Stephen-44-48-
    93
CANNADY,Mark-116
CANE,James-22-25
CAREY-CARY,Edward-21
  Jeremiah-38
  Richard-10-21-69-125
  Thomas-9-10-14
CARLISLE,Alexander-69-
    199-13-18-113
CARNEY,Thomas-10-14-23
CARTER,John-7-8
  Phillip-18-19-27
  Edward-30-100
  George-33-34-49
  Madam-30
CARROLL,Widow-50
CARSLEY,Peter-30
CATHERWOOD,Robert-5-24
    62-74-77-90-95
CATLIN,Robert-2-6-64-
    80-87-104-99
  William,2-6-64-81-
    104
CAVENOUGH,John-57
CAUTHRAY,John-14
CHAMBERS,Richard-14-20
    24-26-32-72-125
CHEESEMAN,Wm.-3-45-101
  John-44
CHAPMAN,Silas-34-111-121
  Edward-121
CHAPWELL,Thomas-48
CHRISTOPHER,John-21-85
CLARK,Jonathan-118
  Rice-119
CLAY,John-84-89
CLAYWELL,Peter-125
CHADWICK,James-121
CLARK,Daniel-16
  Edward-118
  John-37-40-93-100
CLIFTON,Thomas-51-52-71
CLOGG,James-80
CLIFTON,Michael-33
COBB,John-121
COLE,Thomas-38
COFFIN,Stephen-35-86-6
COLEMAN,Ellis-56-67
  John-31
COLEBURN,COULBOURN,
  Ann-6-7-8
  Robert-16

COLEBURN,Wm.-3-6-7
    8-74-114
COCKSHELL,Richard-
    63
COLLINS,George-18-
    71
  Samuel-35-36-39-93
  Wm.-52-63-121
COLLIER,James-44-50
  Robert-43-44-45-
    50-64
COLLBROOK,Thomas-19
CONNER,James-62
  John-97-110
  James-28
  Lawrence088
  Patrick-16
  Phillip-2-3-6-31-
    95-100
COLLINS-John-52-95
CONWAY,Phillip-76-
    84
COOPER-Gabriel-79
  Jonathan-37
  Nathaniel-58
  Richard-82
  Samuel-36-37-39-
    57
COOK,Amos-7
CORD,Joseph-70-81
  Wm.-50-51-60
CORDRAY,John-120
CORNWELL,John-89
  Nicholas-60-65-82
    89
COTTINGHAM,John-94
  Charles-4-5-96
  Thomas-4-5-14-103
COTTMAN, John-122
  Benjamin-13-16-17
    19-42-73
CORNISH,John-30
COSTIN-Henry-36(see
    COFFIN)
COVY,Richard-88
COVINGTON,John-9-19
    75-89-103
  Phillip-9-11-19-64-
    91-96-104-114-115-
    119
  Nehemiah-9-18-74-77
    96-117
  Samuel-16-98-117
  Thomas-15-115
COX,James-16
  Thomas-15-16-18-66-
    74-82-108-117
CRAIGE,Edward-79
CRAYCROFT,John-43-49
CRADEN-Francis, 126

CROCKETT,Richard-
    12-110-16-17-97
    123
CROUCH,Ambrose-98
  John-21-106
  Robert-15-21-78
    89-119
CROPPER,Edmund-60
  Ebenezer-55
  John-55-59-60-61
  Nathaniel-71
  Sebastian-71
CROLLER,John-28
CULHOONE,John-65
CURRY,Wm.-74-84-85
CURTIS,Daniel-100
  James-3-80-87-93
    96-105-98-110
  Martin-71-73-107
CULLEN,John-2-96
CUPMAN,John-52
  Mary-52
DALE,David-35
DASHEILL,George-49
    103-119
  James-21-41-43-44
    45-48-50-94-95-
    106-108-113
  Robert-13-18-20-
    21
  Thomas-8-19-20-
    48-95-102-113-
    125
DAVIES,Elizabeth-26
DAUGHERTY,Nathaniel
    27-64-5
DAVIS,James-22
  John-16-21-77-87
  Thomas-5-7-33-66-
    82-84-99-108
  William-22-26-87-93
  Richard-87-99
  Robert-93
  Samuel-63-97-110-
    123-124
  Sarah-124
DAY-Edward-73-76
  Mary-12-15
  George-67-68
DEALL,John-67
DEALS,James-120
DEERE,Stephen-86
DEAR,John-95
DENT,Robert-26
  Peter-22-23-24-27
    68-96
DENNIS,Daniel,32
  Donnack-5-29
  John-29-30-113
DENEHUE,Wm.-41-120

DERRICKSON, Andrew-93
  Mary-117
  Joseph-117
DENWOOD, Levin -8-11-
  65-55-97-112
  Arthur-22-23-25-65
  97-99-111
DEVERAUX, John-57
DICKENSON, Edward-2-
  18-37
  Andrew-93
  Peter-35-82
  Somerset-2-35-37-
  82-118
  William-35
DICKESON-Wm.71
DIGGS, Edward-70
  William-70
DISHEROON, Lewis-62-109
  John-16-109-113
  Michael-62-85
  William-62
DIKES, Edward-107
DICKERSON, Edmund-38-
  124
DIXON, Ambrose-1-2
  Edward-98
  Thomas-1-3-5-83-106
DORMAN, John-65
DONNAKET, Dorman-33
DONOHOE, Daniel-5-6-
  38-68
  Teague 121
DORMAN-Henry-22-26
  Matthew-22-24-27-69
DORMENT, Matthew-121
DOUGHTY, Peter-44-46-
  63-93(see Body)
DOWNS, George-8-9
DOYNE, Robert-70
DOWNS, Robert-77-79
DRAPER, Alexander-4-24
  98
DRIGERS, Devorez-55
DRISKELL, Moses-124
  Dennis-84-122
DRYDEN, David-97
  John-76
DUNLAP, Ninian-76
DUKES, Robert-4-7-8
DYKES, Edward-30
DYNE, Robert-62
DUNCAN-William-26-38
  John-86
EAYRES, Jessee-65
EASON, Benjamin-125
ELLERY, Henry-99

ELLIS, Corn.-69
  John-29-34-101-
  100
ELLINGSWORTH,
  Richard-123
EMMETT, John-93
  Abraham-62-64-65
  73
ENNIS, John-65
  Cor.126
  William-126
EVANS, Ca.-88
  Edward-61
EVES, George-102
FAREWELL, Richard-
  65
FARNALL, Thomas-50
FASSITT-FAUCETT
  John-63-67-76
  Wm.-27-55-56-57
  60-87-97-111
  Charles-62
FEBUS, George-23
FENWICK-Thomas-65
  67-126
FENTON, Moses-37-65
FITZGERALD, Phillip
  36
  Peter-75
FISHER, John-22-99
FLEMING-FLEMAN
  Phillip-81
  John-120-121
  Lodowick-40
FLEUELYN, Samuel-
  45-71-91-93-95
FOSCUE, Simon-93
FOSTER, Mary-60
  Martha-60
FOLKEN, Simon-63
FOWLER, Edward-77
  Thomas077
FOXON, William-6
FOXCROFT, Isaac-21
  44-50
FRANK, John-72
FRANKLIN, WM.-76
  Ebenezer-58
  John-56-65-98-
  110-111-112
FRENSHAW, Isaac-63
FRIGGS, Henry-118
FREEMAN, Joseph-40
  Wm.-4-117
  John-4-33-65-67-
  68-93-98-111
FOUNTAIN, Marcy-23
  Nicholas-22-23-
  24-25-26

FRISSEL-FRIZEL, John,
  63-65-84-104
FURNACE-FURNISS,
  James-6-23-22-24-26
  Wm.-3-100-101-26-36
  106
FURRS, John-44
GAINES, Mary-29
  Richard-29
GARROTT, John-7
  Thomas-10
GIBBS, Edward-15
GILES-GYLES, Wm.-42-
  46-49-75-85
  Clement-92-111
GILLY, John-42-64-90
  103
  Robert-115
GILLETT, Germon-2-28-99
GIVAN, James-41-50-79-
  81-88-91-105-110-
  111-123
  Robert-41-81-96-
  105-108-115
GILLETT-John-40
GILLIS, Thomas-102
GILLILAND, John-121
GLASS, John-59
  Christopher-123
GLADSTON, John-49-50-67
GLANVILL, Wm.-22-23
GODDIN-GODDEN-John-37
  59-60-66-67-70-75-
  101
  Michael-60-65-71-82
GODDARD, George-13-19-
  106
GOLDSMITH, Anthony-28
  John-105
  Margaret-27
GODDEN, Thomas-62
  William-107
GODWYN-GODWIN, Thomas-
  126
  John-58-126
GOLD, Edward-77-85
GODFREE, Charles-83
GOLDSMITH, Wm.-
GORDON, James-81
  Thomas-49-62-79-113
GORE, Daniel-50
GOOSEY, Nathaniel, 51
GOSSLIN, John-13-74
GORDON, Adrain, 21-63
GRAY, William-120
  James-94-104-109
  John-25-120
  Miles-27

GRAY,Michael-25-79
  Joseph-8-104-101-
  110-126
  James-126
GRADIE-GRADON-
  Francis-24-25-95
GREEN,John-15-56
  Edward-67-87-90-
  91-109-114
  William-6-10-17-
  25-43-46-49-126
GRUNDMAN,Robert-16
GRIFFIN,Enock-56
GUNBY,John-5-120-121
GULLOTT-Wm.-27-28
HACKMAN,Wm.-122
HAFFORD-HASFORT-
  George-51-103
HADDER,Wm.-61
  Warren-61-72
HALL,Alice-2-7-70
  Charles-2-7-70-87
  Henry-50-51
  Richard-79
  John-84
  Thomas-39
  Phoenix-65-81
  Wm.-71-82
HALSE,Thomas-47
HAMBLIN,John-49-58
HAMLIN-George-51-
  52-61
HAMMOND,Phillip-37
  Edward-38-40-56-
  60-86
HANDY,Samuel-1-3-39
  69-72-87-88-95-
  98-100
HARDY,James-14
  Robert-14
HARPER,Edward-36-106
  Wm.-36-38-40-41-106
  Widow-40
HARMAN-Henry-50-77-
  78-107
HARMANSON,Henry-107
HARRIS,John-96
  Richard-61-64
  Wm.,-20-38-117
  David-62
HARRISON,John-35-
  38-40-61
HART,Robert-1
HARWOOD-Thomas-29
HAST,Daniel-13-14-16
  18-20-21-104
HATCH,Abraham-28-38-
  105-111
HAYMAN,Edward-11

HAYMAN,Wm.-84
  Henry-9-10-44-63
HARDING-James-15
  Robert-15
HARVEY,Timothy-88
HAZARD,David-68-
  115-122-123
HEARN,Wm.-51
HEATH-John-1-37
  Adam-16-86-117-
  120
  William-28
  Robert-35
  Mr.-104
HEAP,Francis-69-82
HEMERSON-HERMENSON-
  Christian-64-68-
  80-126
  Christopher-80
HERINORSON,Herman
  95
HEPWORTH,John-81
HEWETT,John-64-76-
  77-78-88
HENDERSON,John-22-
  32-73-90-105-108
  Christian-62
  James-32-76-101
HEATHER,Ephraim-58-
  86
  Abraham-59-63-57-
  126
HESTER,Thomas-64
HAMPTON,Mary-122
  John-56-61-64
HILL,Jacob-51
  James-66
  Abraham-51
  John-4-7
  Richard-58-61-68
  Johnson-54-87
  Thomas-70
HENRY-John-114
HINNING,Phillip-112
HASTING,Robert-122
HICKMAN,Wm.-41
HIGNOLL,Robert-30
HILLIARD,John-32-100
HIGHWAY,Thomas-28-85
HIGH,George-84
HIGGARTY,Dennis-82
HOBBS,Joy-10-11-23
  Thomas-126
  John-126
HOLDER,John-66-122
HOLBROOK,Thomas-12-
  15-110
HOLLOWAY,Peter-74
HOLSTON-HOULSTON
  Robert-34-40-102

HOLSTON-John-33
HOLLAND,Mitchal-7
  John-16-52-53-73
  Richard-51-53-112-
  124
  William-51
HOPKINS,Goerge-4
  Robert-4
  Nathaniel-53-88-
  104-107
  Samuel-71-88-93-
  104-107-114
HOPE,George-34
HORSEY,Isaac-1-109
  John-2-4-5
  Robert-27
  Nathaniel-1-6-8-
  109
  Samuel-8-83-1-2-8
  Stephen-1-2-4-5-6-
  7-0-14-20-49-90-
  99-100
HORSEMAN,Thomas-63-
  84
  Richard-84
HOGINTONS,Thomas-53
HOWARD,David-50
  George-60-115
HOPINGTON,John-118
HOWARD,Edmund-27-36
  Edward-39-126
HOUSTON,John-124
  Joseph-124
HOSEA,Mattnew-117
HUDSON,David-68-
  Henry-114
  Richard-61
  David-58-59-68
  Henry-30-31-32-59-
  61-62-65-87
  Nicholas-32
HOGGINS,Edmund-90
HUGHES,James-77
HUGGETT,Thomas-68
HULL,orphans-14
  Richard-88
HUMPHREYS,Thomas-13-18
  68
HUTCHENS,Charles-43-45
  George-10-14-90-103
HUTCHINSON,Wm.-70
  Robert-88
HYLAND,John-30-31
INGRAM,Abraham-73-78-
  122-123
  Jacob-124
  James-73-78-105
  John-12
IRONMUNGER,Thomas-76
IRONSIDE,Isaac-66
IRONSHAN,Isaac-64

IRVIN, John-81
JAMES, John-53
   Gilbert-11-18
JACKSON, Jonathan-43-45
   Samuel-41-45-48-102
JARRETT, Graves-15-25
JAZARD, John-59
JARRETT, Richard-15
   Thomas-113
JEFFERSON, Richard-106
JENNER, John-77-85
JENKINS, Col.-28-32
   Francis-21-20-41
   46-47-48-50-51-56-60-61-106-112
   114
   William-5-7
JINGLE, Wm.-65
JOHNSON, Affradozi-51
   Benajmin-116
   Leonard-72
   James-27
   Cornelius-11-66-78-107
   George-1-3-4-12-13-98-100-101
   John-2-17-27
   Robert,-51-54-55-60-71-83
JOLLY, James-20-98
JONES, Andrew-48-59
   David-32
   Edward-27
   George-21
   Daniel-8
   Gilbert-46
   Howell-15
   James-12-14-15-16
   44-46-53-59-102
   Charles-27
   Leonard-4-45
   John-52-79-125
   Matthew-95
   Thomas-5-24-30-34
   52-62-74-77-90-107-98-121-122-123
   125
   Robert-10-30-32-40
   William-8-9-11-66
   Samuel-11-88-104
JOSEPH, Wm.-79-80
JOYCE, Francis-53-83
JUNIS, Corn.-56
   Charles-59-65
   Nathaniel-59-65

JUNIS, Wm.-56
KEEN, Orphans-49
   John-13
   Richard-20-49
   William-13-21-49
   75-85
KENNY, Stephen-115
   Lazarus-115-116
   William-60
KELLUM, John-86-104
   107-125
KEMP, John-47-49
KERSEY, Peter-100-108
   Robert-108
KEMPHALL, John-79
KENNETT, Wm.-60
   Martin-60
KILLAM, Edward-119
   123
KIMBALL, Richard-16
KING, C.-22
   Benajmin-28-82
   John-20-23-25-26-27-28-30-31-32-40-58-82-99-105-124-126
   Robert-112-121-123
   Upshur-27
   James-110
   Mary-6-21-25-28
KIRK, John-4-7-8-40
   80
   Bridget-120
KNOX, James-63
   Wm.-27
KOLICK-KILLOCK-Simon-116-118
LAND, John-71
   Walter-71
LANE, Dennis-28
   George-28
   John-37-80
   Walter-35-37-72-80-107
LANGRELL, James-4-44-83
LANGSTON, Wm.-47
LANGSTOR, James-76
LANGSTER, James-40-48
LANKFORD, John-73
LAMEE, John-62-73
   Mr.-66
LARRAMOUR-LARRMER
   James-
   Thomas-42-44-45-46-95
LAMBERSON, Richard-41-93
LAURENCE, John-29

LAWS, George-33
   Robert-33-49
   John-25-33-39
   Wm.-62-118
LAYFIELD, Benajmin-34-59
   George-19-31-89
   Samuel-19-31-34--36-39-40-53-58-66-89-101
   Thomas-31
LAYTON, Henry-90
   Wm.,-20-73-83
LEIGH, David-59
LAURENCE, Wm.-59
LEATON, Henry-25
LEONARD, Josias-5
LESTER, Morris-33
   Richard-35
LEWIS, Richard-104
LIGHTS, Jos.-82
LINCH, John-125
LINGLEY, Jus.-120
LINZEY, Ralph-30
LITTLETON, Bowman-51
   Southy-102-50
   Madam-37
   Susannah-50
LLOYD, Richard-39
LON, William-116
LONDON, Ambrose-13-72-100
LONG, Jeffrey-6
   John-2-7-77
   Samuel-7-77
LOMAY, John-119
LOKEY, LUCKLEY-LOCKEY
   Alexander-123
   John--22-46
   orphans-46
LONSTER, John-40
LOWE, widow-97
LYON, John-45-50-105-106
LOTEN, Wm.-63
LUCAS, Thomas-15-61
LUNN, EDward-10
LYSTEN, Morris-31-100
MACKMORIE, James-12-97
MACNAMARY, Edmund-49
MADDOX-MATTOCKS-
   Alexander-5-25-31
   Thomas-120-100
   Lazarus-3-9-22-25-26-87-121
MACKITT, John-30-37
MAGRAUGH, Owen-22-24-25-28-48-69-106
   Mary-22-24-25-28-69-97-106-111

MARLO,Wm.-121
MAJOR,Wm.-40
MARKS,John-41-53
MANLOVE,Mark-30-38-
  40-46
  George-37
  John-13-24-31-43-
  45-46
  Thomas-23-24-25-
  28-69
  William-34-35-103
MARCOMB-MARKHAM-
  John-9-10
MANNING,Thomas-8
MARROTT,John-13-106
MARSHALL,Adrain-34
MARRETT,John-45-47
MARSH,Paul-54
MARPLUS,Thomas-40
MASTORS,Wm.-39
  Marmaduke-49
MARROTT,widow-45-47
  William-64
MARTIN,Edward-117
  Francis-6-7-81-83
  Robert-119-123
MASON,Wm.-69
MASSEY,Alexander-57
  Wm.-54-57-98-112
MARVEL,John-91-101-
  111
MEARLE,Wm.-121
MEARS,John-28
MELSON,John-69
MERRILL,Wm.-74
MESECK-MESSEX-MESSEY
  John-124
  Jacob-123
  Julian-48
  William-62
MEECH,John-41-42-43
MATTHEWS,Wm.-36-64-
  85-93-100
MERRILL,MORRILL,Wm.
  39-30-33-90
MILES,Alice-26
  Henry-26-27-74
  Samuel-27-74
MILLS,James-52
  John-118
  William-35
MILBOURN,Ralph-29
MILLER,John-64-65
  Thomas-126
MILLWARD,Wm.-68
MINSHALL,Helena-2-86
  Jeffrey-2-31-32-86
MITCHELL,Randall-7
  Alexander-13-17

MC(page 136)

MITCHELL,Robert-41
  Thomas-6
MORE,John-63-69-7
MORGAN,Henry-56-57
  71-46
MOORE-MORE,
  Anthony-105
MORGAN,Rice-2
MORRIS,Cornelius-
  32-34
  Morris-115
  Jenkins-45-49
  Samuel-35-110-111
  112
  Manasses-49-69-73
  Thomas-68-75-76-
  57-61-66
  Wm.-38-104
MURPHY,John-63
  Thomas-51-63
MURRAY,John-120-125
MUMFORD,Thomas-126
NELSON,John-22
  William-41-59
NEARN,Robert-124
NASWORTHY,Geo.-99
NEVILLE,James-81
NEWBOLD,Thomas-3-
  30-32
NESHAM,Benajmin-
  13-17-19-42
NICHOLSON,Charles-
  112
  James-9-23-124
  Richard-14-69
NOCK,William-55
NOBLE,Isaac-12-16-
  17-19-42
  WIlliam-38-41-66-
  89-117
NOCK,William-55
NORTON,John-95-112
  114
NUGENT,Margaret-27
  Christopher-27
NUTTER-Charles,42-
  45-48-104
  Christopher-23-42
  45-65-70-105-125
  John--48-69
  Margaret-27
OBONTON,James-63
OKeen,Roger-36-37
OLANNUM,Dennum-25-
  27-28
OLDFIELD,Charles39
ONORTON,Wm.-67
ORHINES,John-20
OSBURN,orphans-60
  John-63

OUTEN,John-2-3-5-6-
  54-84-85
OWENS,Moses-108
  Robert-120-122
  Samuel-120-122
  William-123
PALMER(Planner) Wm.-
  1-2-6-87-93-105
PARK,John-81
PARKER,George-62-82-
  94-89-109
  John-21-73-76-84-
  93-112
PANTER-PANTHER,John
  9-11-49-74-88-126
PARKER-Peter-65
  Charles-67-92 82
  Phillip-34-67-82
  Matthew-103
PARSONS,Peter-62
  John-15-17-78-69
MARRAMOUR-PARMOUR-
  James-122
  John-46-49-54-73-
  103
  Thomas-54
PATTEY,Richard-68
PATRICK,Daniel-59
  Roger-59
  John-62-119
PEAKES,Richard-64
PEARCE,John-16-43
PEARSON,John-116
PEMBERTON,Thomas-12-
  105-21
PENNOCK,Richard-90
PEPPER,Richard-54
  Tobias-52
  Wm.-116-117-118-
  119
PERRY,James-124
  Robert-72-113
PEYTON,Major-73
PEALE,Thomas,-33
PETERKIN,Thomas-32
PERKINS,John-31-81
PEAD,Timothy-37-38-
  40
PEASY,John-44
PEIRCE,Robert-56
PASSWATER,orphans 14
PHEBUS,George-77-81
PIERRE,Robert-80
PHILLIPS,Henry-27
  Richard-14-85-86
  Roger-43-45-85-
  86-105
  William-81
  Thomas-84-85

132

PIKE,John-52
PIESLEY,Henry-30
PIPER,Isaac-34
  Wm.'s orphans-
    42-45-104
PITTS,Robert-31
  widow-33
POLLETT,Thomas-77
POLLICKEY,John-91
POLKY,John-126
POLK,POLLOCK-
  McDanoll-27
  Ephraim-10-98-
    109-110
  John-36-24
  Robert-126-68-109
  William-23-27-98
    125-28
  Magdalen-68
  James-111
POOL,Thomas-23-80
PLUNKETT,RIchard-25
POINTER-POYNTER
  Edward-56
  Argalas-55
  Jeremiah-55
  Thomas-55-56-60-
    63
  Wm.-63-59
POLLARD-Charles-71
POPPLEWETT,John-60
POTTER,Thomas-84
POWELL,Edward-86
  Rachel-120
  John-37-126
  Samuel-58-62
  Thomas-61-110-50-
    55-60-95
  Walter-37-58-70-
    86-106-126
  William-29-70-106
POPE,John-53-71-114
  Richard-53
PORTER,John-54-72
PRESTON,Richard-100-
  101
PRICE,Edward-83-100
  Alexander-75-85
  John-57-70
  Rebecca-75-85
  Catherine-30
  James-4-8-23
  Jenkins-30-31-35-
    36-39-98-99
  Mary-4-8
  William-29
PRESLEY,Peter,-20
PRIOR,Thomas-84
PROFIT,Thomas-97-51-
  58-61

PURNELL,John-50-51-
  53-55-103-118
  Thomas-51-52-53-
    61-63-79-91-103
QUATERMASS,Patrick-
  48
WUILLAN,Liddia-38
  Daniel-30-34-38
  Thomas-34-119
  widow-32-34
  William-33
QUINTON,Phillip-118
RAIN,Matthew-123
RALPH,Thomas-20-42-
  62-72-73
RAYMOND,Jonathan-20
RATCLIFFE,Eliau-58
  Charles-58-60-61
    86-102-117
RAMSEY,Charles-121
RAWLEY,James-81-83
READ-REED-REID
  John-48-113-120-122
  Percival-10-99
  Walter-52-53-76-
    82-90-101
Renshaw-Renshur
  John-10-12-75-77
REILY,LYLEY-
  Lawrence-39-54-
    36-103-113
REYNOLDS,Christopher
  57-69
REVELL,Randolph
  (Randall)6-105-100-
  103
RHODESON,Joan-3
RICH,Henry-58
RICHINS,John-27-77-
  79
RICE,Nicholas-12-101
RICHARDS,John-48-57
  William-68
RICHARDSON-Angoll-77
  Charles-54
  Robert-54-55-58-
    103
  John-17-18
  Willie-59
RICKETTS-John-54-80
  86
  William-55-68-80-
    112
RIGGIN-Ambrose-36-
  105
  Teague-20-30-31-
    105
  John-29-96
RIDGELY,Robert-14-
  16-46

RIDER-John-122
RIXON-John-17
ROADS,Humphrey-35
ROBERTS,Thomas-60
ROACH,Nathaniel-3
  John-2-6-8-21-81
    87-91-113-120-124
ROCKSON,John-6
ROBINSON-Joseph 81
  Wm.-16-55-56-73-
    80-112
  Richard-103
ROBINS-Thomas-50
  John-36-50-51-58
ROBERTS,Ann-10-110-
  126
  Francis-10-11-15-
    90-110-111-126
RODOLPHUS,Wm.-17
ROE-ROWE-Thomas-17-
  18-24-25-95-109
ROUND-ROWND,James
  41-56-61-64-126
  William-57-58-59-
    62-93
ROGERS,Henry-53
ROLLS,John-88
ROSS,Alvin-62
ROWELL-ROUSELLS
  John-41-35-51
  (ROWSALOE-ROUNDSLEE)
RUGG-Furbey-2-96
  widow-103
RUNSLEY,Bernard-33
RUSSELL-George-40-53
  James-42-46-65-67
  Richard-63-90
RUST,John-51
RUTTLEDGE,Ed.-14-73
SAMUEL,Richard-43-45
  91
SAUCER,Benjamin-11-72
  105
SANFORD,Samuel-57
  Augustin-126
SANGSTER,James-48
SCARBOROUGH,Charles-
  13-31
  Matthew-27-38-51-52
    54-55-56-59-63-68
    71-104-107
SCHOCKLEY-John-112
  Richard-106
SCOTT,Wm.-3-8-33-102
  103
SCHOLFIELD,Benjamin-53
  54-69-95-103
SELBY,Daniel-51-52-53
  58-67-79-85-118
  Parker-52-79
  Phillip-51-52-118

SELBY,Thomas-54-57
  Wm.-52-53
SEAWARD,Josias-5-
  11-34-36-103
SEWELL,Henry-98
  Thomas-6
SHERLEY,Roger-126
SHIPHAM,Edward-67
SHAW,Thomas-11-68
SHOLLITES,Thomas-5
  24
SHARROTT,widow-32
SHIELDS,Alice-45
  John-102-108
  Thomas-102
SHEPHARD,Rowland-53
SHOWELL,Charles-71
  Samuel-71-80
SHILES,John-14-16
  Thomas-12-14-19
SHURMAN-SURMAN-
  Edward-14
  Peter-19
  Thomas-16-42
SHEHEE,David-17-18
SHANK,Thomas-26
SHIPWAY,John-22-26
SIMMONS,Samuel-42
SINGLETON,John-21
SIMPSON,John-60
SLAUGHTER,James-39
SMITH-John-2-13-23-
  41-47-53-64-81-
  94-123
  Archibald-117-122
  Elizabeth-39
  Edward-53-54-56-
  57-58-103
  Arch-35-95
  C.-32
  George-49-85
  Arthur-28
  HENRY-21-24-25-27-
  28-33-36-39-66-67
  70-72-105-99-107
  102
  James-19-51-94
  Mary-22
  Nicholas-11
  Samuel-15-20
  Robert-37-104
  William-27-28-29-
  30-32-101
SMALL,Honner-32-97-
  112
SMOCK,Henry-50-60-
  126
  John-50-55-57-58-
  59-60
SNEAD,Robert-112

SMULLIN,RAndall-36
SOUTHERN,George-15
SOUTH,Oliver-44
SPAT,John-46
SPENCE-Adam-83-114
  David-12-15-16
  John-12-18
  James-12-15-17-74
SPEER-Andrew-91-75-
  89
STANFORD,Jos.-84
STANBY,Christopher-38
STANLEY,Hugh-40
  John-40
STARRETT,Mary-40
STAPLEFORD,Raymond-
  100
STARRETT,John-52
  Sarah-52
STANDORS,John-54
STERLING,John-4
  Robert-126
STEVENS,Edward-29
  John-29
  Richard-12-13-17-
  21-102
  Charles-70
  William-3-4-5-6-7
  8-9-10-15-16-17-
  18-18-23-24-25-26
  27-29-30-31-32-34-
  35-36-37-38-40-44-
  45-46-47-48-49-50-
  51-53-54-55-56-57-
  58-59-61-65-66-67-
  70-95-98-100-104-
  105-106-107-101-
  102-103-126
STEVENSON-STEPHENSON
  Christopher-29
  William-32-56-51
STOCKDELL,Ed.-2
STOCKWELL,Thomas-4
STOCKLEY-John-109
  Woodman-65
  STOCKFIELD,Benjamin
  56
STUCKLEY,orphans-59
STORREY,John-68
STUGGS,Thomas-115
STURGIS,John-54
STUTT,Isaac-125
STRAWBRIDGE,James-27
  125
  Thomas-17
SQUIRE,John-44-21
SUMMERS,Benjamin-2
  8-108
SURVILE,Wm.-51
TARR,John-87-105

TAYLOR,Charles-67
  Christopher-34
  James-125
  John-7-12-36-64-75
  76-115
  widow-30
  Walter-32-33-76-94
  99
  Hope-72
TAYLORD,Wm.-109-111-
  112
TEAGUE,John-62
TEDBURY,Edward-28
THOMAS,Alexander-46-
  67-65-107
  LAMBROOK-86
  Morgan-34
THOMAS,Griffith-38
  William-13-20
THOMPSON,Andrew-6
  Thomas-54
  Joseph-44
  Christopher-82
THORNE,Wm.-13-22-23-
  24
THOROGOOD,Francis-36-
  39-54-62
TIMMONS,widow-34
  Joseph-124
TILLMAN-TILGHMAN
  Gidenn-23-24-35-40
  117-121
TINDELL,Charles-124
  Samuel-1-124
TINGLE,Hugh-58-67-110
TIZER,Robert-67
TOMLINSON,Thomas-5
TOADVINE,Nicholas-19-
  78
TOMKINS,Wm.-55-56-61
TOWERS,Margaret-58-95
  114
TOMLINSON,Samuel-34-37
TOWNSEND,Charles-70-
  126
  Elizab.-33-119
  James-69
  Jeremiah-61-108
  John-35-37-100-70
  Richard-43
  William-35-60-72
TOUCHBURY,Henry-70
TRAIN-James-41-47-77-
  85-122
TROTTER,George-49
TRIPSHAWS,orphans-35-
  104
TRUITT-TROUETT-TRUETT
  George-59-63-79-91
  Jacob-77

TRUITT, Samuel-91
  James-60-110
  John-66-79-108-111
TULL, Thomas-1-70
  George-31-36-125
  Richard-31-65-104
  John-2-35-36-57-104
TULLY, John-73-43
TURNER, Samuel-90
TURVILL, widow-61
  Margery-58
  Presgrave-58-97
  Wm.-56-58-61-112
TURPIN, Wm.-10-21-24-26-66
  John-26
TULLY, Stephen-43-47-86
TURRVILL-John-61
  Thomas-62
TUNSTALL, John-36-119
TWERLEY, Robert-47
TWYFORD-TWIFORD
  Wm.-38-120
TYLOR, Nicholas-107
UNDERWOOD, Anthoy-21
VALENTINE, Luke-22
VENKACK, John-8
VENABLES, Joseph-13-17
WAINRIGHT, Wm.-4-71
WAITE, Wm.-53
  Nathaniel-53
WALE-George-32-99
WALES, Benjamin-13-16-20-98-112-124
WALL, Edward-55-58
WALL, George-29
WALLACE, James-85
  William-84
WALLACE, Richard-113-10-19-90-95-120
  Matthew-18-80
WALLBURN, John-30-40
WALLEY, Thomas-13
WALLER, John-9
  William-9-90
WALKER, John-102
  Thomas-11-12-15-16-18-20-21-25-43-62-82-83-90-104-123
  Susanna-20-21-14
WALTER, Thomas-11-43
WALSTON, Thomas-2-73-95
WALTON, John-37-66
  Fisher-50
  Stephen-50

WALTON-Wm.-50-51-57-112
WALLIS, Thomas-39
WARD-Thomas-82-100
  Cornelius-2-4-5-8-100-108
  Bonnard-28
WAPLES, Wm.-69-115
  Peter-39-40-69-107
WARWICK, Wm.-38-41
WARREN, Richard-61
WATERS, Gabriel-70
  John-1-87-96
  Richard-1-50-87-108
  Sampson-21-43-widow-43-44-45-50
  William-1-101
WARRINGTON, Ste.-94
WATSON, John-56
  Robert-125
WATTS, Edward-58
  John-36-39-52-54-56-57-89-103
WEIR, Robert-122
WEATHERLY, James-25-41-42-43-44-45-47-49-72-73-77-88-89-90-91-104-107
WESTLOCK, John-22
WEST, John-6-39
  Thomas-87
WEBB, John-10-54-62
  Richard-38-44-53-57
  Mark-116
WESTLAND, John-53
WELLBOURN, Thomas-53
  Daniel-53
WHARTON, John-117
  Daniel-115
  Richard-35-36
  Charles, 69-117-120
WHEATLEY, Sampson-36-86-100
WHITEFIELD, Wm.-100
WHITTINGTON, Southy-122
  William-21-50-96-110-112-114-115-116-119-122-57-63-70-82-94-105-109
  Andrew-25-26-27-64
  Ursula-24
VAUGHAB, John-28-29
WASEY, Nathaniel-51

WATSON-Robert-69
  Peter-51-52-71-
  Robert- 69
WHITE, Ambrose-57-60
  Phineas-39
  Alexander-36
  Stevens-30-32-36-54
  Thomas-31-39
  William-36-39-54
  Wrixum-55-57-86
WHEELER, Edward-36-75
  John-77
WHITEMARSH, Richard-41
WHITTY, Richard-12-14-21-49-66-68
WESTLOCK, Magdalen-46
WHITE, Ambrose-50-55-125
  John-94-109-113-125
WILK, James, 73
WILLIN, James-22
WHITE, John-6-7-9-10-16-17-25-26-27-37-46-54-56-57-58-62-90
WILLETT, Ambrose-122
WILLIAMS, Charles-11-103-111
  Edward-11-66
  Michael-1-42
  Thomas-1-39-88
WILSON, Jane-99
  John043-50-96-111
  Robert-28-43-113-124
  Ephraim-14-22-24-26-55-68-99-109-111
  George-2-104
  Thomas-24-26-48-78-79
  William-2-75-104-119
WILKINSON, Wm.-2
WILLIAMS, Henry-73
  Elizabeth-103
  John-40
  Francis-51
  Alexander-54
WINDSOR, John-25-42-45-91-95
WINSLOW, Wm.-39-40
WITH-James-49
WILLIAMSON, David-10
  William-38
WINDER, Thomas-46
  John-12-14-18-20-23-24-37
  William-20

WINN, John-36
WINDERSON, James-55
WOOD, John-17-80
  Robert-31-_121_
WOODCRAFT, Ro_g_er-95
  Richard-55-67-69
    70-86-95-113-11_4_
WOODHAVE, Wm.-56-_67_-
  68-126
WOO_D_WARD, John-37
WOOLFORD, John-13-26
  Mary-10-23-32-38--39
    67-91
  Roger, 23-26-32-38-
    67-91
WORTH, Robert-30
WOODGATE, Wm.-43
WORTHINGTON, Samuel-15
  23-49
WOODER, Richard-114
WOOTEN, John-124
  Edward-124
WOOD, William-60
  Ann-60
WRIGHT-Edward-36-62-
  73-79-109
  Abell-6
  Bloice(Bloyd)_9_-11-
    71
  William-18-42-_71_
YAULDING, W_m_.-85
YOUNG, Laurance-63
  Samuel-31
  William-119

MC
MaCALLY, John-58
McCARTY, John-107
MaCLANY, John-60
MacCLEMEY, Woncey-77
McLOYSTER, MacCLESTER
  Daniel-120
  Elizabeth--113
  Joseph-113-123
  John-13-43-76-93-_94_
MacLEAR, Richard-66
McCOLLON, Alexander-64-93
McGRAUGH, John-125
MacGUNIS, Daniel-43
McMANUS, John-58
MacMORRIS, James-110
McNEALE, 73
McWILLIAMS, James-91

136-end of Book

Made in the USA
Coppell, TX
14 June 2020

28202892R00079